AGENDA

Tread softly…

Irish Poets in the UK

AGENDA

CONTENTS

INTERVIEWS

REVIEWS OF LIVING POETS

POEMS

ESSAYS ON DECEASED POETS

POEMS

CHOSEN BROADSHEET POET

CHOSEN BROADSHEET REVIEWER

NOTES FOR BROADSHEET POETS

Front cover, and artwork: **Sarah Longley**

Born and raised in Belfast, Sarah Longley studied Drawing & Painting at Edinburgh College of Art where she lived and worked for many years before moving to the West Highlands. She has exhibited in the R.S.A, the R.H.A and the R.U.A. and has recently been made an Associate member of the Royal Ulster Academy. Her work is in several public collections including the Arts Council of Northern Ireland. 'My recent work has been inspired by my new surroundings and I've been particularly drawn to the salt-marsh close to our home and the mysterious hill behind (Angel Hill) which provides an excellent promontory for sketching. The plein air studies are developed in the studio into oil paintings or very large charcoal drawings, where memory and emotion start to take over.' Sarah runs a popular life-drawing group near her home in Kirkton. www.sarahlongley.co.uk

Introduction – Patricia McCarthy

This double issue has taken quite some time to put together. The very title 'Irish Poets in the UK', which seemed so straightforward at first, threw up quite a few complexities and led to bigger considerations, such as what is national identity and is it, after all, important to being a poet. Most people know of the troubled history Ireland has had with England.

In terms of poetry, however, it seems that 'home' is often a place in the head – the 'Lake Isle of Innisfree'. Grey Gowrie puts this well in his poem 'Marches': 'the mind's secret: to live, live, walking against a wind / in Wales, in the mind, that lets you live in Ireland'. Michael Longley, in his *Sidelines: Selected Prose 1962-2015* (Enitharmon), calls his 'soul landscape' his 'first glimpse of wilderness in the Atlantic light' from the cottage in the remote Carrigskeewaun in County Mayo, his preferred home. And the landscape around this home often 'looks like a sodden Ithaca', the two places overlapping irrespective of time. As a well-versed classicist – he very modestly says, ' It was Homer who spoke to us across the millennia. I was only his mouthpiece' – he continues the comparison: 'The magical simile with which Homer compares the campfires on the plain of Troy to the night sky has often reminded me of County Mayo where, in the electric-light-free-darkness, I can gaze up into the depths of the Milky Way'. He enlarges upon the notion of 'place' and 'home':

> Carrigskeewaun provides me with the template for experiencing all other places and keeps me sensitive… The bones of the landscape make me feel in my own bones how provisional dwelling and home are. In 'Remembering Carrigskeewaun' I say: 'Home is a hollow between the waves,/ A clump of nettles, feathery winds'…

How could anyone say it better?

This issue of *Agenda* draws together not just the Irish and English, but also groups within these two general groups such as Irish poets brought up in Ireland but who come to reside in the UK, poets brought up here but whose parents were migrants of one sort or another. And then, of course, there is the great band of Northern Irish poets who are differently Irish in the UK, since Northern Ireland remains part of the UK. Here there are two splinter groups: poets (such as Heaney, Montague) brought up in the Catholic religion, and those linked to the Protestant ascendancy such as Derek Mahon, and Michael Longley English by birth but brought up and a long-time resident in the North of Ireland – all of whom, of course, transcend the limits of their tribe.

I myself am someone who writes poetry in the UK but who was brought up from the age of eight in the Republic of Ireland. I am half-Irish but feel more Irish than English. I had an Irish father (from West Cork), and an English mother who hailed from Yorkshire. The poems I wrote in my twenties were published in the main places in Dublin, especially in *The Irish Times* – and in Hayden Murphy's famous *Broadsheet* (see his essay in the following pages). Brendan Kennelly was, for many years, my mentor. He got me to send him every poem I wrote and he would comment on it and send back a letter in his distinctive black-ink handwriting – I have a whole bundle of those letters to this day. Now I have lived in the countryside in England for so long, my poems have been adopted here, after a big gap when I hid them away in drawers, though the *Irish Times* (that published my very first poem ever) still honours me by choosing one every now and then, and I would like to offer this elegy that was in *The Irish Times* fairly recently:

There, still

to Annie

Along the rush-lined boreens of Brackloon
I see you still, your long evening shadow
strung between glades pulled around you
like shawls after a bald mountain spell.
As if you have forgotten, simply, to phone –

and are there, about to pick up the receiver,
raging with me for not keeping in touch.
I hear you confess how scared you felt
at the ticks from the bracken, stuck
to your skin, sucking the blood's weather

from your body over penitential stones
in the descent on Croagh Patrick's steep side.
When kittiwakes cried out for you, my hand,
I said, would hold yours, pull you back
from the cliffs of your high cheekbones

that in the past you had fallen over, spattered
with Atlantic salt. I can't wait for your voice
to come through again, crackling along a line
wild with fuschia whose red bells you ring
at close-calling times. How I chatted

7

about my visit, perched on a breath – soon,
yes soon, promising to swing with you in trees,
on tides, in hammocks of green light.
The silence between us, softly familiar, creeps
along the rush-lined boreens of Brackloon.

Dennis O'Driscoll, a great ambassador for poetry and a great personal friend, wrote quite some time ago about the unique situation Northern Irish poets find themselves in with their hybrid culture, facing across the Irish Sea to England and at the same time looking across to the border with the Irish Republic; then also looking into themselves. They can embrace, he inferred, and get their work published in all three territories. This brings us to another way Irish poets can 'be' in the UK, via their own published works. For example big names such as Heaney was always published by Faber, Longley by Oxford and Cape, Peter McDonald by Carcanet. Many poets from the Republic are transferring their loyalties, now, it seems, from excellent Irish publishers such as the Dedalus Press, The Gallery Press, Salmon Poetry, the relatively new Doire Press, the Blackstaff Press in Northern Ireland – to big publishing houses such as Bloodaxe, and Carcanet. Perhaps they feel their work will get a wider readership here. However, with numerous small poetry presses springing up almost from nowhere, including online, and, dare I say, too much poetry (some not of very high quality) being published, with too few readers, I am not so sure that this will be so. In this issue, I cannot take on Southern Irish poets published over here but will include some and have reviews of poets such as Eiléan Ní Chuilleanáin, Pat Boran, Moya Cannon, Mary O'Donnell in the next more general anthology issue of *Agenda* due out before the end of this year. I always encourage poetry from Ireland as Seamus himself endorsed when I took over the editorship of *Agenda* not far off twenty years ago.

Indeed, *Agenda* the journal brought out a special Irish issue in 1996, guest-edited by me in William Cookson's time; there had been a Heaney at 50 issue, then, later we brought out Montague at 75, and an Atlantic Crossings issue in 2008 (with work from both the US and Ireland, including a 50th Birthday Celebration for Greg Delanty). Nearly every journal since I took over the sole editorship in January 2003 has been sprinkled with Irish poets. Then Agenda Editions (*Agenda*'s separate small publishing house for individual collections) has published Montague's *A Smile Between the Stones*, translated from the French of Claude Esteban, Desmond O'Grady's *Seven Arab Odes*, and his *Kurdish Poems of Love and Liberty*, Steven O'Brien's first collection *Dark Hill Dreams*, Joseph Horgan's *An Unscheduled Life* with pictures by Brian Whelan. Gary Allen's *Iscariot's Dream*, followed by *Mexico* – as well as collections by myself. All these can be found on *Agenda*'s website www.agendapoetry.co.uk

Time, now, to let the contributors here speak for themselves in their own unique voices, but let us conclude with the singing voice of Michael Longley who shows in this moving poem 'Greenshank' from *A Hundred Doors* what the place, or 'home', has meant to him, means still to him and will mean hopefully to someone after he has gone:

> When I've left Carrigskeewaun for the last time,
> I hope you discover something I've overlooked,
> Greenshanks, say, two or three, elegantly probing
> Where sand from the white strand and the burial mound
> Blows in. How long will Corragaun remain a lake?
> If I had to choose a bird call for reminding you,
> The greenshank's estuarial fluting would do.

* * *

W. B. Yeats inspires a work of art proposed for London

The great Irish poet grew up in Bedford Park in west London, and lived there as a young man with his family. Bedford Park became a model for the Garden City movement, and a place of Bohemian enlightenment, egalitarian, spiritual, feminist. Cahal Dallat, the poet and critic, has taken the lead in commissioning a sculpture from Conrad Shawcross. R.A. Conrad's design is called *Enwrought Light*, from Yeats' poem 'He Wishes for the Cloths of Heaven':

> Enwrought with golden and silver light
> The blue and the dim and the dark cloths
> Of night and light and the half-light

'The artwork will catch ambient light, day and night, picking up on the theme of light which runs through Yeats' poems.' It is to stand outside St Michael & All Angels' Church. The funding has been generous, but more is needed: pledges are welcome until 20 July. https://www.spacehive.com/yeats-bedfordpark-artwork/pledge

Note:
By a strange coincidence the title of this issue, *Tread softly* comes from the first two words of the last line of this memorable poem, 'Tread softly because you tread on my dreams'.

Portrait of my father (i) by Sarah Longley

Michael Longley

A Bouquet of poems for *Agenda*

Quatrains

i

What did they talk about on picnic trips,
The concentration camp's senior staff?
To whom did they post their happy photos,
'Lots of love from all of us at Auschwitz'?

ii

They put up a Christmas tree in Auschwitz
And stacked as presents underneath the tree
Bodies of prisoners who had died that day.
Then the assembled ranks sang 'Silent Night'.

iii

The deadly smoke belching night and day
And screams from the tortured and dying
Meant that birds stopped singing at Auschwitz.
Sanity was remembering their names.

Ravine

In a quiet Polish ravine
Two German soldiers with rifles
Can murder so many women.
Oh, their ageing breasts look sore.
Keep your blouses on, my dear ones.

Lullaby

When a ghetto baby dies
the mother sings a lullaby
lullay my child lullay lullay
her breasts are weeping milk
lullay my child lullay lullay

Amateur

In his last years my dad took up painting,
Imagined landscapes to begin with – yachts
That snuggled in their harbour, overwhelmed
By a huge geranium in the foreground –
'I want to grab hold of the stem,' I said.
We hung it cheaply framed above the piano.
Then, a re-arranged Donegal – haystacks
Where they were needed, a red wheelbarrow,
A yellowish towpath going nowhere.
Prognathous, chain-smoking, an amateur
Leaning into perpetual summertime,
Squeezing rainbows onto a dinner plate,
My dad painted to please himself and me,
For eternity a weekend painter
'Should I move Muckish a little to the left?'

Takabuti

in the Ulster Museum

My granddaughters stare down at her,
A petite fashion-conscious Egyptian
Not much older than they are, her face
Darkened by incense and time, her linen
Eyeballs returning their gaze, her hand
By her side as though to welcome them,
Her foot poking out of the bandages
As though to follow them to the exit
And accompany the rest of their lives.

Origami

Why shouldn't they make use of my failures,
Early versions, outlines, my granddaughters
Conjuring frogs and birds out of scrap paper
And laying my lost words on a swan's wing?

Scrimshaw

The tooth of a sperm whale,
A walrus or narwhal tusk,
Space enough for scrimshaw –
His sweetheart's portrait
Scratched by a mariner
In the smelly fo'c'sle
Onto the loneliness
Of an oceanic voyage
Through bloodstained waters.

Winifred's Flowers

after Winifred Nicholson: a found poem

My paintbrush always gives
A tremor of pleasure when
I let it paint a flower – and I
Think I know why this is so –
Flowers mean different things
To different people – to some
They are trophies to decorate
Their dwellings (for this plastic
Flowers will do as well as
Real ones) – to some they are
Buttonholes for their conceit –
To botanists they are species
And tabulated categories –
To bees of course they are
Honey – to me they are the
Secret of the cosmos.

Seascape

You followed our father towards the end
And painted this picture of the ocean,
A mariner's desolate horizontal.
Is it up to me, Peter, to name the hue –
Lapis lazuli, spring gentian, larkspur
Or sapphire (our mother's engagement ring)?
I want to call the white streak spindrift.
The yellow horizon could be dawn or dusk.
Our father and you are dead, a soldier,
A sailor, the three of us amateurs
Looking out to sea for inspiration
And making it up as we go along.

Four Hearts

You were playing bridge on the day you died,
Catherine, my twin's widow, sister-in-law.
So, did you win or lose bidding four hearts?
I was listening to Mussorgsky's death songs
When I heard, and through the kitchen window
Watching a wren near the watering can
Search the brickwork of our home for spiders
And, balanced on suet-filled coconut shells,
Little birds putting on weight for winter.
Bird-gossip was part of our friendliness
As well as fags and gin 'n' tonic mischief
(Until I gave up both, 'traitor to the cause'
You joked, though in your way half serious).
Six long-tailed tits keep coming and going.

Bouquet

Your whisper on the phone
I cannot understand
Though I pretend I can.
Soon I shall send a wreath.

These words in the meantime
Are just a wee bouquet:
Rain-bent autumn crocus,
Honeysuckle tendrils.

Funeral

The day Catherine died
Sarah found a dead wren
Outside her studio:
She lifted it up
On a teaspoon and
Carried it with care
To its bracken grave.

Beech Bowls

Roger Bennett, woodturner,
Has turned into four bowls
Storm-damage, the long arm
Gale and old age removed
From our mighty beech, bowls
With inky contour-lines
And spalting scribbles for
Great-grandchildren to hold
As though at a picnic
Underneath the canopy.

Portrait of my father (ii)

Michael Longley

A Ghost Among Ghosts

In 1998 I wrote 'A Perpetual One-Night Stand', an essay about four of
my favourite jazz musicians. Bix Beiderbecke came from a white middle-
class family who lived in Davenport on the Mississippi. He was the first
white man to play great jazz. My parents came from Clapham Common in
London to live in Belfast twelve years before my twin and I were born in
1939. When I wrote my tribute 'To Bix Beiderbecke' in my mid-twenties I
wondered if I might be the first Englishman to write Irish poetry.

Ireland has provided me with most of the data from which I try to make
sense of experience. My cultural hinterland takes in my hometown of Belfast
with its embracing counties Antrim and Down, and the island's western
seaboard, most especially counties Mayo and Clare where I have found my
soul-landscapes, Carrigskeewaun and the Burren. So, I am an Irish poet or
I am nothing. Nevertheless, there is no way I would disown my Britannic
background, the nobility of my father's old-fashioned patriotism (he served
in both world wars) or my mother's lovely accent and enduring English
viewpoint. For me, the Good Friday Agreement of 1998 was a relief. It
allowed me to feel Irish and British, either or both or neither.

'Where is my father's house, where my father?' I ask in 'Second Sight', a
poem I wrote in the late 1970s about visiting London to search for traces of
the relatives I never knew:

> I have brought the *Pocket Guide to London*,
> My *Map of the Underground*, an address –
> A lover looking for somewhere to live,
> A ghost among ghosts of aunts and uncles
> Who crowd around me to give directions.

Peter McDonald

Abroad Thoughts, From Home

I am, I suppose, pretty much against labels of all kinds when it comes to poetry and poets. By now, after some decades of being both a critic of poetry and a published poet, I am not at all sure what most of those labels really mean. I have been told, for instance, that I am a 'formalist' poet; but this leaves me at a complete loss, I'm afraid. It strikes me, for a start, that all poets are formalists of one kind of another – but I don't think that's really what is at issue in deploying this particular term. Often, perhaps, 'formalist' is just useful shorthand for boring, dutiful, or simply old: and I'm perfectly willing to be called all of those things (the last, come to think of it, isn't really in question). The term can also, importantly, describe the kinds of company (living and dead) that a poet keeps, as though it were the name of a gang. Yet I've never (so far as I know) sat down determined to write a poem in a specific form, and the specific forms that have cropped up in my poems are not – I hope – mechanical templates. As a poet, I am no more a formalist than I am an avant-garde experimentalist. What's more, a poet (when she or he is writing a poem, anyhow) shouldn't be any kind of '-ist'. They should be far too busy for that.

So yes, I'm uneasy about labels. This is more acutely the case once we move past those faintly academic '-ist's and '-ism's into the world of labels which plenty of people besides poets are compelled to wear (and which, sometimes, they try to remove). I have a pretty unenviable collection of these (for starters, just try using 'male', 'middle-aged', 'heterosexual', 'academic', and 'white' as parts of a blurb, and see how far you get), but again I feel the need to make some kind of weak protest against them, in the knowledge that any struggle against such labelling is utterly in vain. And it may be in itself, well, utterly vain – best to admit that before going any further. I am – another admission to get out of the way right now – the author of a book about poetry called *Mistaken Identities*, published as long ago as 1997, which tried to resist identity-labelling as part of critical routine (and as bad politics to boot): with hindsight it's safe to say I picked a fight there, and lost. Identity – let's make this sound better by slamming it into the plural, *identities* – comprehensively won. So far as I can see, identity-driven art, like identity-driven politics, is by now more or less the only show in town. I'm contented enough not to be in any poetry-show, so this doesn't bother me overmuch; though I do deplore it even so, and feel obliged to maintain (still) that in the long run no good can come of it.

(Nobody's listening, I need hardly add.)

All of this is something of a run-up to a very difficult issue indeed, another issue of name-calling where straight responses are *de rigeur* and yet also – for me – next to impossible. Am I 'Irish' (which, if I want to be described as an Irish poet in Britain, I would have to be)? This needs to be faced, for I do feel, as a matter of fact, increasingly Irish as a poet: or at least, I can't very well see what else I am. Still, though, *am* I 'Irish'? And in that case what kind of 'Irish' am I, exactly?

From some angles, I'm not very Irish at all. That 1997 book, for example, elicited the response (in *The Irish Times*, no less), 'The man's a Brit!' And that was true enough, in its way. I could try beginning my answer with the facts: I was born in Belfast, to Protestant (and Unionist) parents, and lived there for the first eighteen years of my life, through the most intense years of the Troubles. I grew up on a fairly deprived housing estate, from which I and my family were burnt out by the local paramilitaries in the mid-1970s (my father had gone to work during the Ulster Workers' strike, being more anti-strikes than he was pro-Paisley), and I was fortunate enough to have a grammar school education on the other side of town, which in turn delivered me to the undergraduate place in Oxford which I took up in 1980. I spent the next three years between Oxford (where I worked unfashionably hard) and Belfast (where I fell amongst poets, and worked not at all). By the mid-80s, I was a graduate student, still at Oxford but now for more of the year, where I wrote a thesis that was to grow into a book about Louis MacNeice. Then I tried – when jobs were thin on the ground – to get a job. I managed that, and have been working in English universities ever since. I married an Englishwoman, whose father was half-Irish and half-German: he regarded identity-labelling with long-habituated irony (a historian, he was once introduced at a seminar by David Starkey as someone who combined the wit and charm of the Germans with the methodical rigour and seriousness of the Irish). Over the last thirty years, I have spent a good deal of time in Ireland, and I did my best to see my parents securely through their old age: as an only child, I had a lot to do, and now that I am finally an orphan, there are few reasons to go back.

So, am I Irish? Well, I've been called that often enough, and many times not with charitable intent. I'm temperamentally unsuited to the world of slighted dignity and cultivated resentment, but I do have to conclude that, to the English, I'm as Irish as makes no odds: in Oxford, at the very peculiar institution of Christ Church, where I've worked for over twenty years now, I've certainly been on the receiving end of anti-Irish remarks from people in positions of authority, and probably (if I cared enough to think about it) it's true I have lost out professionally on this or that as a result of the subtle

– but real, and deep – prejudices of senior English 'colleagues' over the years. But really, I've done all right: I've done much better, anyway, than might ever have been expected of someone from my background, and I'm not going to start complaining.

And yet, since we're speaking of backgrounds, my own sense of myself was not ever an 'Irish' one – to put it mildly. I grew up thinking of myself as Northern Irish, Unionist, British (and Protestant), not as Irish, nationalist (and Catholic): from the beginning, I was trained in attention to and cultivation of difference, and in a kind of deep, historically proud belief in aboriginal, inalienable identity. All of that was, I now think, in the nature of a willed mass hallucination, both historically conditioned and historically flawed, and yet it was undeniably real at the time. (From time to time it can become real to me even today.) But now, as I near the end of my fifties, I feel more definitely Irish than I ever did when living in Belfast all those years ago, in that lost and frightened time.

Are there 'political' aspects of all this, ways in which I can be newly labelled? I hope not, and yet I expect so. In truth, I myself have no great interest in poets' political beliefs or affiliations: these are usually irrelevant to their art (if the art is good), just as they are (sadly) essential to their art when the art is something other than good. This is not a widely shared view. But, for what it's worth, I'll put my cards on the table – the hand I currently hold, at any rate. I feel on the whole that events are drawing Northern Ireland into a position where unity (of some kind, and doubtless a constitutionally complicated one) with the Republic of Ireland is inevitable; and I think that this would be more a good thing than a bad thing, if handled in the right ways. It could not be a victory for one 'side', any more than it could be a defeat for another. But England is headed somewhere else, somewhere that does not have room (or funds) for Northern Ireland, or indeed for Scotland. Brexit may or may not turn out to be economically crazy, but it's undoubtedly an act of collective self-harm in cultural terms, a closing of the doors that is also a closing of the mind which a majority of the English have desired, consciously or not, for several decades. It's a triumph of identity, and it was completely foreseeable. From all of this, I don't need to ask to be counted out, for in some ways it counts me out already.

As I say, though, the political musings of poets strike me as basically irrelevant; almost always, they are banal, and either arrogant or weakly self-serving. I shouldn't be too hard on poets, I know, for poets are no worse than most people (and certainly no better). Still, my unscientific sense of contemporary poetry engaged in its modern equivalent of table-talk, on social media and sometimes traditional media too, is that many, many writers are all too eager to be labelled, and to label others; that politics have a large role to play in all this (political allegiances being so easy to announce and broadcast); and that poetry itself is often the last thing to surprise, upset, or bewilder all of those identities, busily firing off the right opinions about whatever is in this week's news, braying solidarity with things they barely understand, and generally congratulating themselves on their uniform – often, regulated – uniquenesses.

My own poetry isn't something I write about. I hope, in any case, that it can speak for itself, even if what it has to offer is disappointing for some (as I'm sure it is). Yet I suppose *not* writing about my own work could be taken as a sign of arrogance, too, when really it's just something I can't do very well, and in which I see little point. Life is too short for literary self-analysis, especially when there are poems to be written (and, for someone like me who is also a critic, great poems of the past to be done justice to). Despite all this, I think I can say one or two things about what I've done, which may not be too far off the mark. (Though of course, I'll not be bound by them: next week's poem could nullify the lot, for all I know.)

In poetry, my 'voice' (remember that term? a slippery one always, but still necessary) is very specifically a voice from Belfast – east Belfast, from the 1970s or so onwards. This is how I hear the rhythm of a line, the pitch of its diction, the timing and direction of its syntax: it won't change. Beyond this, the things I write 'about' (careful with that term too: a poem 'about' a sunset isn't the same thing as a sunset) are Irish things, insofar as they come from my own memories and experiences, and from my interests and obsessions. Following from that, the poems are caught up in feelings (love, hope, grief, delight – the usual things that may well be common to us, but which matter for the poems because they happen to *me*, and not to anyone else) so completely that they don't have the leisure to fret about an intellectual dimension: no true poem can ever be concerned about what it 'means', in that intellectual sense. So, compared to the flashy, academically hyper-alert and assiduously streetwise poems out there, I expect my poems are – well, a bit stupid, and certainly not up to date with their reading or their breadth of contemporary reference. That's OK, though: I'd far rather be able to make someone cry or feel happy than drive them into debt for a doctoral thesis.

This is all partly a matter of ambition, or getting ambition right. My heart sinks every time I encounter someone who announces their ambition to become a poet, hungry for tips on making it to that position (an all too unexalted one, if they but knew). Yet ambition should rest in the poetry, not the writer. The truest ambition for any line of poetry is not, surely, to be studied, or to chime in with a slogan, but to be remembered; and lines of poetry, I suggest, are remembered less for what they're 'about', for what they're supposedly saying, than for their rhythm, rhyme, diction, their sense of being inevitable and irreplaceable; and for the new things which, by that process, they can make you see and feel. A real line of poetry, like a real poem, puts something new into the world, by placing language that wasn't there before among the resources of individual minds, where it can make itself come to life, repeatedly in all kinds of circumstances.

Saying all of this, I realise, puts me in a contemporary minority. Plenty of 'British', and plenty of 'Irish' poets would want to disown such sentiments; and plenty of academics would feel the need to 'interrogate' them (what a sinister word that is, and how often they use it: but of course the really advanced people are all post-liberals, and probably feel some kind of affinity with users of aggressive interrogation techniques).

I don't especially mind being in a minority of one, if need be. In terms of the work of writing, though, the real question is whether or not it makes a difference to have some kind of national context within which you could place that condition. Is it better to be 'British' in your isolation, or 'Irish' in the same situation? Maybe it's possible to be just as productively alone under both designations? In the end – and yes, we are (and I am) getting to the end now – the whole thing may come down to a question of what's more comfortable, in that it makes fewer demands on attention that should be spending itself on the proper work. Just at present, I'd feel more comfortable *in* Ireland, and do rather wish someone would deliver me from the clammy grip of Christ Church, though I suspect I'm too old to pass as Cinderella: this doesn't mean that wearing an 'Irish' label is comfortable for me (patently, it's not), but it does perhaps make that less of an issue, less something to be worried about. And there is, we know, already more than enough in the world about which we can all agree to worry. Poetry, though, can be relied upon to take care of itself – quietly, with its labels off, and untroubled by the fact that almost nobody is looking.

Bernard O'Donoghue

An Irish Poet in the UK

The term 'Irish poet in the UK' seems an unduly grand definition for me; I became an Irish person in the U.K. when I was 16 in 1962 when my father, a farmer from the north of County Cork, died, and my mother came back to teach History in her native Manchester. I came too and was fortunately allowed to join the sixth form at St Bede's College grammar school where my grandfather and his brothers had been students at the end of the nineteenth century. One of them, John McNulty, taught there before being appointed as Catholic Bishop of Nottingham in 1932. I mention this not in a vaunting spirit but rather the reverse: without having some ulterior connexion of this kind, it is hard to see how I could have been admitted to that school in the competitive era of the 11+. It also indicates a way in which I was an untypical Irish immigrant to Manchester; most of my contemporaries that I met in St Brendan's Irish Club worked in the building industry. So there was a Manchester pre-history; my mother had studied History at the University of Manchester in the 1930s, taught by Lewis Namier and A.J.P.Taylor, and with her father George McNulty she watched Manchester City at Maine Road and the Lancashire cricket team at Old Trafford. Her father sang in the Halle Choir at the Free Trade Hall, and she was pictured on the steps of the Manchester Central Library the day it was opened in July 1934.

In my life of course all this *is* pre-history. I was born in Cullen, Co Cork, in December 1945 and had a very contented childhood there. The Manchester connexion was operative there too though; when my two elder sisters and I were growing up in Cullen, we were sent children's books by my mother's sister and her mother in Manchester, so we grew up balanced between the curriculum of the Irish National School (my sister Margaret did Irish in her degree at UCC, and we were all thoroughly taught in the language at the local countryside primary school) and the classics of English children's literature: *Peter Pan, The Wind in the Willows* and *Alice*. The school texts were divided across English and Irish subjects: Thomas Davis's 'The Geraldines' celebrating the Norman-derived Fitzgeralds (the name of several of our schoolfriends)

> These Geraldines! These Geraldines! – rain wears away the rock,
> And time may wear away the tribe that stood the battle's shock;
> But ever, sure, while one is left of all that honoured race,
> In front of Ireland's chivalry is that Fitzgerald's place.

side by side with Walter de la Mare's 'Listeners' –

> 'Is there anybody there?' said the traveller
> Knocking on the moonlit door.
> And his horse in the silence champed the grasses
> Of the forest's ferny floor.

At the same stage we were learning poems in Irish, like Douglas Hyde's 'An Gleann inar tógadh mé', 'The Glen where I was reared'

> 'Ó áit go háit ba bhreá mo shiúl' ('Fine was my walk from place to place').

I often reflect on how strange it was that we were simultaneously taught in our cradle language, English, and in Irish which linguistically was new to us without any sense of its relative unfamiliarity.

When I joined the sixth form in Manchester, I was in a curious position. Having previously existed in an Irish world with a greater than usual contact with England through my mother, I was now an Irish interloper into an English setting. What made this particularly difficult was the fact that I shared a culture with the parents of many of my student contemporaries who were not particularly excited by the arrival among them of someone who belonged to a past world they associated with their parents. I was Irish to a distinctive degree that I hadn't been before. So, in doing English (my joint favourite subject with Latin which I loved and knew very well from being taught by Joe Garvey from Brosna, Co Kerry), I did *King Lear* and Donne and *Wuthering Heights* for A Level, while leading a private reading life of my own: the stories of Frank O'Connor, Yeats, Joyce, Kerryman Brendan Kennelly's *Penguin Book of Irish Verse*. Like my mother before me, I went to watch Man City at Maine Road; but in the long summer holidays, back in Millstreet parish, my obsession was with the Cork football team.

When, at the next stage I came to Oxford in 1965 to study English at Lincoln College, there was a remarkable turnround. The Irishness which at St Bede's was an unofficial thing between consenting outsiders and nothing for young people to flaunt suddenly was culturally fashionable even amongst the young in the age of the Beatles (Liverpool Irish), Bob Dylan and the Dubliners. One of my friends at Lincoln, Keith Bloomfield, became the British Ambassador in Nepal; but in student days he and I went together to Irish music sessions in the pubs of Oxford, run by Mick Henry, a musician and builder from Mayo who became one of my closest friends. This complicated heritage was reflected in my first ever publication in the school magazine *Baeda*, called 'Irishman at Oxford' which ended

'It's a very fair country', referring to my adoptive country. I remember a BBC television programme in 1964 made by the English-born *Observer* journalist Patrick O'Donovan called 'I'm a Stranger Here Myself' which expressed the Ireland-England dilemma with great eloquence. Much later it was the subject of poems of mine like 'Westering Home' and 'Bona-Fide Travellers', and of the volume *Here Nor There*.

Back in 1965 the English literature curriculum at Oxford ended in 1900 and was strictly confined to 'British' writers. Americans were excluded; Irish writers were admissible for as long as Ireland was part of Britain. I rather riskily wrote on Yeats in my final examination: risky both because he ceased to be British in 1922 and because he doggedly went on writing for another 39 years after the cut-off date of 1900. When I returned to Oxford in 1969 to do a postgraduate course, I briefly considered researching on Yeats, my favourite poet. But I worked on Middle English: both to incorporate my other favourite poet Chaucer, and to play to a kind of cultural strength, the writings of the Catholic tradition – Dante, Langland, lyric poems and the medieval mystics.

In 1970 came my first active encounter with modern Irish poetry. Tom Paulin arrived at Lincoln College to do graduate work (on the poetry of Thomas Hardy). He introduced me to the poems of Seamus Heaney which before that I had seen only occasionally in the pages of *The New Statesman* or *The Listener* or Irish journals like *Fortnight* or *Hibernia*. The next year I started to teach Old and Middle English at Magdalen College where the tutor in modern literature, already an established poet, was John Fuller who ran a college poetry gathering, the Florio Society. I began to submit poems to it in 1972, mostly on Irish themes. The first poem I ever published was called 'Morning in Beara', set in the beautiful Beara peninsula in West Cork (which I visited every summer) and with a title translating a celebrated Irish language poem, 'Maidin i mBéarra'. It was further confirmation of the acceptability – fashionability even – of Irishness in English culture at the time, despite the fraught condition of political conditions in Northern Ireland of that era. I became increasingly aware of the contemporary Irish poets, though I wouldn't have dreamed of describing myself as one of their number. My friend Tom Paulin was published by Faber; Heaney came to read in Oxford. Other names became prominent: Muldoon, Boland, Longley, Mahon, and Irish Language poets at University College Cork who followed Seán Ó Riordáin: Nuala Ní Dhómhnaill, Liam Ó Muirthile and others.

In 1982 John Fuller, who was a tireless promoter of the poetry of his students and friends, published a pamphlet of my poems called *Razorblades and Pencils*. It was one of a series of beautiful little books which John published in his Sycamore Press, printed on an ancient printing press in his garage. During the same period, I was (briefly) one of the editors of *Oxford Poetry,* published from Magdalen. In that capacity I was in touch with various Irish poets and authorities on poetry, notably Dennis O'Driscoll who was, like John Fuller, an extraordinarily disinterested proponent of poetry. He introduced me to the work of Richard Murphy and we published two of his sonnets from *The Price of Stone* in *Oxford Poetry.* Murphy had been a student of C.S.Lewis's at Magdalen in the 1940s.

In 1985 Craig Raine published some of my poems in Faber's *Poetry Introduction* 6. O'Driscoll also put me in touch with Peter Fallon who published my book *Poaching Rights* in Gallery Press in Dublin in 1987, the most prominent of a series of strokes of good fortune. I am giving this extensive account to illustrate the fact that I had it both ways from the first: combining the very considerable literary advantages of professional life in Oxford with the more surprising advantage of being Irish there in the 1960s and onwards. I had become 'an Irish poet in England': an improbable outcome from where I started. After *Poaching Rights,* I was published by Chatto and Windus from 1991 onwards; my ex-student and fellow-editor of *Oxford Poetry* Mick Imlah had become poetry editor there.

It was a similar case of 'being in the right place at the right time' in my teaching career. I was employed by Magdalen in 1971 as a lecturer in Medieval English (which I loved, for the reasons I have given) and I remained in that post until 1995 (when I moved to a Fellowship in English at Wadham College). But from the 1980s onwards, the relatively new field of 'Irish Studies' was rapidly growing. The Yeats industry in Oxford was thriving, through the presence there of Richard Ellmann, Jon Stallworthy and especially John Kelly, the editor of the magisterial edition of the poet's letters. But what was not so available on the strength in the English faculty there was someone with a knowledge of the Irish language for the growing number of graduate students arriving from Ireland and elsewhere. I had done school Irish for eleven years in the distant past (when it was of course just the norm in Southern Ireland), so I got involved in the supervision of graduates in topics like 'Yeats and the Irish language' or 'Douglas Hyde and the deanglicizing of Ireland'. And of course in 1989 Heaney arrived as Professor of Poetry.

In more recent times, there is a galaxy of writers who grew up in the Irish Republic publishing poetry in England, as the lists of English publishers like Carcanet and Bloodaxe: writers like Martina Evans, Tara Bergin and many others. But when I was first published in England, the only other writer of that background who was publishing in England that I was aware of was Matthew Sweeney. I suppose the moral is that writers very commonly belong to a culturally mixed heritage. But I think I was an unusually fortunate instance of that because my material – what I wrote about – was life in County Cork, present and, more commonly, past. My real life in the modern world stood at a distance both from Ireland and from the Middle Ages – a distance which I think may be salutary in operating between two polarities. It has been essential for me to travel to and from Ireland as often as possible (along with my Ireland-loving wife from the Danelaw in the North-East of England who is a Professor of Icelandic literature and my Ireland-loving children). The 'here nor there' principle still applies, and the prohibition on travelling in the current crisis is as painful for me as it is for everyone else. The batteries are waiting to be revitalised as they approach their last charge.

Broadsheets 1967-1978, Poetry, Prose and Graphics

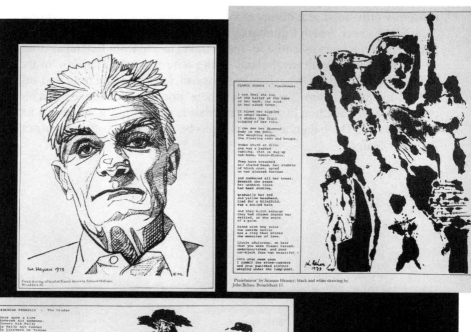

Pencil drawing of head of Francis Stuart by Edward McGuire.
Broadsheet 20.

Punishment' by Seamus Heaney; black and white drawing by
John Behan. Broadsheet 17.

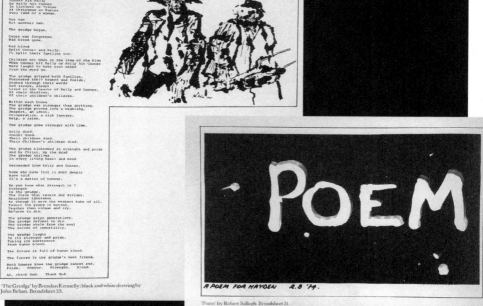

'The Grudge' by Brendan Kennelly; black and white drawing by
John Behan. Broadsheet 23.

'Poem' by Robert Ballagh. Broadsheet 21.

Hayden Murphy

Broadsheet Years in Dublin and Edinburgh:

My Coming of Age in the summer of 1966 coincided with two events that have had long-term consequences in my adult life. In July, on the basis of one poem published in *Icarus*, the literary magazine for Trinity College Dublin, I was invited to 'represent Ireland' at *Arlington Une*, a prolonged five-day weekend gathering to celebrate Concrete, Spatial and Sound Poetry in a converted water mill in Bibury, Gloucestershire. Surrounded by William Morris artefacts were typographical and verbal conundrums from all over the globe. I became introduced to a new literary world, new cultural attitudes, alternatives to the somewhat sedate Dublin of my birth. Friends were made, addresses exchanged. I was actively encouraged to go to Edinburgh the following month where further readings and introductions would be made. The wonders of the Edinburgh International festival were revealed to me in that summer of Culture. Since then the treat has become a tradition. Festival is my annual cultural seminar in the self-designated Athens of the North.

I returned to Dublin rejuvenated, adrift and ambitious to create 'a new platform for the arts'. Literary Dublin was in a lull: James Liddy's *Arena* (1963-64) was shut, Brian Lynch had closed *The Holy Door*, John Jordan was attempting to span generations in *Poetry Ireland* and the courageous Michael Smith was still to draw *The Lace Curtain*. I teamed up with street-wise Benedict Ryan. I had become fascinated by the broadsides and chapbooks of the early 19th century which were sold on street corners, in pubs and theatres. I suggested a slight adaptation: a two sided sheet, 18" x 15", in a print run of 1,000, with a minimum charge of 6d. Prosaic and pedant that I was, I called it *Broadsheet*.

The first issue appeared on 14th February 1967. Twenty six contributors from six countries in three languages (Irish, Welsh, English), ranging from the traditional to the concrete. There was a typographically experimental translation of André Breton's *Le Porte Bat*. The latter came from Jean Paul Pittion, junior lecturer in the French Department, TCD. He welcomed my 'adjustments', declared our collaboration 'the new surreal'.

The first issue was well received. Ben decided his work was done and left for northern France. I had surplus contributions, sufficient for a second issue. I put No.2 together in late May. I then began a routine way of selling the issues. I went on a pub crawl. The historian Roy Foster noted this vendor as being an 'inspirational part' of his youthful pub-life in the late 60s (*TLS* 24th October 2019). I then took it with me to readings in London, placing it in bookshops with Bob Cobbing and Bernard Stone. In Norwich its arrival in Giles Bristow's legendary bookshop in Bridewell Alley led to weekly readings in early August before I left for Edinburgh. There it became a word-of-mouth best seller and I left the remaining copies in Richard Demarco's Gallery in Melville Street.

For the third issue I became ambitious and produced five sheets bound in silver ribbon. Graphics and illustrations marked every side. Artists ranged from John Behan and John Furnival to a two-sided sheet devoted to exponents of the Concrete art from around the world. The frontpiece was a striking image of a collapsing alphabet by French artist/poet Julien Blaine. Prose pieces from John Jordan and James Liddy sat with more traditional poems from over seventy poets. These included five lines from Patrick Kavanagh affectionately addressed to me. His biographer Antoinette Quinn (2001) believes these may have been the last lines he wrote. He died November 30th 1967. Broadsheet Three, dedicated to him, appeared in the shops of Dublin three weeks later. It has become a collector's item, if a somewhat messy one. In 250 of the run of 1000, on the concrete page, I had inserted a reversible highly coloured sachet of real honey.

The next issue came with five sheets safely tucked and folded into a brown envelope. The same mix of poems, prose and graphics. Notably it enclosed a poster size version of Julien Blain's dramatic *To Have the Evil Eye of the Dragon Fly*. On 16th June 1969, when visiting Julien and his family in Paris, I inserted a small reproduction of that piece into the stones of one of James Joyce's Paris residences in the 30s. So Bloomsday became allied to Broadsheet.

For practical and financial reasons the multi-page editions had to stop. I reverted to a single sheet with No. 5. John Behan' dramatic Toreador embrace headed Luke Kelly's declamatory ballad *For What Died the Sons of Roisín*. The singer/author summoned me to bring all unsold copies to a *Dubliners* concert in the National Stadium. Bespoke tailor and fellow regular in Mc Daids, Liam Brady, helped me with transport. When we arrived we found Luke had set up selling stalls for us at the entrance/exits to the mains bars in the packed arena (5000). As the interval approached he stopped the music to 'tell' the verses and announced he would only give autographs on purchased copies of Broadsheet. Within half-an-hour we were sold out. The future, financially, looked sweet.

I challenged the optimism by devoting a full side of No. 6 to the 'reversibles' of the Benedictine monk Dom Sylvester Houedard. He advised they be read 'in a fine drizzle of small frogs'. It was not a seller in the pubs of Dublin or indeed anywhere though it did have an afterlife. In December 1974, when I had agreed to address the first International Gay Rights

Congress in Edinburgh, the organisers asked if I had any copies. I had them left right and centre propping up tables and chairs in my small mews house in Herbert Lane. I posted bundles of them ahead of my arrival in Scotland where I found they had already sold out. Apparently the monk had become a cult figure among the Gay community following his dramatic appearance at the Albert Festival Hall *'Wholly Communion'* poetry readings in 1965.

Irish artist Pauline Bewick's line drawing accompanied Eiléan Ní Chuilleanáin's poem *Pictures* in the next issue. It was an easy sell. However a one-off Prose issue (8a) attracted Police attention. Sales were prohibited. It contained a single short story of a vulnerable homosexual in Dublin. At the time people told me it was 'an expensive folly' but I have no regrets. It too had an afterlife in Edinburgh in 1974 when the so called 'clandestine' issue sold out at readings connected to the actually Congress.

I reverted to bad habits with No 10. I suspect I was thinking of stopping. I set up six sheets, pasted down over a hundred contributions, introduced colour on three of them and folded all in an envelope carrying a portrait by Edward McGuire RHA. It was going to be costly. Rescue came from an unlikely source. Sean Bourke's memoir of how he had 'sprung' British spy George Blake was a best seller in Ireland. The journalist Rosita Sweetman approached him and he agreed to 'pick up' the printing bill (nearly £500). This was fortunate as it did not sell well and attracted criticism with John Jordan describing 'Broadsheet a most improper publication' (Irish Press: 3rd April 1971).

For the next ten issues I reverted to my original format and endured hangovers for literature. No. 17 featured Seamus Heaney's poem *Punishment* illustrated by John Behan. Professor Adrian Frazier of Galway University speculates in *John Behan: The Bull of Sheriff Street* (2015) on how the artist may have influenced the poet to make changes to the text I received and published. It may be of interest to *Agenda* readers that No.19 (October 1973) featured the poem *Search* by one Patricia Mc Carthy.

Broadsheet 21 was a splendid six sheet, calendar style, production. With over 100 contributors it attracted praise from both *The Irish Times* and *The Sunday Times* and nominations for press awards. It was launched, Bloomsday 1974, with an exhibition of the original art works in Grogans of South William Street, Dublin. The festivities were interrupted by two member of the Arts Council (Eilis Dillon and John Behan) arriving to announce that the printing bill would be covered by the Mandarins of Merrion Square.

The real Final Issue appeared on June 16th 1978. Composed of six double-sided broadsheets stapled together. It carried contact addresses in Dublin (Grogans), London (publishers Martin Brian & O'Keeffe) and Edinburgh where a year later I was to settle.

In February 1983 the National Library of Scotland mounted a retrospective exhibition *Broadsheet: 1967-1978: Poetry Prose and Graphics*. In an editorial for *Poetry Ireland* (No.7, 1984) John Jordan now spoke of Broadsheet as 'a valiant, wayward, outrageous and off-gold enterprise'.

In December 1999, in Kings College London, it was the subject of a lecture on its role in Irish Literature in the 60s/70s. The speaker was Dr Jean Paul Pittion, emeritus Professor Trinity College, Dublin and Tours.

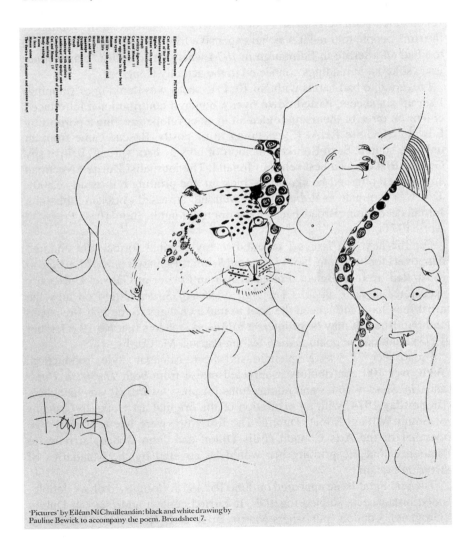

'Pictures' by Eiléan Ní Chuilleanáin; black and white drawing by Pauline Bewick to accompany the poem. Broadsheet 7.

Edna Longley

The Currency of Poetry

[The following article is reprinted from a special issue, in September 2020, of the Northern Irish magazine *Fortnight*: born 1970, died 2012. The special issue – or resurrection – marked the half-century since *Fortnight*'s founding. It included reflections on those difficult years, together with updates on matters such as 'Evolving Irish attitudes to Brexit Britain and to Northern Ireland'; 'The on-going Bill of Rights debate'; 'What next for dealing with the past' (Northern Ireland's perennial paradox). It should be said that, like all such journals, *Fortnight* had its ups and downs, and its temporal title would soon prove over-optimistic. Yet it survived for a long time, perhaps powered by faith in a better future. To quote a former editor: 'almost every significant political and literary figure in Ireland wrote for it', and 'some of its analysis and proposals influenced political developments in Northern Ireland'. The thinking of *Fortnight*'s editors and contributors, perhaps its very existence, had a role in the Belfast Agreement. Further, *Fortnight*'s subtitle, 'politics, arts and culture', indicates that not all the thinking was political. It might also suggest that this triad had/ has an unusual proximity in Northern Ireland. The angle of my own article on poetry reflects that proximity, as do the poems – by Leontia Flynn, Stephen Sexton, Colette Bryce and Michael Longley – with which their authors allowed me to accompany it.]

***

When an anniversary issue of *Fortnight* was mooted, contributors were asked 'to avoid too much of a historical rather than a forward-looking approach'. We all know that the hand of history is liable to seize Irish pens. But history particularly complicates my own topic: 'current poetry'. 'Current' poetry includes the *Iliad*, whereas yesterday's Lockdown lyric may already be out of date. So, in this impressionistic catch-up, 'currency' will not only signify how some of our poets position some of their poems in socio-cultural terms. It will also cover the position of poetry itself since *Fortnight* shut up shop in 2012. Introducing their anthology, *New Poets from the North of Ireland* (2016), Sinéad Morrissey and Stephen Connolly were upbeat: 'In spite of its small size and population, the North of Ireland, it seems, has a knack for *continuing* to produce celebrated poets.' (It would be vulgar to list the poetry prizes won since 2012.)

Poetry does pick up Zeitgeist-shifts, even if its prescience can't be gauged for years or centuries. In *The Parkinson's Poems* (2016) Frank Ormsby says: 'I suspect that I have already finished writing my Parkinson's poems (in the same way that I have written my poems about the Northern Ireland Troubles).' Yet Ormsby's 'Troubles' poems, like those of other poets, remain current. To talk of 'post-Agreement' poetry (or post-Viral poetry) is to categorise prematurely. Poems about war are also poems about peace. Contrasting the time-zones of poetry and 'the news' (in *Poetry and its Others*, 2013), the American critic Jahan Ramazani argues that in poetry the 'present' can be 'multiplied, echoed, and stretched into the past and future by poetic form and memory'. Ciaran Carson's last poems, in *Still Life* (2019), underscore his unique ability to align the rhythms of a present-tense poem with the movement of time and history. His poem on Poussin's 'A Landscape with a Calm' traverses various pasts before ending with the poet's self-image as a 'musician driving the stock-still moment steadily into the future'.

Back in the day, Carson said that his poems might be 'of the Troubles' rather than 'about' them. '*Of*' suggests how civil war invades and intensifies every cranny of life; and thus might reconfigure the traditions, genres and forms of poetry itself. Northern Irish poetry since 1968 has still been only partially read for its aesthetic or metaphysical import. Fran Brearton wrote in 2003: 'Poets from Northern Ireland have been the focus of extensive academic and media attention over the last thirty years, sometimes to the detriment of proper consideration of their work in the island's poetic traditions as a whole, and in the context of British, Irish and American cultural exchange and influence.' It's a good sign that more recent critical overviews feature matters like 'theology', 'classical presences', 'domestic space', 'ecology'. The extraordinary four-page list of 'Credits', which Stephen Sexton attaches to his long poem *If All the World and Love Were Young* (2019), implies how much can get into any poem: Damselflies, Dante, eelgrass, Hale-Bopp, the Albert Bridge, MacNeice's 'Snow', 'The Omagh Bomb (15th August, 1998)', cancer, 'stone-throwing, dismay, enmity, a future'. Sexton's elegiac sequence, despite its structural debt to Super Mario World (1990) – now history too – takes its title from Sir Walter Raleigh; while its deepest structures (like those of digital games) hark back to the *Iliad* and *Odyssey*.

Yet dark history remains in the poetic kaleidoscope. Poetry broadly mirrors society here in that the Troubles have not ceased to figure as an uneasy collective unconscious, which can, unpredictably, rise to the surface. The trees of Ormsby's 'Willow Forest' 'hang their heads/ over a history that, now memorialised,/ could be forgotten'. Carson's poem on Velasquez's 'Old Woman Cooking Eggs' recalls a Belfast pub in 1973 as a 'chiaroscuro' where 'Every so often of an afternoon we'd hear a muffled thunder'. The reproduction of Velasquez's painting behind the bar now becomes indelibly highlighted with hindsight: 'How close to life, the texture of the blood red, papery dried red/ Pepper pods!' Poetic memory (as in Wilfred Owen's 'elegies') also criticises less complex memorials. More than any other poet, Carson has exposed a Belfast unconscious; while also turning the city into a matrix of metamorphic possibilities – city-planners, please note. Poets continue to remix Belfast's seismic historical strata, from the Titanic to the Titanic Quarter: not without peaceful epiphanies. In 'The Singing Gates' (*On Balance*, 2017) Morrissey uses an accidental Aeolian Harp on Divis mountain to symbolise getting difficult history into poetic perspective. In *Still Life* Carson's walks through the Waterworks Park (a pastoral locus for Ormsby too) counter some of the darkness. But perhaps Paul Muldoon's 'Belfast Hymn', 'commissioned by the Grand Central Hotel', is a trifle too heart-warming: 'We rejoice in .../ gooseberry jam, Nambarrie tea/ Irwin's malt bread ...'. Are those really on the menu?

The Troubles may surface as brief allusion or enter a poem's foreground. Gail McConnell's 'Type Face' (2016) harrowingly exemplifies the latter. This sequence represents McConnell as researching the death of her prison-officer father. Once again, 'poetic form and memory', poetry's critique and renewal of language, question other ways of formatting history. McConnell begins: 'The thing I notice noticing's the font/ in the Historical Enquiries Team Report./ It's Comic Sans ...'. And: 'The word I've tried hard not to use is *murdered*'. McConnell, Morrissey, Sexton, Colette Bryce and Leontia Flynn are among poets who variously speak as 'children' of the Troubles. Bryce's Derry sequence, in *The Whole & Rain-domed Universe* (2014), starts with the poet falling into memory as into an ominous snow-drift: 'I stepped from my skis, and stumbled in, like childhood,/ knee-deep, waist-deep, chest-deep'. The title-poem of Flynn's *The Radio* (2017) filters the language of 'the news' through personal experience in a stanza that switches between discursive and evocative effects:

> The radio hoots and mutters, hoots and mutters,
> out of the dark each morning of my childhood.
> A kind of plaintive, reedy oboe note –
> Deadlock ... it mutters, *firearms ... Warrenpoint*;
> *Just before two this morning ... talks between ...*

Poetry is a good place to look for that problematic concept 'legacy' – or post-traumatic syndrome.

In a more positive sense, there's still something 'collective' going on.

Poets who now mainly live across the border, the Irish Sea or the Atlantic – e.g. Bryce, Muldoon, Gerald Dawe, Alan Gillis, Miriam Gamble, Nick Laird, Peter McDonald – will home northwards in their work. This may confirm that a return to origins (Heaney's Mossbawn unconscious) is intrinsic to the poetic impulse. And 'new poets' don't displace old poets. Ormsby, after long silences, has had a creative Indian Summer, despite calling one book *The Darkness of Snow* (2017). The title-poem of Derek Mahon's *Against the Clock* (2018) enjoins: 'Don't give in or give up, Sophocles, obviously,/ who wrote *Colonus* in his ninetieth year/ is our exemplar'. (Mahon, who has died since this article originally appeared, followed his exemplar by publishing a last book, *Washing Up*, at the last minute.) Few poets have written more powerfully against the clock than did Carson, whose resurrection as a poet was indexed to his dying from cancer; who proved Wallace Stevens's dictum: 'Death is the mother of beauty'. More closely than other literary modes, poetry entangles the generations in 'tradition'. Sexton salutes '*il professore*, *il maestro*, Ciaran Carson to whom I am indebted and to whom language itself is indebted'. Tradition ramifies temporally and globally. But, to quote Morrissey and Connolly:

> A pre-existing place-specific poetry canon with which we all remain in conversation, and the education provided by a dynamic poetry culture, arguably unrivalled in these islands, are hugely important in challenging and sustaining succeeding generations of poets. The Seamus Heaney Centre for Poetry at Queen's University Belfast, founded in 2003 … has also played a decisive role in fostering new poetic talent.

Heaney's death was a huge local as well as global shock. Giving his imprimatur to the Centre named for him and his art, he had endorsed 'the intent, self-sustaining, unpredictably liberating activity that goes on at a centre for poetry'. The Centre now commemorates Heaney; as does the enterprising Bellaghy Homeplace. Radiations from the Centre include the Sunflower poetry readings, organised by Stephen Connolly and Manuela Moser, who also publish the impressive series of 'Lifeboat' pamphlets (named for a poem by Michael Longley). These pamphlets mark the dedication to poetry amongst younger writers such as themselves, Padraig Regan, Caitlin Newby and Scott McKendry. Directed by Carson for a decade, the Centre also nurtures other modes of 'creative writing'. But it has primarily and crucially exemplified the 'conversations' that remake poetic tradition. Flynn's moving elegy for Heaney, 'August 30th 2013', is precisely that: a conversation in which she clears her own aesthetic space: 'But this is *my* idiom'. Flynn also clears some critical space: 'waxing operatic/ about how Lit-Crit culture's getting sick/ still makes me seem a touch arthritic/ if not potentially undemocratic'. Flynn's irony attacks literary influencers who put 'diversity' before verse in a way that devalues poetry's currency. Himself a very fine critic, Heaney wanted the Heaney Centre to involve criticism, in all its guises, lest conversations about poetry should degenerate into cosy chats. Poems are not selfies. Poetry has largely weathered – and often mediated – our indigenous 'identity politics'. This may induce wariness when other brands are uncritically invoked.

Conversation between *poems* is ultimately aesthetic. Northern Irish poetry has long been noted for its renovations of 'traditional' form: line, stanza, rhyme. In *Frolic and Detour* (2019), we find Muldoon still ringing the changes on rhyme and sonnet as structural principles. Yet poets remain open to all formal possibilities. Witness Regan's and Jan Carson's distinctive prose poems. Before the Troubles, a few northern poets were obsessed with poetry itself: with its aesthetic essence. This actually stood them in good stead during the Troubles. It may also explain the persistence of poetry here. Simon Armitage recently called poetry a 'marginal' medium (although that's why he likes it). Poetry has a little more 'currency' in these parts. But perhaps what matters is poets' continuing faith that it matters.

The Troubles

Think of the children
Behind the coffins.
Look sorrow in the face.
Call those thirty years
The Years of Disgrace.

Michael Longley, from Angel Hill (2017)

Malone Hoard

In coffeeshops on the Lisburn Road we eat with mobile phones beside our plates: our shiny black talismans. Sixteen-year-old girls *LOL*-ing, hoarding our trove of digital images: text and symbol. Uploading, but less loading up treasure – not to grind an axe – than laying the present moment, heavy and useless, ceremonially in the thick dust of itself. Our lives, bright relics.

Leontia Flynn, from The Radio (2017)

Butter Bridge 2

The traffic on the Albert Bridge crawls stubbornly from the city.
Crews are coxed along the river by a voice through a megaphone.
This is I suppose what faith is a voice that steers into the dark.
A murmuration of starlings is a smudge on the setting sun
or the huge and happy thumbprint of Shigeru Miyamoto.

> Stephen Sexton, from *If All the World and Love Were Young* (2019)

The Analyst's Couch

I was not there when the soldier was shot, so I didn't see him
carried up the street and manoeuvred
through our propped front door.
Who took his weight, the women or the soldiers?
Blood, seeping into the cushions, dark brown stuff
like HP sauce, soaking thoroughly into the foam, the worn
upholstery of the enemy. *Laid out on the sofa
of eternity*, its faded tweed, its sag, its hoard
of household smells, fluff and pens, small change
and lost buttons. *Am I making this up?* Its animalness.
Paw-footed, it pads from the room, the soldier lying bleeding on its back.
No it doesn't.

> Colette Bryce, from *Selected Poems* (2017)

Belinda Cooke

From the 'Back of Beyond' to Westland Row

> *You go back, but the flower of youth is gone: you've got*
> *grey hair; and you're goin' down the little boreen, to*
> *see your mam again; but your mam is gone and the*
> *crows is flyin' in the bloody chimney and your house is*
> *open to every cow in the village, to use it: nobody's*
> *there anymore...*
>
> John Neary, Swinford,
Memories of a Long Distance Kiddy[1]

When young, we don't know the questions to ask, older, there is no one left to answer them – just ever shifting memories and lacunae as we piece together the lives that went before us....

'Home'...

...it starts simply enough, arriving late evening to the small scattering of houses lights that made up Johnsforth, our family's village, near Swinford, Mayo, on to two weeks trailing our grandfather in new wellingtons through muck and rushes; nights him warming our clothes by the fire; morning, kicked out of the 'outchat'[2] by our grandmother, in his Long Johns to ignite the turf with bacon rind, boil eggs in tin cans on the open fire beneath that great black kettle – *Radio Eirean*'s brogue waxing lyrical on the merits of *Kerrygold* butter, our eyes drawn to a train motion lamp always travelling, always going nowhere....

Granny and Grandad? No. Only grandad was the larger than life survivor of history – The Easter Rising, single-handed builder of the *Waldorf Astoria*[3] – she just a fellow traveller, a minor subplot, but for her gold front tooth, her animal-like cry when we'd arrive and depart, and her *Flight of the Valkyries* sweep down, to click off the newly acquired television set

---

[1] (London, 1994), cited in Ultan Cowley, *The Men who Built Britain: a History of the Irish Navvy*, (Dublin, Wolfhound Press, 2001), p. 29-30. A seasonal worker circa 1910 who transferred to nomadic labour in the 1920s.

[2] The outshot (or hag) was an area protruding from the main cottage wall, just enough for a mattress. It was beloved of the older generations who even if bedbound could still take part in the storytelling and gossip.

[3] Knocked down and rebuilt 1929-1931 to make way for the Empire State Building (1931).

protected by its tri-coloured screen: 'That's enough of that!' It would take my mother's tantalising, shifting memory fragments, for these two small lives to transform to a grand shared story, punctuated with departures and home-spun wisdom: 'Don't be complaining about the mess, when the mess is gone, they'll be gone'.

But wait a little. Let's, for the moment, keep with us Babyboomers as we recall the wider Irish landscape of the sixties, envying the inhabitants of this rural idyll of welcoming relatives and Irish 'characters' far from our urban streets and country walks blocked off by 'Trespassers will be prosecuted' signs – an alienation well captured in these lines of Carol Ann Duffy:

> I remember my tongue
> shedding its skin like a snake, my voice
> in the classroom sounding just like the rest. Do I think
> I only lost a river, culture, speech, sense of first space
> and the right place?
>
>   'Originally'[4]

So… it could be our first car, the *Popular*, it could be the train to Holyhead – my father corralling us in to back 'big' money on poker or pontoon, licking his thumb as he dealt the cards: 'Come on Blin – you're the banker' – me, eight or nine, feeling like some hardcore crony down the local *Granby*. The ferry crossing has us vomiting around him: 'Jees, it's awful rough, I nearly spilt these pints bringing them back from the bar'. Next stop, Dublin's main conduit *Westland Row*[5], its taxis like *Doctor Who* Tardises, cramming in our family of five with two more adults on top: 'Sure they'll be plenty of room when we shut the door!' Finally, we are stopping off at various watering holes on the road west, with locals pouring forth at the bar: 'Shakespeare came here once – he said they were the best days of his life.'

To get inside small towns like Swinford with their cathedral-like Catholic churches read Maeve Binchy[6], read Alice Taylor[7] – books that did the rounds of female family members when first published – portraying an idealised community of comfort and safety. So, for us that is what it was. Everyone

---

[4] *Meantime* (London, Anvil Press Poetry, 1993).

[5] Now Dublin Pearse Railway Station, renamed in 1966 during the 50th Anniversary of the Easter Rising, in tribute to two brothers who took part. Its most famous image is that of crowds welcoming returning prisoners of that conflict. This has always been Ireland's sole route between all parts of Ireland and the boat.

[6] *Light a Penny Candle, Echoes, Firefly Summer* (London, Arrow Books, 1982,1985,1987).

[7] *School Through the Fields, Quench the Lamp, The Night Before Christmas* (Dingle, Brandon 1988, 1991, 1994).

attended mass. Everyone bowled out afterwards into *Mellets* and other local pubs, doubling up as grocers, where children were allowed to drink inside, treated with pink and white ice creams and red lemonade – ours to own till the last day when neighbours and relatives would see us off, with fly looks, shoving bright orange fifty bob notes into our fists.

With equal ease we accepted the unacceptable: 'Travellers' on the margins of the town and society, great tarpaulin tents direct onto tarmac – one of their women with a powerful weathered face, flaming red hair and a great tartan blanket wrapped up to feign a baby in arms – to my mother's wry amusement, exclusion well captured in my brother David's late night encounter with my grandfather's words echoing: 'you couldn't trust a tinker / who would steal both eyes / from out the back of your head':

> Out late one night in our teens
> with no lift home, my brother and I
> walked past them, making our way
> along an unlit road. The night
> country-dark, a black sky welded
> to earth, our ears were suddenly filled
> with the yelps of their dogs untethered.
>
> Panicked, we stood directionless
> till one of the men came over
> to leash them, his coaxing voice
> like a neighbour's as he asked
> which part we were from, our visiting
> accent sounding alien to us
> in the shock of re-established quiet.

'Travellers'[8]

Was it my brother or was it the traveller who was the greater outsider here?... Fitting prelude, perhaps to so many questions....

Heading for the Boat...

'God bless Holy Ireland! – What use is Ireland to us!' My father, the pragmatist's oft repeated words, in spite of the tacky carthorse statue on the fireplace as a reminder of 'home'. Departing feet, and a weak economy

---

[8] *Workhorses* (Wardwood Publishing, 2012).

propped up by cash-filled letters home was the norm from the Famine to the late eighties when my cousins were still leaving, for England, America and elsewhere. Woe betide a family member who sent an 'empty letter'. It was to take the Civil Servant T K Whitaker's[9] creativity to spearhead a shift from Eamon Devalera's isolationist policies, to The Celtic Tiger[10] of the later eighties. We may have resented the sounds of our own English voices, yet we were the successful diaspora free of a stagnant, repressive Ireland of limited choice, employment, or possibilities of marriage.

My family's emigration covers two postwar waves of emigration – its causes both simple and complex, with land at its heart: a mix of Ireland's struggle for independence along with outdated traditions and 'ways of going on' that turned Ireland into a nation shooting itself in the foot. Mayo's Michael Davitt founded The Irish Land League[11] where he campaigned with some success for tenants to be able to own their own. A fitting hero, given both my parents came from 'The Back of Beyond' – Mayo and Sligo – offering some of the poorest land in the country, and with it the largest economic exodus for all but the few who would inherit the farm.

Ironically, though seasonal migration was the norm, the main trigger for mass emigration was the post famine shift from tillage to grazing. Previously the bottom rung of peasantry could eke out a living with a patch of potatoes repeatedly subdivided among children who would go on to marry at will. However, later avoidance of overdependence on the potato led to single inheritance ownership, to help increase farm size as well as large families as an insurance policy of financial support for parents, with most non-inheriting children forced to emigrate. Women required substantial dowries to marry into land, to help increase farm size, or to provide a dowry for a prospective husband's sister. Thus marriages were late, and, along with mass migration, led to population decline and with it a repressed society of forced celibacy and segregation of the sexes. Arthur Hughes's sickly hue of the couple in his painting *The Long Engagement*[12] is an apt image of such repression.

Such social stagnation, combined with unremittent political turmoil helps fill in some of the blanks of my grandparents' early lives. Like a mirror

---

[9] (1916–2017) Irish civil servant who served as Governor of Bank of Ireland 1969-1976 and a Senator 1977 credited with a pivotal role in the economic development of Ireland.

[10] Mid-1990s late 2000s boom fuelled by foreign direct investment, dampened by subsequent post 2008 crash.

[11] Irish political organisation which sought to abolish landlordism enabling tenant farmers to own the land they worked on, period known as the Land War. The Michael Davitt Museum is located in Straide in Co Mayo on the N58 route between Ballyvary and Foxford.

[12] *The Long Engagement*. Arthur Hughes, 1859

image of World War One recruitment itself, things started out upbeat enough, with the town's proud commemorative postcard of its willing Irish Volunteers in 1914, ostensibly defenders of the realm – a kind of Home Guard – but in fact (knowingly or not) being trained for the forthcoming Easter Rising. My grandfather and a cousin there at the front. Two years later – just weeks before the Rising itself, they would be married. Much may be surmise, but the unimaginable, unrelenting suffering after 1916 is not. Universal disgust at the executions of its leaders triggered the War of Independence – the Tan Wars – exacerbated by the arrival of Royal Irish Constabulary Auxiliaries[13] and the Black and Tans whose atrocities shocked even the English public, Prime Minister Lloyd George included. An all too brief truce led to the Home Rule Treaty and the formation of the Irish Free State (1922-23), which had little chance to thrive due to the onset of the heartbreakingly divisive Civil War (1922-23) over the terms of that Treaty. County Councils and brigades became divided over Collins' Home Rule, versus Éamon de Valera's demand for full independence – contentious to this day – resulting in even more men heading for America, sickened at so much blood and even more so at this final act of killing their own – why am I no longer surprised at my mother's words: 'They never talked about it.'

The Easter Rising: 1916 Myth and Reality

MacDonagh and MacBride
And Connolly and Pearse
Now and in time to be,
Wherever green is worn,
Are changed, changed utterly:
A terrible beauty is born
'1916'[14]

Was it someone famous who said: literature is our compensation for mortality? – books, if not exactly that, can often be a comfort against the disappointment of debunked family myths. Yeats above – though criticised for it at the time – offers a vexed approach to the Rising leaders' heroism: whipped up by his glorious tone so we almost miss the sting in the tail of

---

[13] Resident RICs came from within the communities they served so there was initially much condemnation of the 1916-1919 attacks on RIC constables and barracks. However, in mid-1920, the arrival of RIC auxiliaries (ex UK army officers) hand in hand with war-hardened Black and Tans transformed public opinion into seeing the war as direct attack on Ireland by England.

[14] *Collected Poems* by W B Yeats (London, Macmillan, 1933).

what such single-mindedness might trigger – but books are good at taking us away from the black and white, allowing the 'do' of 'What did you do in the war daddy'[15] to become a much more weighted word. In *War and Peace*, Leo Tolstoy gives Napoleon a bad press in favour of the peasant Platon Karataev, who is the novel's real hero due to his simple life – history driven not by 'great' leaders' decisions but by the cumulative choices of each individual – take it as read, war's a messy business. George Eliot tops this with her gentle satirising of Dorothea in *Middlemarch*, for her naive attempts to perform heroic acts on behalf of the poor, before transforming her into a spiritually finer hero, encapsulated in these immaculate concluding lines:

> But the effect of her being on those around her was incalculably diffusive: for the growing good of the world is partly dependent on unhistoric acts; and that things are not so ill with you and me as they might have been is half owing to the number who lived faithfully a hidden life, and rest in unvisited tombs.

These words resonate strongly as I piece together the social and historic push and pull factors that increasingly highlight the ease of my life built on the tough labour and extended partings of theirs.

This said, everyone loves a hero and lacking facts, it's natural to create your own – I'd always assumed some dramatic dash from the provinces down to Dublin for the main event; the reality was far from that... after all the mythology it is a little disappointing to learn how the last minute cancellation of orders due to the capture of Roger Casement's arms supply[16] meant few of the Volunteers outside of Dublin took part at all. Indeed, even without this confusion there had never been an intention for full participation for county brigades, but rather non-combative roles such as disrupting communication links. It is also shocking to discover that many of the poorer inhabitants were not at all supportive of the Rising, looting shops at every opportunity, while Dubliners in general were annoyed at the disruption to the everyday workings of the city.

---

[15] Famous war poster of WW1 much castigated later.

[16] Roger Casement's idealism was seen in his earlier UK diplomatic career, in particular his work on behalf of the Congo rubber workers. He subsequently transferred his total allegiance to Irish Independence. He had been in Germany since 1914 liaising with Germany to organise Irish prisoners-of-war into a brigade for the Rising, as well as raising arms. He arrived in Tralee Bay on board a German U-boat midnight on Holy Thursday, only to be arrested. This had a significant impact nationally, leading to the Volunteers leader Eoin MacNeill's countermanding order calling off the mobilisation of his men for the Rising. Casement's 'Speech from the Dock' before being hanged as a traitor goes down as one of the greatest speeches in history.

Its success, however, lay in the long-term effects, largely due to Britain's ill-chosen decision to put the leaders to death. It was only this that enabled Yeats' 'terrible beauty' to be unleashed, reflected in these prophetic words of Tom Clarke to his wife on the night before his execution:

> All of us going out tonight believe we have saved the soul of Ireland. We have struck the first successful blow to freedom. Freedom is coming. But between this and freedom Ireland will go through hell. But Ireland will never lie down again.[17]

These executions of the leaders and other known associates dramatically turned public opinion away from the slow constitutional change to a demand for full independence, transforming what set out as a hit-and-miss affair into Ireland's bloody yet finally successful liberation.

With respect to my grandfather, the period between the Rising and that mythological sole construction of the *Waldorf Astoria*[18] in New York one can only imagine[19]. My grandfather, aged twenty eight at the time of the Rising, would have been part of the East Mayo Brigade of the Irish Volunteers, but how far he continued to participate throughout the period up to 1922 is unknown. The towns were very proud of their volunteers so one would assume he still took part in the illegal marches during the War of Independence. Though the Rising had been a missed affair, in and around Swinford there was no shortage of violent conflict that neither fighter nor civilian could be free of during this awful period. By the time of the Civil War itself he would be well into his thirties with a family of six. All the same, as a Michael Collins'[20] man, one can't imagine that he wasn't among the many who headed across fields to avoid road blocks to hear Collins

---

[17] Dominic Price, *The Flame and the Candle: War and Mayo 1919-1924* (Cork, The Collins Press, 2012), p. 272.

[18] The building of the Waldorf and the Empire State Building are part of the same story; with respect to the latter, the role of Irish (and Scandinavian) construction workers is well documented. See Tom Deignan's *Irish men who built the Empire State Building* in Irishcentral.com, Dec 14, 2009. Deignan emphasises the impact the Irish Civil war had on providing this new wave of Irish immigrants keen to put the past behind them and help create an American icon. He also flags up an interesting novel on the subject, Tom Kelly's *Empire Rising, (*New York, Farrar Strauss and Giroux, 2005).

[19] The most in-depth account of this period in Mayo is Dominic Price's book noted above. See also Cormac O'Malley, *The Men will talk to Me: Mayo Interviews by Ernie O'Malley (*Cork, Mercier Press, 2014*).* largely focusing on the Independence side of the Civil War. Conor Mcmamara's *War and Revolution in the West of Ireland: Galway 1913-1922 (*Dublin, Irish Academic Press, 2018) is also close to home.

[20] The Neil Jordan movie *Michael Collins* (1996) claimed by some to be a little too generous towards the iconography of Collins is nevertheless a great way into the story for newcomers.

speak when he came to Castlebar.

But, perhaps now is the time to recall George Eliot's words – the 'unhistoric acts' of those 'who rest in unvisited tombs' – namely the hard fact of the Irish emigrants' lives: work and money sent home from fierce family loyalty. Nothing can airbrush away my grandfather's five years away from home from 1925-1930 in New York labouring – a reliable man, not a great drinker, faithfully sending the cheques home as my mother tells us: 'When daddy posted the cheque to mammy, he was happy, he could relax.' A certain irony that he was rebuilding a luxury hotel having left a three-roomed cottage that housed both parents, a wife and six children and uncomprehending to us how such long-term relationships could be maintained. Gugliemo Marconi was transforming the world into a wireless network, but still there would have been only letters and no chance of a short trip home during that time. Even harder to picture the life of our grandmother, living with in-laws and running the farm – the one single lining in that cloud possibly being the five year gap from childbearing – what would be an almost regular event with that added bonus of some financial support.

The Invasion of the 'Biddy tribe' from the bogs of Ireland[21]

And, it is just at this very moment that, out of the shadows, comes another Keatsian 'Looking into Chapman's Homer' moment with a very recent utterance from my mother: 'Well, of course, mammy and her sisters went to America as well' – so it turns out my grandmother was in America well before her marriage to my grandfather, heading off around 1909-10, for five years. The story of Ireland's Mayo women is heroic in the extreme, given the drudgery of their lives, harrowingly documented in Maureen Langan-Egan's social history, *Women in Mayo: 1821-1851*[22] where she emphasises the degree to which they were treated as economic commodities. Whether they thrived depended on their ability to establish some independent income on top of their hellish workday trapped in badly ventilated cottages that defy description. After the collapse of Ireland's textile industry, no longer able to rely on craft skills, apart from selling eggs, those without a dowry were often seen as a liability.

No surprise, then that women outnumbered men in emigrating, working largely as live-in maids, and one can only be amazed at their earning capacities, often sending the bulk of their earnings home. Hasia Diner's

---

[21] Lynch-Brennan's *The Irish Bridgets: Irish immigrant women in domestic service in America. 1840-1930* (Syracuse Univ Press, 2009). p. 70

[22] (Galway, Galvia, 2016).

Erin's Daughters in America: Irish Immigrant Women in the Nineteenth Century[23] and Lynch-Brennan's *The Irish Bridgets: Irish immigrant women in domestic service in America. 1840-1930* – both thoroughly researched social histories – are a glorious paean to these women who combined fierce family loyalty, and *a carpe diem*, Sylvia Plath-style 'thumbs down on the dode's mode'[24] to counter the serious odds life had set against them. Both books take delight in digging out great, often hilarious, stories of these women's doings, particularly during periods of servant shortage... surely we, as readers, should have a little sympathy for these poor American ladies who simply 'can't get the staff these days' but who, nevertheless will still rather do anything than have an Irish – and worse *Catholic* – maid, can our hearts not go out to them trying to maintain the upper hand: 'No Irish need apply' or 'good Protestant girls only'. For these maids were such a trial, so badly trained in the niceties of serving at table, so unscrupulous as to hide broken crockery, yet having the nerve to demand high days and holidays off – surely they should realise live-in means *live in* and be at hand at all hours of the day and night and not to take shortcuts when blacking the stove, but above all no one with a heart could fail to agree that they should *at least* know their place – it simply isn't done to spend any money on oneself, getting decked out in the latest American fashions indisputably... it *must* be clear who is the mistress and who the maid.

One can only relish and admire, the way they didn't take life lying down. Living-in enabled them to save money, as well as develop and integrate more readily into American society than the men, leading to many success stories. Some became part of trade union movements. Then there is the 'unhistoric act' of Emily Dickinson's insubordinate maid who failed to burn her mistress's poems. Others went home with a dowry, having forewarned their parents to fix them up with a suitable partner. Some opted for an independent single life as preferable to a restrictive marriage back in Ireland. One of my great aunts ran an American boarding house before returning to buy property of her own, while my grandmother did indeed save a dowry before marrying my grandfather though when I asked: 'Was it arranged?' – 'Well they were neighbours...' came my mother's suitably ambiguous reply.

So, clearly, both my grandparents both did their part in establishing a safe and economically sound start for my mother. My grandfather's return in 1930 with a boat fare carefully saved for the event of his mother's death led to the births of first Helen and, then my mother, Noreen. But, though buffered by his American work, the farm alone was still not enough to live

---

[23] (Baltimore, John Hopkins Univ. Press. 1983).

[24] 'Morning Song', *Collected Poems*, Faber and Faber, 1963.

off, leading to more departures – this time England – only cut short due to compulsory evacuation of children during the Blitz. For this reason they headed back to Mayo. Clearly my grandfather had had enough of partings...

'If the man didn't drink it was ok, but if he drank the family had no chance'

This my mother's assessment of the haves and have-nots. Aged seven in Mayo, rather than a school girl in London, restored to us the idyllic *Johnsforth* of our childhoods for the future, as well as memories of her own childhood – filtered down to us in fragments... held together by the above dichotomy. Given the time, she had it pretty good but saw those around her who didn't: she had a father who'd be up to sort out the abusive teacher, but observed daily the suffering of the child who hadn't; she actually had shoes for school – but hid them in the hedge to 'keep down with the Jones'.

Her positive experiences coincide with those of Helen Taylor mentioned earlier: the transformative arrival of electricity; the magic and scariness of walking home late after the storyteller's late night tales[25]; austerity that made treats all the more special – smells of the special Christmas cake along with the Christmas Night[26] light in the window, her father sending gift oranges down the chimney because as she tells us: 'Daddy really believed in Father Christmas', and her mother's comfort at the sounds of so many children voices always playing in the fields outside – a presence more meaningful after so many partings.

But she also witnessed wretched poverty endemic to the forties – even when interspersed with hilarious asides: the woman above them who refused to send her children to school, forcing my mother home to fetch them to no avail. Regularly drunk on her homemade *poteen*, she finally made a trip to London to the amazing discovery that the London Tube 'wasn't made of rubber at all!'. Helen remembers visiting the family of a drunkard on the very day his wife died in childbirth – not one crust of bread in the house and the midwife holding out the newborn to her relatives: 'Who will take this baby'? – this the same house where the other children were minded by a disabled uncle and my mother's dread when duty called: 'Mammy wouldn't let me pass without going into offer help' — given her memories of his unwanted attentions. So many stories... of a more brutal time, of institutions and inadequate schooling: the young woman who broke out and headed back to her home now derelict and simply rolled there weeping in

---

[25] See Peig Sayers, *And Old Woman's Reflections: The Life of a Blasket island Storyteller*, trans. W.
   R. Rogers (O.U.P, 1962) to get a good example of the Irish oral storytelling tradition.

[26] Christmas Eve

the stinging nettles; the abusive master hogging the turf fire, and keeping a daily lookout in case the inspector came to call; the good master who did his best though education past primary would have to be paid for – and thus rationed for the few with a serious gift; stories of saving up for the kit to join the nuns, stories of late marriages, of old folk who still lived in houses shared with livestock who still believed in fairies....no end to the stories.... of a frozen if not decaying world, and in the midst of this, our grandfather, always they'd insist, 'a man before his time': generous to the Travellers, demanding the priest stop castigating people from the pulpit if they failed to contribute to the great stained-glass windows; pleading the case of a disabled neighbour stuck in the asylum: 'Payther! Get me out of here!' 'Oh yes,' says Helen, 'It was daddy who got him out'. Mayo in the forties, take it as read, an idyllic place...but only if you had someone to speak up for you...

'O, but we had a great time in those days in Camden'

Finally, it was time for Noreen and Helen to head for the boat, this time to London, for mum aged 16 initially working with her older sisters, at Onslow Court Hotel, Kensington, renowned for its macabre associations with the 'Acid bath murderer' John George Haigh,[27] before moving onto a farrier's in Camden, sharing a 'cosy' digs with Helen consisting of a single room completely filled by its put-up bed, where you could make tea without getting out of bed. Camden placed them into the heart of London's little Ireland – along with Kilburn, Cricklewood, Archway, Kentish Town and Shepherd's Bush, places long associated with Irish migration, initially where men came building roads and railways, later Irish nurses – thus enabling a home from home for newcomers. Here, they found continuing financial pressures and prejudice, only lessened with the arrival of the *Windrush* generation because then the landladies' 'No Irish' signs could be replaced with 'No Blacks' since, as my mother put it, 'At least we were white'. In spite of the expectations to send money home when earning a pittance, it was a heady time where you met Irish wherever you went, with men aplenty without all the restraints of the place they'd left, though for women smoking and drinking was taboo, 'in case it got back'. But, fixed up with the 'financial necessity of a boyfriend', you'd be able to scrape together the exorbitant half-crown for the great *craic* of the Irish dance halls: Camden's *Buffalo*, Cricklewood's *Galtymore*, Archways, *Gresham*, or the all-important *Round Tower* on the Holloway Road where my mum

---

[27] Convicted of murdering six, but claimed to have killed nine, which he disposed of using sulphuric acid before forging their signatures so he could sell off their substantial assets.

and dad were to meet.[28]

Enter John Cooke from Sligo, following the work, looking dapper with his spiv suit, Fairisle sweater, Brylcremed curls and temperance pioneer badge (for the benefit of his mother!), an image gleaned by us from our family photo of dad and Uncle Jim striding out across O'Connell Bridge in Dublin, energetic, ready for anything, and so, so young looking. It was only in 2016 I discovered that this was one of the thousands of photos, of people on the move caught by the street photographer Arthur Fields, son of a Jewish Ukrainian immigrant amazingly working there for over fifty years, creating a unique documentary of the 1930-80s Dublin era. These men would also be on the look out for women as part of the plan, yet, in the face of such practical necessities, men and women still managed to meet much-loved life partners, as Helen said, 'I'd see your mum and dad walk out in front and they'd always be in perfect step'. To this day mum also talks of the wonderful freedom of that time, as she made London her own, liberated by her bicycle racing about the city, with the courting side-benefit that dad could easily make up after rows, as he'd have to return the bike borrowed for late rides back to his digs. Later, we see Helen still to meet her perfect match meandering along with a relationship going nowhere, dad, five years older, also taking her under his wing: 'Now Helen, you want to be getting out of that relationship... ' Advice she took, but that's a story for another time...

What do you do for a living? – Tell them I'm a shorthanded shovelist!

> *I can only note that the past is beautiful because*
> *one never realises an emotion at the time. It*
> *expands later, and thus we don't have complete*
> *emotions about the present, only about the past.*
>   Virginia Woolf

So now, we the second generation 'outsiders', with our more vexed sense of identity, suddenly discover we are insiders after all – our lives entwined with these loving couples 'making it' – either in London's 'County Kilburn' or following the work to the nearby satellites of our home in Reading and the like. So, what did this mean in practice? – An extended family and community network all close by; Camden-style Irish dances and lessons in traditional Irish dancing; a fair share of alcoholism and an abundance of

---

[28] For an insight into this era see Catherine Dunne, *An Unconsidered People: the Irish in London* (Dublin, New Island, 2003) which covers ten interviews of various Irish immigrant experience in London, and in the dance halls.

Catholicism with its Sunday mass and Catholic primary schools dominated by Irish, Polish and the occasional Italian, where we learnt we had guilty, sinful souls, as well as lungs and hearts, and were trained up for First Communion before going on to secondary schools run by mainly Irish Nuns and Brothers... But all such cultural markers are just shadowy reminiscences set against the glorious, colourful impact of construction sites, for all of us, almost without exception, had dads who 'worked on the buildings'.

You didn't need to be Irish to know how central these road workers were to daily life, for they were everywhere on the street, in cast off suits for work clothes, often naked from the waist up, working shovels, pneumatic drills, and concrete mixers, with time to give young girls the 'glad eye' and older women a respectful passing of the time of day. And they might have remained there in our memories as just background, part of the (street) furniture, were it not for Ultan Cowley's labour of love, *The Men who Built Britain: a History of the Irish Navvy*[29], in celebration of their major contribution both to the industrial revolution and the postwar reconstruction of Britain. He provides fitting evidence, before automation, of their sheer shovelling power, combined with nerve and skill in many high-risk situations, such as the Manchester Ship Canal. Significantly he notes, also, their specialist knowledge as groundworkers and in their efficient running of sites, all taken very much for granted rather than financially rewarded. More tragically, Cowley also offers insights into the exploitation of these same workers due to the cash in the hand culture of the 'lump' which centred around pubs as employment exchanges, keeping many of these men outside the long-term protection of national insurance, the fall-out of which remains today with such men now marginalised both in the UK and Ireland.

Fortunately, in recent years, along with the many verbal testimonies in Cowley's work, a number of the more resilient of these workers have taken to writing about their experiences,[30] painting lively portraits of their rich cultural heritage, known above all for their *craic*, their wit – providing ample evidence of a trait Virginia Woolf noted on a trip to Ireland, describing it as a country full of poets. And it is this poetry that they passed down to us – either as wise pseudo-philosophical mores, or colourful utterances rising as naturally as air such as this explanation for leaving Ireland: 'Why does a man go anywhere?... He's got to go somewhere. What's the difference?

---

[29] See also his *McAlpine's Men: stories form the Sites*. (Co. Wexford: Potters yard press, 2010).

[30] For two notable ones see Sligo's Bob Kennedy, *On the Strength of a Ten Bob Note: A memoir of an Irish Emigrant*. (2014); and Donal Machamlaigh trans. V*alentin Iremonger, An Irish Navvy: the Diary of an Exile* (Cork, Collins press, pbk 2003). This last is particularly enlightening on the Gaelic speaking Connemara group of workers renowned for their brute strength as workers, and tendency to get into fights with Dubliners in particular.

He's got to live somewhere!'[31] My father's own job description was a complete mystery to me at the time, and has haunted my dreams ever since – 'Tell them I'm a shorthanded shovelist!' What lay at the heart of the banter was often a kind of heartening, inclusive cutting down to size – evidenced in nicknames that acted both doubled up as pseudonyms for tax purposes, and also attempts at keeping men from getting 'up themselves'. Thus we'd heard tales of 'Shtiff' ever insisting on some nice 'shtiff' concrete, or 'the ex-creamery manager' who spent too much of his time letting people know he'd come down in the world. My father was, by nature, fundamentally a gentle soul, but he loved to 'sound off' about 'shisters, toe rags, gobshites, latchikoes, boyos', with disdainful reference to 'yer man', 'your one' 'himself'– learning early that the world must be filled with those who might be out to get you – yet this wasn't what it was about at all, because no matter how vitriolic his abuse or character assassinations, it would always conclude with a dramatic volte face – 'Ah sure he's as good as gold, as sound as a pound'... Everyone's foibles were ultimately to be endured, enjoyed and absorbed into life's rich tapestry and nothing in life was to be taken too seriously.

So on reflection, mellow and ageing ourselves, it becomes clear what this inheritance from both parents and grandparents meant: an insightful psychological training in what made people tick, we were taught early to get 'copped on' to life's hurdles and the colourful humanity around us. We became givers and takers of advice – learnt our own homespun wisdom – and most importantly, particularly for those of us who love to write – we became if not bi-lingual at least bi-dialectical. Though deprived of a brogue as children, as adults we know we own our 'Father's voice' and how inseparable it is from a certain empathy, a certain humanity. My father died too early from a work-related accident in the fifties, shortly before the collapse of the Irish monopoly on building work, but he remains permanently now in my memory as a larger than life dark presence who moved in and out of the house with his dreamy easy-going personality and magically strange quirks – his idiosyncratic trait of being able to be asleep and awake at the same time. I still see him waving at us through the window when we were locked out but not awake enough to open the door – lifting his arms in a kind of dozy acknowledgement, relaxed there in his chair.

I went back to Ireland shortly after the anniversary of the Easter Rising in 2017, during the time of the referendum for same-sex marriage, and it

---

[31] John McGregor, *Arise You Gallant Sweeneys* outsidefilm@mail.com. See also a more recent short film: *We Built This City*, a project by the Irish Architecture Foundation as part of Irish Design 2015, by David O'Sullivan Dyehouse Films available to view on vimeo.

was transformed since my last visit at the end of the seventies. But step into *Mellets* for a Guinness and I am back there in spite of the shock of a Tesco's supermarket and murderous three-laned roads crisscrossing the old boreens. Heading back to Dublin with the wrong bus ticket, expecting problems, all I got was 'no you're grand, you're grand'. In Swinford itself, somewhat stunned at the sight of new parking meters (though no sign of traffic wardens) on asking which side of the road was safe to park, I was told: 'Well I think it's this side – but I wouldn't take it too seriously' – and all the Celtic Tiger monsters dissolved away and I was 'home' once more.

Sean O'Brien

Waterworks

Indifferent to sorrow as to time,
the rain is bouncing off the outhouse roof
to meet itself, for added emphasis.

If proof were needed, here is proof:
the sheer redundancy of days like this:
les très riches heures inside the glut of rhyme –

long days of impotent hyperbole and death,
dank-shadowed laurel-arch and dripping trellis,
while a mountainside collapses on a train

and we sit waiting for the minister to tell us
what's wrong now. We know he'll blame the rain
for raining and the poor for drawing breath,

but 'science shows' that we are the disease.
We cannot heal ourselves, nor wish to:
witness the pale rider writ in lemon juice

across the bottom of the contract, seen
only when you've put a match to it. Who knew
that all the *M & Ms* in Hell are brown?

The balsa mermaid in the bathroom
gazes with approval at her glass – it's been
brim-full forever but will never overbrim:

Unlike non-swimmers such as you and me,
she animates the world by being seen
at home in her *cathèdrale engloutie*.

It's raining in the library too, a drizzle
made of dust and all the dreaming hours
we used to think we could embezzle

from the stern recording angel on the desk.
Now even she must wipe her specs and ask
what odds it makes to exercise her powers

or not. Though poems should not mean but be,
all information tends to entropy:
What was the Word is emptied of itself

and speechless water rises through the stacks,
engulfing like a continental shelf,
implacable as death or income tax.

Precipitation looms on every front.
Life, it appears, is quite impossible
as well as everything that is the case.

Poor pelting slums and summer palaces
alike endure the rain, convinced that this will
all be over soon, although it won't.

   You style yourself an inner emigré,
sequestered till the whole thing goes away.
You spend your mornings burning loaves of bread,

and then begin the reading you have planned
With Heraclitus and Chateaubriand,
till downtime, 'Box of Rain', the Grateful Dead.

At three a.m., when other people drown,
you're sick of Nemo's submarine romance.
You search the bathroom for a sleeping pill.

The mermaid turns to look at you askance:
where is the optimism of the will?
Go to your desk and drink your poison down.

Rain seethes like tinnitus inside the ear
and floods the chambers of the mind, as though
with hydra that will feast upon the brain

at leisure, but not kill it. You will undergo
an incomplete noyade, and you will hear
each time the creatures set to work again.

And do beware the demon of analogy
when casual similitudes invoke
the facts at which you merely meant to glance:

rain equals plagues and plagues R us. You wake
between the Devil and the deep blue sea
to find the nightmare real. You had your chance.

Yes, we'll be happy and good from now on
and get an education while we wait,
then starting on the day of our release
we'll banish evil, re-enchant the state
and make a point of loving everyone
until we find them spreading a disease.
Renaissance meets Enlightenment – that's us,
an apothegm for every blessèd day,
all clean and sober, patient and benign,
and if we see some bastard in the way
we'll simply throw him underneath the bus:
so everything is going to work out fine.

If proof were needed, here is proof:
the sheer redundancy of days like this:
les très riches heures inside the glut of rhyme –
while rain is bouncing off the outhouse roof
to meet itself, for added emphasis,
indifferent to sorrow as to time. Indifferent
to sorrow as to time.

58

Nemo Submerged

Inside the iron whale: the varnished ribs,
The drinking fountain and the orrery; inside,

O Captain, close as permanence can come,
In your *cathèdrale engloutie*,

You draw the curtains on the bursting dark
Where flailing monsters take their exercise.

Depth without pressure, cork-lined silence.
You have almost ceased to act, though still

You dress for dinner. Your moustache
Is a philippic and your monocle glares white

With too much seeing, while you turn
Another page of your redundant journal

And commit it to the stove. You ring the bell.
The ancient prisoners are admitted. *So, my friends,*

What news from the mouth-breathing upper world?
Say, Mr Land, if you've grown opposed

To cutlery, or still profess indifference?
Give us a tune. I'll burn your blue guitar to ash.

Caitríona O'Reilly

Fireweed and Mullein

at the Musée de Cluny
      (for Niall)

A thousand flowers on a screed of ground
described in silk on wool; botanically exact
as in herbaria or *hortus siccus*
or clustered round a Christ child's painted foot,
agape in the impression of his heel.
The rosebay willowherb disparpled, during August,
on high stretches of the M62, us driving
into the (pink) dawn, the field of the cloth of gold
it might have been: sudden with fireweed.
Its prodigality astonished me.
More than the ringing silence in the frigidarium,
the stacked silence of centuries
that saturates the air, that might at any second
topple into sound –
it was the flower entering notice and everywhere.
Rife inside the tanning vats at Rievaulx,
but rare until the railways first broke ground,
you named it for me, telling of how
flower following fire
fire dissolving into flower
it rinsed the iron networks with its colour;
how, strafed into life, it blanketed the craters of London
from seed asleep for decades under houses;
how it was named bombweed, but in truth
deserves a place alongside mullein
with its forty common names
in the curious *materia medica* of Dioscorides –
among which are hag's taper, candlewick, and torches –
since it too sends up its tapers into smoky darkness,
its silken seed-pods like stitching on rough wool,
its flowers turning into words: à *mon seul désir*
it could be, its language of possible balm.

Wood Avens

Its flower's a polite five-sided star
the yellow of pastured butter,

its leaves the shape of strawberry leaves.
The avens on my lawn, out of its woodland habitat,

makes me wonder if it got here
hooked to a fox's fur, or tumbling

out of the sky, a bristled snowflake,
the fruit-head spiked like a virus.

In May we stood in the Guadarrama,
in the sun-black squares of Segovia,

watching swallows nest between
the mastodon bones of the aqueduct.

I thought: *this is their inheritance.*
It has travelled far out of the territory of the human,

a burr clinging to the pelt of time.
And I remembered the pike rising

through the darkness of the moat at Bodiam,
their barbed mouths swallowing silence.

Perhaps, even then, the roots that smell
of damp earth and cloves were forming,

months before the architrave of stem
could construct itself in space,

as while, upstairs, I woke to the grey, abortive light
of mornings – oh, countless of them –

a burr stuck in my throat, to learn again
the word must lie in us a while

avens, avens
a knot in tissue nothing can dislodge or scan.

Gall

Those from Aleppo were bitterest,
yielding the vividest ink. More permanent
than lampblack or bistre, and at first pale grey,
it darkened, upon exposure,
to the exact shade of rain-pregnant clouds,
since somewhere in the prehistory of ink
is reproduction: a gall-wasp's nursery,
deliberate worm at the oak apple's heart.
We knew the recipe by heart for centuries:
we unlettered, tongueless, with hair of ash,
the slattern at the pestle, the bad daughter.
But all who made marks on parchment or paper
dipped their pens in gall, in vitriol; even
the mildest of words like *mellow fruitfulness,*
of supplication like *all I endeavour end*
decay equally in time with *bare, barren, sterile;*
the pages corroding along all their script
like a trail of ash (there is beauty in this)
as the apple of Sodom, the gall, turned
in the hand from gold into ashes and smoke.

William Bedford

Talking to Marina

for Sarah

'Tell thy story'
   Pericles, William Shakespeare

Child

I breathe your cries,
a wild distress
flung at the clinical stars.

The window is an eye
that blinks with other eyes.
What is out there
that disturbs you so?

Your sobs subside.
The stars still stare
across their universe,
regardless,

their cries like ours...
unwise,
unheard.

Sloe-Moons

Your eyes
are sloe moons in disguise,
waiting for dawn's cold coming
to lift the fog's smother.

Arcadia

Teaching again, at sixty-five,
I expect to find you here,
and find you here,

blue speedwell
fastening your hair
like an eighteenth-century gardener,
surprised by the picturesqueness of weeds.

Parisienne

You wanted me to translate Baudelaire,
take you to another country
of café lights and cobbled mews,
the dance of love like wine in mountain air.

Les Fleurs du Mal tells the true story,
where broken vows hide bride and groom,
the sleeping infant unaware
as darkening shadows call for news.

The Conference of Birds

Wisdom flies on red wings,
but lapwing and curlew disturb the night
with their slow deliberate cry,
drawing the light from the sky.

A farmer looking up
will sow the wrong seeds.
I know there is nothing to say,
but say it, all the same, the way we used to.

This is a morning like any other

This is a morning like any other –
cobwebs in the hedgerows –
hares dreaming secret desires –
but the taste is of arsenic green.

You did not bring me
this tinny taste of morning,
but a memory of blue eyes,
a longing that will never be satisfied.

Bernard O'Donoghue

Cargo Cults

We crossed the step to take the milk to Nora
every evening before the dark set in
and crossed back with the owl's call in our ears.
Why was the dog barking? Was he hearing
the fox on its careful exploration
of the ditch by the hens' field? From further off
the call of the heron we'd never seen
outside the pages of a children's book,
sent by our grandmother from England.
Some birds, we learned, had never made it
over the seas: the woodpecker, the nuthatch
or the jay. But we had ours to barter:
the bonnán buí whose cold laying out
presaged the grace of a happy death
but sorrow too; the snipe that drummed down the air
to the deep marsh, out of her element;
or the drowned blackbird for whose tragedy
the daughter of the O'Neills wept day and night.

The Crow's Funeral

Not a mark on its sheer glossy blackness,
its wings still swept back, its whole frame bone-light.
Heart failure maybe, or a silent blow
from some insidious predator. Then,
in the early evening they began to come
in numbers from all directions, as if summoned
by a bell to pay observances, crying
in harsh protestation and lament.
They circled and swooped before finally
they perched at the gable, reaching forward
to call as if their lives depended on it.
By the time night fell they'd all departed
on their various errands, northwards
to Taur or southeast towards Mushera
where I picture them settled again,
ready for sleep on their dark pinewood heights.

Elizabeth Barton

If Grief were a Bird

it would be a kite
       hovering above our heads –
              pick-flesh, carcass-thief –

unseen but always there,
       circling in ragged disbelief,
              not caring where it's blown,

tossed from street to street,
       tilting and twisting,
              the air its element.

Up there, no comforting,
       no platitudes to soothe,
              no rites to ease the ache,

only the whirling dance of death,
       pain untethered, sighs spiralling.
              It plummets out of nowhere –

tattered wings outspread,
       feathers red-gold, holy –
              sucks breath from our lungs,

feasts on our wounds,
       guts us clean, exposing
              bones shining with loss.

Rupture

That night, we didn't expect
to leave without you,
to walk in silence through the endless,
strip-lit corridors, our bellies clawed
with grief, clutching your empty shoes,
your overcoat rolled up by the nurse.

We didn't expect the receptionists
in A & E to lower their eyes as we passed,
the sour-faced man in the parking booth
to waive our fee. We didn't expect
to be wrenched from your sheltering arms,
your patient gaze, the calm in your voice,

to stumble into the cold, fatherless
dark, look up at a sky frenzied
with stars, the full moon roaring
your loss. Death licked you
with its rough, wet tongue, tore
your great heart open.

Spring Burial

No Requiem for you,
no grand procession through the town,
no horses draped in ostrich plumes.

They lowered your coffin in the ground
even before your funeral began.
I held my mother's hand.

We stood six feet apart
from the undertaker in her black top hat,
the priest in his violet stole;

the gravediggers wore masks.
Your choir was a ragtag gathering
of sparrows and starlings.

Your altar was the sky,
the light your incense;
your candles were the primroses;

your psalm was the green of hedgerows,
fields, the river's quiet rejoicing.
Love does not come to an end,

my brother read from St. Paul;
the great tits chimed their bells
and a woodpecker drummed.

Your gospel was the naked oak,
its giant arms outspread,
its buds about to break.

A cold wind stirred
among the pines and cypresses.
We went our separate ways

and as we left the cemetery,
a masked man waved,
padlocked the gate.

Peter McDonald

Mothers

for Elise Paschen and Rosanna Warren

i

The one and only time I meet your mother
my knowledge of you is a good three-quarters
'On a Plane Flying down the Coast of Florida'
and twenty-something glamour; now here we are
pushing sixty, and talking about her
when she had to cook for Auden or Stravinsky
(or was it Auden and Stravinsky together?)
in a little apartment in New York City
though nearly all of her twenty-three years
had been spent dancing, dancing, dancing
from Fairfax Oklahoma, and the Osage,
to California and Monte Carlo, dancing
against her parents' wishes into marriage
a long time before happiness, and you.
She fiddles about in that tiny kitchen
as the great men talk their talk, and it's taken
all this time for me to know what to do,
to fetch clean knives and forks out of the drawer
then clear a space and stack away the saucepans,
so she can move as gracefully as ever before;
and she dances again now, precisely weaving
through your poems, on points, abolishing gravity
and so balanced there that she can never leave.

ii

Peering like experts into the oven, we
check on the vegetables and roasting salmon,
till I turn and there on the wall behind me
is the face of the most beautiful young woman
I already knew: she was twenty-one
and orbiting close in to the *Partisan Review*

70

when he fell – collapsed – in love with her, then
wrote letters where his heart, brimming with ice,
cracked into torrents. And you know all this,
remembering her memories: how she
had liked him well enough, but – as our children
might say – she just wasn't that into him.
The apartment windows are Chicago at night time,
but even this long away, we flinch. You send
me your poem about the snake, that great sum
of small pain we absorb and move on from,
which lessens us, or doesn't, as the case
may be; it's March, and I'm shivering; I see
you both at the end in Judith's photograph,
and imagine your hands clasped cold in hers.
As a girl, she almost died once in the snow,
but now her twenty-odd, encumbered years
leave her to quarrel with the Irish poet
about politics, and how it all matters
apart from love: when he dreams of her, she
is a skater, and she has another name,
dancing across the lake when the lake is frozen.

Belinda Cooke

With Our Own

For Paul

You gone, and the high winds blowing,
all the little girls in their white, white dresses,
petals dropping one, two, three, all along
the trail, as they make their genuflection,
following the path past the ancient ruins,
dropping rose-pink petals, calling to the
bridge for echoes, before heading to the
fountain and the amazed and wide-eyed
sightings of the flash of darting goldfish,
mindless mouths forever opening, closing.

You gone, and the high winds blowing.
Where is God? – is he lost in the moans
of the big girls sighing? *Optima Deo!*
Optima Deo! The Sister cries. It's such
a drag, but we'll do it for you, we'll say
a little prayer, as we're gazing through
the glass, at these waxy sainted bodies,
our eyes glued to the screen, on our own
Big Holy Brother, only to discover in
the flesh, that he's such a tiny wizard.

You gone, and the soft winds blowing,
blowing through the rushes, blowing
through the barley, lamenting the lost
voices, – *Return. Return. Repeat. Repeat,*
you the last and youngest: Please stay,
they say, we need you here – No, I must
be away, so our own will know they're
always welcome, voices many voices,
beyond the edge of silence but none ever
returning, when are they ever returning?

You gone, and the cold winds blowing,
blowing where bare knuckles scrubbed
those fag-stained bed-sit floors to shining,
gazing out on your Mayo Hill, seeking
the life that would make you, dreaming
the Lost City of Learning, the geography
of absence, your only finishing school.
God is everywhere. God is nowhere.
Listen close for the voices of our own
and we'll l never stop hearing their cries...

Travelling up the Blue Nile[1]

My mother too travelled up the Blue Nile,
the master's pointer, tracing the route, while
she chanted the scenery in that frozen stagnant land.

Lucky to have a teacher to recount such journeys, always
himself and his brother together - 'And that's when
I got interested, that's when I'd have liked to learn'.

Victim of a mad Irish Pol Pot, in the early days it was
the kind but ineffectual master's wife, middle years
the abuser – no other word for it – till the

halycon year of – the Master, with his white bread
for the extra classes, and his wondrous pointer,
tapping out these journeys through the big world,

no limits to what might lurk in the water's depths
or among the pagan peoples they met: 'And, myself and
my brother, we always had a great time altogether'.

He was the teacher you would have pointed to as having
changed your life, if it had, but in spite of this little holy light
beneath your breast – even then, the doors were shut on you:

while your father had the last word:
'Sure, he never went beyond the end of his own *boreen*'.

---

[1] First verse includes an echo from Carol Ann Duffy's 'In Mrs Tilscher's Classroom': 'You could travel up the Blue Nile /with your finger, tracing the route/while Mrs Tilscher chanted the scenery.'

Patrick Lodge

Listen

Listen…

When we lifted the box,
though there were two inside,
it was light, almost floating,
you'd think we were holding it down
not raising it to our shoulders.

Listen…can you hear it?

The wood still bleeds; pine resin reek
in my nose. Saw-mill lumber
hauled from Waco in my wagon;
the only plank floor in Palo Pinto County,
for my bride's pleasure.

Listen…can you hear it?

Wedding day, I carried her into the cabin
from Loving Pasture; the floorboards sang
all that night with our two-step.
Now all is ripped out, chopped, hammered
into angles, corners; nailed shut.

Listen…can you hear it?

Rain dripping off the pecans, that's all.
A faucet leaking out back, that's all.
Wind flapping a shutter, that's all.
There's nothing to be heard here
but the wind's dirge through the pines.

Listen…I hear it…tap, tap tap…

that beat pure – her favourite polka, my beloved
and her new-born dance to their grave.

Listen.

Note: In 1857 John Davis homesteaded on the Brazos River in Palo Pinto County, West Texas.
To impress his new bride he wagon-hauled floorboards from Waco to have the only cabin in the
county with a proper floor. When she died in childbirth, he ripped up the floor to make her coffin.

slán abhaile

always I am the emigrant   at sea   fathomless
no questions   no answers   sea

buoys me up   as long as I move   gives me passage
can't see land   stern or bow   I sail

never arriving   can't recall leaving   I am not alone
ghosts of those I knew

(some I never did)   stare as I leave   as I approach too
I have a claim to stake

there is the blood litany to chant   one drowning (chased
the herring)   one marching

to fife and drum   he took the Queen's shilling   and more
the women too   stunted in exile

like the scrap of shamrock flown in annually   buried
in foreign earth   never rooting

they were short-changed   exchanging the Long Quay
for Dock View Road   a wild Atlantic way

for a channel going nowhere   those ghosts call   waving
shreds of histories   scraps of charts

like handkerchiefs   fluttering at a quayside   they mouth
Slán abhaile Slán abhaile

as if I might comprehend   as if arriving I should know
I'm there   home

If I was lost on this sea   what would they look for
the cleft on the chin   the green eyes

must have come from somewhere   the quick red temper
the sadness seen in most things

whose are these   I have always found a way out
never a way back in

Terence Dooley

The weather house

Sunshine brings the little woman forth,
idyllic in her dirndl and white coif.
Come rain, come hail, the little man storms out,
killing in leather hose and feathered hat.
Never the twain shall meet to chew the fat,
eschew the lean, here on the polished step.
Surely this indifferent greyish day
suffices to unite them within doors?

He turns his back, her smiling eyes alight
elsewhere, elsewhere, beyond the frozen alp.
A cow-bell strikes the melancholy hours.
Like riders on a carousel they glide
together a diameter apart,
hale, hearty, ailing, prosperous, bereft.

Background music

Remember, she said, and she spoke of a house
with blue shutters, drawn almost to, so the light
spilt on the turkey rug, and a blowsy scent
of jasmine blew in on the lucid breeze,
and beyond was the all-remembering sea.

Remember, she said, and she spoke of a time
out of time, a blip, an interval, a spell –
sweet music, tall strangers dancing each with each,
a glitter where the waves flirted with the shore,
and beyond was the all-remembering dark.

Remember, she said, and I was unsure:
had she invented these remembrances
to torture me with my forgetfulness?
Yes, I remember, I said, for what else
could I say, with the sea and the dark beyond?

Colette Bryce

The Griefs

The external examiner visioned your past
as a mammoth on a leash,
resistant behind you.

Weary to the bone,
you'd come to depend on the toil
not least for its muscle-tone advantage.

One might envy more confident modes,
the oak-carved utterance,
other humans.

A piano extended
its wing like an unhappy thought
and changed the nature of the room.

A waterlogged sibling charged up the beach
and a dolorous voice in your ear
repeated

the family story,
a primitive summons
back to the sinking earthworks of the cemetery.

The flowers you left were devoured by rabbits
nobody could see,
and you kept

bringing more
like a timeworn definition
of madness, hoping for different results.

(The master of art in the past)

The master of art in the past
had weighed and measured our obscure melodies,
wild in the eyes like Saturn
fed on paltry agonies and raptures.
Once, I'd swelled to find the image,
one to equate to the angle between
my upbringing and something vital,
songs the soprano wouldn't sing.
The master is lately attended by carers.
The tyranny of his famous ear,
its delicate claptrap stirrup particular
enough to petrify the spirit,
sports a mosquito-frequency device.
Young girls biro his progress in a ledger.
He is waiting for the gavel to fall
on the roof of the house.

Cathy Galvin

The Seaweed Factory

Seán has worked in the seaweed factory for forty years,
and remembers when he used to cut the weed by hand.
Wonders what he will do when he retires, now there is no currach,
no needy fields.

                                        The Countess offers soup
with a view from the window where Ted Hughes watched his Crow,
where Assia Wevill watched him as the children played near Cashel.
It suited them well; the stark proportions of a house built by the seaweed agent;
so much profit in a tonne of back-break sold for saltpetre, exploding in gunpowder.

Gráinne Ní Mháille

My hair is gunpowder.
I took a ring from
the finger of the battlefield.
Hid it in my child's clothing.
The English queen had a stench
to rival the fish boats of Bunowen;
The child, grown on granite and grass,
steps aboard. Our men fill the hold,
lower the sails, steady the oars.
My guns are ready.

Breaking Waters

Stroke my brow in the cot.
In your cloak of pitch and ice, unmake an ocean bed,
throw boulders at the wide-eyed, headless cabins,
flare fingers
of phosphorous white into the drumroll of the hurricane.

You are alone in a tower wreathed in cigarette smoke
where the city washes below:
I am away, getting it wrong,
not hearing the doctor's footsteps, not seeing what they cut from you and throw to the pail.

Swimming in rain within murmurs of Maria's, of grá mo chroí's,
you storm. Not a song – the wind's roar.
Not a song – an ecstasy. Not a song –
a birth moan broken over my feet. Fish, in a bucket,
left by the door. Shoals of breathing silver
abandoned by the tide.

Put on the island as a dress, and when you wake,
put on a coat of fathoms. What does the water want?
O ... the O ...
the O of a child's face crowning
the eye of the moon. The opening ...
opening ...O...
breaking on the shore.

Kevin Crossley-Holland

Your Sea-Voice

in memoriam Richard Murphy 1927-2018

When I heard you'd died, I'd no idea
we would meet for a second time.
I'd called in fifty years ago
at Derek's bidding (or Michael's?)
en route for Inishmore. All morning
we devoted to monks, penance, islands
and then you jolted me over to Omey
and Saint Fechin's pink granite ruins.
That's where you told me, and wept
as you told me, about the double sorrow.
We sheltered in a sandy hollow
under the first stars, weighed by all
that's fated and inescapable.

You're younger now, you say.
All day I've been scouring this trove
of your early verse for tell-tale signs
– dark histories, nightmares begun.
night drinking dark bog-pools
and drowning is quick and *wild graveyards;*
the soaked faces of the burnt out men
and their charred Armada wreck
plunges its rusty flukes into my heart,
but there's no more than I expected.

The wind's at worst boisterous,
showers spark, then they're gone,
and what I hear so very clearly
is your persuasive sea-voice,
what I watch is your hand steady
as *the boom lifts, and the boat*
drops, and above my knees the surge departs, departs…
Yes, much younger, you say, and sailing
to Tír na nÓg before nightfall.

Patricia McCarthy interviews David Cooke

David Cooke was born in Wokingham, although his family comes from the West of Ireland. In 1977, while still an undergraduate at Nottingham University, he won a Gregory Award and since then his poems and reviews have appeared in many journals in the UK, Ireland and beyond. He has also published seven collections, the latest of which is *Staring at a Hoopoe* (Dempsey and Windle, 2020). He is the founder and editor of the online poetry journal *The High Window*. Married with four grown-up children, he was for many years the Head of Modern Languages at a large comprehensive school in Cleethorpes. He is now happily retired and lives in Swindon.

P McC: As a young poet, you won a prestigious Eric Gregory award, were silent for quite a few years, but now have a very impressive body of poetry indeed. Have you any explanation for the way your gift comes and goes for such long periods?

DC: Well, first of all, Patricia, I'd like to thank you personally for the support and encouragement you have given me for many years now and for giving me this opportunity to reflect upon my relationship with poetry. Yes, my poetic 'career', if that is not too grandiose a term for it, has been quite sporadic. There have been years, decades even, when I wrote nothing. I did, however, start quite young. Unfortunately, though, during those first ten years when I was learning my craft, I did so in almost complete isolation. I just had one friend who used to read my poems and give me feedback. Then, a few years later, my sister, Belinda, was to become my regular sounding board. When, eventually, I went to Nottingham University, it was to study Modern Languages, so again I wasn't really part of any literary scene, although I did publish a couple of poems in a magazine that was edited by some English students, one of whom said that I should show my stuff to Tom Paulin. This was about the time Tom had just got his own Gregory award. To my great surprise, he was very encouraging and even suggested I should think about a Gregory myself.

P McC: Many people now go to workshops to try out poems, but I always think writing poetry is, or has to be, an isolating process initially at least. In a way you are writing each poem for the whole world. Looking back, Brendan Kennelly was my wonderful mentor for many years…

DC: You were lucky with that and I do agree that the actual writing is an intensely private affair. I also think that ultimately you have to be the final judge of your own work. However, I suppose I have still needed some sense of recognition or maybe just reassurance that I wasn't kidding myself! Of course, it's obvious also that my need to earn a living didn't help. My wife and I got married young and we soon had a family. For many years I worked as Head of Modern Languages in a somewhat 'challenging' comprehensive school in Cleethorpes. However, I retired early and then, out of the blue after a chance encounter with the poet Peter Robinson, I started writing again. In fact, the poems seemed to more or less write themselves. In the words of Derek Mahon, they seemed to be flowing 'from the heart unbidden'.

P McC: How special. And do you believe, as Brendan Kennelly once told me, that you should carefully look after your own original voice, once you have found it, and that it doesn't need necessarily to change over time.

DC: Yes I do. I was lucky enough to find my own voice quite early and this seems to be confirmed by those who are familiar with my work. Although my range has widened over the years, I hope that the poems still sound like me and that new readers would be hard pressed to say whether any given poem was written recently or forty years ago.

P McC: I totally understand that, as I'm the same. I sometimes slip some very old poems into new work as, like your work, my voice is the same.

DC: Well, I'd like to think that across the years there's been a consistency of tone and outlook. It's probably also safe to say, given the erratic trajectory I have followed, that I have never been what you might call 'fashionable'. So if I have any claim to authenticity, it probably stems from this. I can also say quite honestly that I have never tried to force my poems into existence. I've never seen the point and I'm not a great believer in 'keeping my hand in'. Others may disagree, but I think you have to be patient. In terms of my technique, I tend to be quite confident and feel that if a poem needs to be written it will be.

P McC: Absolutely. You can always tell when poems are forced – they have no engine behind them and usually leave the reader cold. Back to your Irish roots, though, Derek Walcott said he felt 'divided in the vein' – would you say this applies to you regarding nationality? In the sequence, 'After Hours', no 16, for example, you say 'England/ Ireland: it's one life'.

DC: Although I was born in England, my parents come from the West of Ireland. Growing up, I was very much part of an Irish community. I went to Catholic schools where most of the teachers were Irish and many of the kids, like me, had Irish parents. As children, we used to regularly spend our summer holidays on our grandparents' farm in Mayo. For me, it will always be my 'dreamtime', a rural idyll in which I was given total freedom to run wild and explore. Of course we were also spoiled rotten by larger-than-life characters like our grandfather. In fact, the first proper poem I ever wrote, aged nineteen, and which was eventually published in The *Honest Ulsterman*, was called 'Visiting' and is dedicated to his memory. I suppose you could say it was my 'Fern Hill' moment. However, in a poem I wrote many years later called 'Fenians', I hint at a certain artificiality in all this, or at least I poke fun at it. This was most obviously expressed in the cod Irish accents we tended to pick up. It was all too obvious that we weren't Irish in the way our cousins were and they used to think we sounded like Cockneys.

P McC: *Does this mean that your own sense of identity is still problematic for you?*

DC: I'd say I am less concerned with it now than I used to be. I tend to think of my 'identity' as a question of culture. I am certainly drawn to Irish writers, but then Shakespeare is English. I voted to remain in the EU, but now we have left it doesn't change my love of European music, art, literature. In fact, these days, I'm increasingly uncomfortable with the way in which the notion of 'identity' is so easily politicised. This is part of what lies behind the image you quote from 'After Hours'. It's from a sequence I wrote in memory of my Irish father-in-law. In marked contrast to my father, who was a pragmatist and never had a bad word to say against this country, my wife's father was a sentimental Irish republican. Although he had lived in this country for fifty years, he did have a slight chip on his shoulder. We used to argue quite regularly about Irish politics. He was a lovely man, but took great delight in winding people up with his outrageous pronouncements, even though he had settled here voluntarily and knew on which side his bread was buttered.

P McC: *In your poem 'Migrants', there is a line 'Home is more than the house you live in'. This is deeply philosophically true. Can you expand on this? Where do you feel is your home? Or do you feel you are always an outsider wherever you are?*

DC: Whenever my parents or any of their friends used the word 'home', it always meant Ireland. Of course, for me, it did more obviously mean my family home in Reading, that is to say 'the house I live in'. I do, however, think you are right in picking up on the 'philosophical' overtones. One of the other themes that has been important to me over the years is my lapsed Catholicism. Without wanting to sound too angst-ridden, I do suspect that a sense of alienation or 'homelessness' is part of my psychic landscape. This was exacerbated in the 70s when, as a student of French literature, I read a lot of Sartre and Camus. I also read everything by Kafka and was obsessed with Samuel Beckett. Deep down, it probably has its roots in my loss of faith and also the loss of that rural paradise I have just described. Come to think of it, I was probably making that connection, quite unconsciously, in a poem I wrote in the 1980s called 'Connacht', where I have the couplet: 'knowing now that Eden / is only a fierce nostalgia.' In fact, 'homelessness' is an idea that underpins quite a few of my poems from the 80s. 'Travellers' is a poem about those people who, in less politically correct days, we used to call 'tinkers', but it also describes my younger brother Martin and me as outsiders.

P McC: I suppose reading Sartre etc as a young man you imbibed a lot of existential thought which must indeed have challenged a lot of your old Catholic beliefs. We have extracts from your sister's memoir in these pages. She seems to be on a real roll and it looks as if her wonderfully detailed memoir is growing into a full-sized book. Would you say that your memories coincide with hers? Or perhaps you recall other details or aspects. After all it is surprising how two people's memories of one event can be totally different.

DC: I'm always impressed by how much Belinda does remember and she spent far more time than me quizzing our mother about her early days. We maybe also see things from a slightly different angle. She is four years younger than me and I stopped going to Ireland in my teens because I used to spend all my summer holidays working with my dad. Looking back, I think my Irish 'idyll' also got a bit tarnished by the Troubles in the late 60s. It seems slightly irrational now, but I do remember feeling quite worried in case the violence in the North might spill over into the South. Still, in 1961 we'd had the Cuban Missile Crisis and in 1967 the Six Days' War. Back then, it was quite easy for an impressionable teenager to think that Armageddon was around the corner. So, gradually, I lost contact with Ireland and many of the relations I grew up with. I suspect, also, that Ireland has changed out of all recognition since then. All but one of my many aunts and uncles have died and there are younger generations that wouldn't know me from Adam.

P McC: Do you think that gender plays a role here: that your being Irish in the UK as a male impacts on your work differently from the way it impacts on Belinda as a female poet?

DC: I think there are differences between what we remember and this is obviously reflected in what we have written. Gender may have some part to play in it. As I've just mentioned, I used to work for my dad as a labourer and wrote about it in my poem 'Working Holidays'. There was also my relationship with my father-in-law, which gave me a different perspective on Ireland. Recently my sister has written lots of poems about our mother, whom she nursed through her final illness, while my wife and I were at home in Swindon 'shielding'. On the other hand, I have written many poems about our father, who died forty years ago. Then, when my father-in-law died, I wrote poems about him. For me, my mother was mostly a sane presence in an increasingly mad world. I'm pleased that before our mother died I did manage to write poems like 'Songs He Sang Her', 'The Leaving Cert' and 'Lives of the Saints'.

P McC: They are very fine poems. And now, let's move from gender onto class. You write about your father's working class origins, with fine portraits of him, and others. Do you think this is perhaps what gives your poetry its gutsy, unadorned approach?

DC: Well, I'm certainly pleased if that's what comes across. As a reader and a writer, I'd say that I have quite a visceral, instinctive approach to poetry and don't tend to 'overthink' it. I just write the poems that come to me. We are who we are and I feel lucky to have had the upbringing I did. I was certainly shaped by rural Ireland but maybe even more by the experience of working on building sites from my mid-teens onwards. Then in my early twenties, as a student in Nottingham, I used to work during my vacations as a dustbin man and general labourer for Rushcliffe Borough Council. I loved the experience of doing hard manual work and enjoyed what my dad would have called 'the craic'. Going back to the poetry, I do tend to be drawn to work that is rooted in real experience and focuses upon particulars. I have little patience with poetry that seems pretentious or fuzzy around the edges. Maybe that's why, in spite of my degree in French, I don't get on with modern French poetry, which, since Mallarmé, so often seems abstract and mannered.

P McC: Indeed, in putting together the fairly recent French issue of Agenda, *I had a hard time trying to avoid those abstract, mannered kinds of French poems, all too fashionable there. In contrast, your own poems, say, on Cleethorpes and a Grimsby in decline, where you lived for many years, are very vivid and alive and again give the reader the real, harsh experience of what went on. Striking images abound in this memorable section of more recent poems from which there would be too much to quote. For example I recall, in 'Braider', the portrait of a skilful yet tough young woman repairing nets 'she views the world/ through a puzzle of knots/ and meshes'…*

DC: I lived in Grimsby for thirty-four years and for a large part of that time I wrote nothing. So I am pleased that before I left I did manage to write some poems about the people involved in the fishing industry. Once the inspiration started coming, I didn't really find it that difficult to connect with the lives of teenage apprentices, the hard-drinking men who ribbed them, or the hand-to-mouth existence of their long-suffering wives. Much of this was replicated in the precarious lives of the men I'd worked with in the Sixties and Seventies, who were employed as casual labourers 'on the lump'. There were parallels also in the dangers associated with work on both the trawlers and on building sites back then. My own father died as a result of an accident on a building site in 1981, as did his older brother a year or so later.

P McC: How terrible. I like the way you write from your own personal experience, yet broaden this out to include exiles, migrants... For example in the poem 'Going Home', the man described, reduced to being 'Stage-Irish, for sure, and patriotic/ to a fault, you were self-styled Irish John' – seems to assume a kind of act in allegiance to the country he has left which has diminished to 'a place that doesn't exist/ beyond exiled memories'.

DC: Again, I'm pleased that you have picked up on that poem. 'Irish John' was my father-in-law. To be honest, you couldn't really write a dull poem about him because he was such a lively character. On the wider topic of migration, I'd say it's the underlying theme of my 2010 'comeback' collection, *Work Horses*. In particular, there's a poem there called 'Empty Nests', which I tend to think of as my definitive statement on this subject. It re-examines my parents' experience at a time when many Polish immigrants, co-religionists of my parents, were also establishing themselves in the UK. However, my original intention was simply to write a poem for my wife about our own children growing up and leaving home. Three of them have spent time working abroad, while the remaining one has married into a family that hails from Sri Lanka. So it just happens to be a theme that's close to me.

P McC: At the end of the above poem, you weave in some words from the Irish language, or Gaeilge: 'how one who leaves says slán agat / and one who remains slán leat!' I know you yourself have studied Gaeilge quite considerably. Is this your way of getting into the soul of the Irish people, and, indeed, into your own soul?

DC: To a degree perhaps, but actually, from a very early age, I have been obsessed with foreign languages, so it was inevitable that I would have a go at Irish. You will recall that I dedicated to you my poem 'Learning Irish', in which I described my first faltering steps and took the opportunity to describe a lovely aunt of mine, who was a primary school teacher and who died of cancer in her thirties. However, I'm pretty sure that my interest in languages must have started with the Latin Mass when, in my boredom, I tried making sense of the Latin in our mass books by comparing it with the parallel English text. I'd say also, in passing, that I consider myself lucky to have been able to study Latin at school. So at quite an early age I had made some kind of a start on what might be considered my two ancestral languages. That got me going and since then I have been a serial language learner all my life. I did French at school and taught myself German, which I also ended up doing at university, then I moved on to Italian, Spanish, Russian and many others over the years. Where Irish is concerned, I am said to have the *blas,* which means that my accent isn't too bad, but I'm never going to have any need or even opportunity to speak it fluently. Still, I have read a fair bit of it over the years and do make a point of acquiring any bilingual books of poetry that come my way.

P McC: It's interesting how you have found for yourself, and savoured, the Irish language, even teaching yourself that tongue. Yet so many born in Ireland had Irish forced down their throats at school, and if you failed Irish in the Leaving Cert, but got honours in every other subject, you failed the whole thing. I don't know if it's the same nowadays as when I was at school there. But this set up a real resentment of the language among many.

DC: Yes indeed and, as a teacher of Modern Languages myself for the best part of thirty years, I'm afraid I know all about this. Languages are not the easiest subjects on the curriculum and most British kids don't feel inclined to opt for them. As a result, it seems that even in our universities the number of students taking quite mainstream language courses is in serious decline. Irish kids don't need to know Irish to function in the workplace and most English kids will get through life quite happily without a foreign language. It's sad but I'm afraid it's true. I can't imagine not being able to access the poems of Baudelaire, Montale, Cavafy, and so many others, in the languages in which they were written.

P McC: You sound as if you are a bit of a natural polyglot! Now that I come to think of it, you recall, very touchingly, your mother's displaying of her own 'Leaving Cert' in the poem of that name, and show how she was much cleverer than her limited background would suggest.

DC: As you know, my mother died last year. I'm particularly pleased with the one you mention because I think it does give a good idea of what she was like. Neither of my parents had any education beyond the age of thirteen, but they didn't let that hold them back. I have always admired her for her selflessness and her inexhaustible common sense. I think I may also have captured something of her spirit in my poem, 'Songs He Sang Her' where I say she was 'all go / and focused on living.' Yes, she always had bags of energy.

P McC: The influence of Catholicism, presumably your inherited religion, is evident in some of your poems that capture an era with Sunday Mass. I think of poems like 'Lives of the Saints', and 'Going to Mass'. You did mention earlier that your 'homelessness' probably stems from when you lost your faith. In general, though, how important has Catholicism been to you?

DC: I have no resentment whatsoever at having been brought up as a Catholic. It probably still shapes my thinking in various ways and I don't think it did me any harm being brought up within a clear moral framework, even though I don't believe in the theology that underpins it. I suspect, also, that it may have given me what I'd call a 'philosophical' or at least a thoughtful outlook on life. I also received an excellent education at both of my Catholic schools, so I don't really have anything to complain about and of course, back then, I had no inkling of the scandals that have since come to light. In fact, sometimes it still has its uses. Catholicism shaped European thought for centuries and was itself shaped by the Classical and Hebraic traditions that preceded it. During lockdown, I have been immersing myself in Dante's *Commedia* and it's amazing how much of that theological stuff I still have at my fingertips. It must have been drummed in very efficiently!

P McC: Well, they say 'once a Catholic, always a Catholic'. If nothing else I think it leaves one with vestiges of mysticism. It is interesting how, enfolded in all the above influences, you are very much a European as seen, for example, by your interest in French poets and artists. Baudelaire, Proust, to name only two. And by your travels in Europe. Music also is important to you, particularly jazz.

DC: Yes, music, too, all kinds of music, has meant a lot to me and, poetically speaking, has been important because of its mnemonic significance. My poems about people like Miles Davis, Aretha Franklin, Joni Mitchell, are always rooted in particular moments; quite often they go back to the first time I heard them. That is why there is a specific reference to Proust in

'Chasin' the Breeze'. That 'little phrase' taken from Vinteuil's Sonata, which always reminds Swann of the first time he met Odette, is one of my literary touchstones. Travel has also been important for my poetry, but there does need to be some kind of meaningful connection between the place and my various 'obsessions'. That is how I have managed to write about Russia, Sri Lanka and Malta, and, more recently, Paris where, as a nineteen-year old, I went off on an ill-conceived adventure to perfect my French after I had wasted two years in the Sixth Form studying sciences.

P McC: Is translation also important to you? Is this a growing interest? I note in the poem 'Ships' how your interest in etymology was evident even as a child, when taught by monks:

> *I had always known since schooldays*
> *that* navis, navis, *feminine,* ship
> *was how we got to* nave,
> *its pews aligned in shipshape rows,*
> *its congregation, facing east,*
> *like pilgrims on a voyage*
> *toward the promised land.*

DC: As far as translating is concerned, I have done a few bits and pieces at times when I had no ideas for my own poems. The problem is that I'm not a very committed or disciplined translator and tend to stray from the original text. For example, I thought I'd have a go at Rimbaud's 'Le Buffet', but very quickly lost interest, until Rimbaud's sideboard reminded me of another piece of furniture: the old dresser in my grandparents' cottage. The first line or so came from nowhere: 'The shrine and archive of those who had gone, / the dresser loomed imposingly ...' and then I was off, writing about something with which I had a real connection.

P McC: It would be another interview altogether to talk to you about the High Window, but could you just say a few words about the challenges of editing and running such a project.

DC: I set up my own press in 2015, initially to republish a much revised collected edition of my earlier poems. I then started tinkering with WordPress and set up a website, not knowing exactly what I was going to do with it. However, around this time, my son introduced me to Anthony Costello, a friend of his who ran poetry events in Calderdale. That was the push I needed and we started the online journal together for which I already had the name. However, because it was difficult to work by email across the geographical divide between Calderdale and North East Lincolnshire, I decided after three years I would go it alone. The journal and the press definitely involve a lot of work and I will almost certainly have to publish fewer books because it really can get to be too much. Still, it is very satisfying and I enjoy it. It's good also that the costs involved are minimal which is the way I like it, because it means I have complete editorial freedom and am accountable to no one.

P McC: Even if you are not working on any poems at the moment, you have published several collections in the last few years. Is there still more to come?

DC: To date, I have published seven collections, five of which have appeared since I started writing again in 2008. They have all been surprisingly well reviewed, which is of course quite gratifying! Towards the end of this year, my next collection, *Sicilian Elephants*, will be published by Two Rivers Press and I am also sitting on another one called, *The Metal Exchange*, for which I have a publisher lined up who will bring it out when the time is right. So that's surely more than enough from me or anyone else, for that matter. In fits and starts, over close to half a century, I have created a body of work that does at least mean something to me and which I'd like to think has some kind of unity and coherence. At the moment, I don't feel any desperate need to expand it and I certainly don't want to dilute it with anything that is half-baked or inauthentic. Maybe poems are like heartbeats and you only get so many. For some people they come slow and steady. For me it's different. As Michael Longley once said, 'If I knew where poems came from, I'd go there.'

PMcC: David, you have a remarkably exciting, fine body of work as evidenced in Slippage, Selected Poems *2013-2018, from three of your collections (The High Window). So many poems are memorable, wonderfully worked in terms of form, for example the poem 'Biscuits' is a very clever working of a sestina, with the end words of each six-line verse all being the same throughout six and a half stanzas, yet unnoticeable (as in Thomas Hardy's poem, 'The Haunter'). Your own unique voice, its 'lack of showiness' as John Greening has said, and its very fine achievement deserve to be much better known. You are up there with the very best of them and thank you for allowing me to interview you.*

Peter McDonald in conversation with Matthew Campbell

Peter McDonald was born in 1962 in Belfast, Northern Ireland. He is the author of seven books of poetry. The first five were brought together in his *Collected Poems* in 2012. Since then, he has published two further volumes of poetry with Carcanet, *Herne the Hunter* in 2016 and *Gifts of Fortune* in 2020. His verse translations of *The Homeric Hymns* came out from Fyfield in 2016 and Agenda Editions have just published his versions of Psalms 8, 25, 94, 98, and 114 as *Five Psalms* with accompanying 'Paraphrases'. He is the Christopher Tower Student and Tutor in Christ Church, Oxford.

Matthew Campbell teaches Irish and English Literature at the University of York. He is the author of *Irish Poetry Under the Union, 1801-1924* (2013) and editor of *Irish Literature in Transition, 1830-1880* (2020).

The following conversation took place by email towards the end of lockdown, April 2021.

MC: You collected your poems in 2012, and in the same year published a book on 19ᵗʰ century poetry, Sound Intentions, *that you had been working on for a number of years. Since then, you have continued to manage a career as a poet, a translator, a scholar, a reviewer and a teacher. I could invoke an old-time profession – man of letters – but it seems a broad-enough notion that is suitable in your case. The translating and editing do seem like jobs for a poet, if time-consuming, and many poets have been critics and editors. But if asked, which would you say was the day-job?*

PMcD: It's odd to think that 2012 is almost a decade ago, isn't it? The reasons for the *Collected* were various, and most of them to do with publishing. My first two books were long out of print, but with another publisher than my regular one (Carcanet), so it seemed to me like a good idea to get them back and, in the process, enjoy a little bit of revision. Which I did, by the way. Anyhow, the upshot was a slim enough book and – I figured to myself – the chance to draw a line under my first fifty years on this earth. I turned fifty in 2012 you see, and had a strong urge to get things tidied up a bit, and finished – hence *Sound Intentions*, which I'd actually been working on, in one form or another, since the mid-1990s.

As to day-jobs and jobs, poets and men of letters, all that – I'm not at all sure I have a meaningful answer. I've earned a living in universities, and that's certainly been a job. I'm old-fashioned enough to believe that my writing life has to be kept separate from what you might call the life of teaching. Although I have dabbled in the 'creative writing' side of pedagogy, I was never whole-hearted about that, and abandoned it altogether at least ten years ago. Besides, the grim world of workshopping really did make it harder for me to write poems of my own: how good poets manage to manage *that* as their job and still produce their own work is frankly beyond me. I admire them – for their courage, apart from anything else. But on the whole, I suspect real work is safer, in terms of keeping the creative spirit going. If more poets were bankers, engineers, taxi-drivers, policemen – or whatever job you can think of – there might be more good poetry around. Well, more poetry that I like: which, in fairness, isn't quite the same thing. Or perhaps there'd just be less poetry around. A shame, maybe, but I'd settle for that.

I suppose that sounds frivolous, and partly it is. But I'm perfectly serious when I claim that my work as an academic has been undertaken as professionally as was in my power over – what? – the last thirty-five years. I haven't been doing it all as a way to boost my profile as a poet. And just as well: I think I was better known as a poet in the late 1980s than I am now, when I am somewhere beyond the little-known, and closer to the completely obscure. Whenever people have asked me about my poetry, I've been inclined to play it down. Though the trouble with self-deprecation, I've found, is that people are all too willing to take you at your word. I'm committed to being a literary critic, and am quite proud of what I've done in that line; proud, too, of having taught useful things to people, and of having made things happen in university environments that have had positive results, or at least prevented some negative ones. Maybe when I'm sixty I'll stop having being an academic and – at long bloody last – become 'a writer'. A man of letters, yes: a nicely out of date term. Another decade, another line drawn.

MC: Many congratulations on the publication of the first two volumes of the 'Longman' (now Routledge) Poems of W.B. Yeats. Such an editing project would be a massive task for any academic, particularly a series which asks for annotations which require allusions or explanatory glosses as much as textual variants. I'd like to ask how difficult that is for your writing as a poet – both in the everyday sense and in the sense of pitting your ongoing career against such a predecessor? Even leaving aside the question of editing a writer as heterodox in his beliefs, how do you as a poet find yourself committing to spending many years trawling through the guts of the text? Who is being modified in whose guts, the living poet or the dead text?

P McD: You're kind enough not to point out that WB and I have only got to 1899 together so far. By my reckoning, four or even five more volumes lie ahead –though I'm pretty far along with the next instalment, as it happens. But we need to face facts here: WB and I are in it for the long haul now. Till death do us part.

I thought long and hard before taking on the Longman. I already was well enough aware that WB was central to all I knew about poetry, and thought about poetry; and that he was vital to whatever poetry I might myself try to write – for better or worse: that's not at all for me to judge. Even so, this was taking such commitments to another level altogether. Every single line he ever wrote would need to be examined and explained. The level of intimacy there is potentially dangerous, and I was on my guard against it, as best as I could be. I hoped, I think, that I had had time enough already to know what I was as a poet, and what he was, and to know how to keep these things in a good working relationship, rather than one side bloodsucking the other.

It's hard work. On a purely technical level, I've had to learn how to do a lot of things, and how to look in some very dark corners. I have spent more time editing these poems than he spent writing them, and I've annotated things that I'm sure he forgot ever having written or read. I haven't come to worship Yeats. The *arcana* of magic and the like are a real challenge, I will admit. Temperamentally, I find such things very alien and – to be frank – a bit boring. They worked for the poet, so we certainly need to know about them. But really, they couldn't have worked for anyone else, in my opinion. Naturally, I might be quite wrong about thousands of things in the edition; I hope, though, that I'm right about a few things too, and that I'm starting to make it possible for people to see Yeats in a new light. Yet another new light. And there will be other, newer sources of illumination on the poetry after my time, I'm sure. But then again, I do believe that he's worth that kind of attention. Few poets are, really. I mean, in English there are Chaucer, Shakespeare, Milton, Wordsworth, and Yeats. That's just how it is. It's indecent to set limits to the gratitude each one of them is owed: you *can't* study them too much. Many other great and important poets, yes; but these are the ones to whom most is owed. Scholarship, I think, is my way of starting to pay this particular debt which, as a poet, I have run up with Yeats. It won't be enough – of course it won't – but that's no reason not to give what I can.

MC: You have also recently published a number of translations from the not so recent past, from what we understand as the Classics, within at least a century of translating in the Irish poetic and scholarly involvement with classicism, a number of poets and professors have been there before you: E.R. Dodds appears in 'Mud' one of the poems in Gifts of Fortune, *but Michael Longley, Eileán Ní Chuilleanáin, Seamus Heaney have been had long and rich engagements with versions of Homer and Virgil. Leontia Flynn has recently brought together her versions of Catullus. These are Irish Classics derived from the classics – although the interest may very well be accidental, international even, in the way that the 'classical world' is a sort of lingua franca (albeit disappearing) for 'world literature'. And you have been for some time, a supporter of the writing of the American poet A.E. Stallings. Do you think your own versions of antiquity, of Homer or the Psalms fit into that lineage – modern, contemporary – or can they be like a Tennysonian monologue, a sort of prosopopoeia?*

P McD: In the end, I've a feeling that it's difficult for me to separate translation from original poetry. I suppose that in a translation the poetry's sources are more directly acknowledged, and in plain view. Translating a poem means – to put it very bluntly – that you don't have to make the poem up. The meaning, the theme, the references, the turns of thought – you can blame all of these on the other guy. You get to be the cuckoo in the nest, which is fun, and I think you get to discover things creatively in the process.

I'm aware of a lot of the discussion which has taken place about Irish poets and the classics: I've even engaged in it from time to time. My own orientation was inevitably towards Greek and Latin, owing simply to my having been educated in these languages (though my Latin is and always has been very poor: *nota bene*). As a reader, as a critic also, I am deeply aware of how fundamental classical material has been for really significant Irish poets: I'm thinking here especially of Louis MacNeice, Seamus Heaney, and Michael Longley. They knew the languages they translated, and knew them well. (Longley's pose as a 'lapsed classicist' has never convinced me: he hasn't lapsed all that far, and he approaches Homer, for example, with a lot of (well-hidden scholarly training). Heaney's grasp of Latin was excellent, and his intellectual acuity about Greek drama, to go no further, was very considerable. And MacNeice, as we know, was for a time a functioning academic classicist – Dodds's protégé, indeed. Dodds was a decent minor poet, but a very major classical scholar. I'm fascinated by him, and impressed. Yes, he does turn up in that sequence of mine called 'Mud'. I should perhaps point out that I never met him – and that's something I very much regret, for I only just missed him. Is it too much to claim some kind of affinity? I mean yes, obviously in many ways it's much too much: in terms of Greek, he was alpha double plus to my gamma double minus, and in terms of social background he was from a world that was a long way above mine. But in other ways, I sense a bit of a kindred spirit. Well, that's fanciful really, but I think there's something about the Ulster/ Classics/poetry interface (horrible term, but you know what I mean) that resonates. Plus biographical coincidence (very much the point of 'Mud'): Belfast, then my undergraduate college, University College Oxford (where he was brilliant, but prone to getting into trouble), ultimately Christ Church, Oxford, where I've worked now for over twenty years, and where in his day as regius Professor of Greek the nastiest kind of English snobbery enjoyed sneering at him. Dodds's autobiography, *Missing Persons*, is a wonderful book: self-aware, humble, affectionate, wise

Still, you want to know about translation, and not hero-worship. Maybe the point lurking beneath what I've just said is that I think good poetic translation means you have to know the language, and be willing to know it more and more well. *That's* how the cuckoo can get into the nest. You don't just bring your 'poet' qualifications to bear, and transform something in a language you don't know into poetry. I know there are exceptions, yes. But that's the rule. And I've taken advantage of exceptions myself, for *Five Psalms* isn't done from any real knowledge of Hebrew: I did go over the poetry word by word, and tried to gauge the vocabulary and diction, while I also took pains to hear the lines read aloud, measuring this against the Hebrew texts; but I had no real insider feel for the dynamics involved. As I say though, that was my exception, and I still hold to the general rule about having to know the language. I feel bad about how few languages I know; but it's too late to mend these things now. As a translator, I have to work with what I've got.

The working, though, is hard to describe. I'm glad you mentioned Stallings: I think of Alicia as someone whose poetic reflexes, when it comes to translation, are similar to my own. She's a very, very good poet quite apart from her translation work, I should say. But her version of Hesiod in rhyming couplets is a marvel, and it gave me the confidence to push on with what I think may take most of my effort in poetry over the coming few years, a version of the *Odyssey*, also in couplets. I wake up at night thinking this is a completely mad thing to do. I've finished about a quarter – some people who have read this are very enthusiastic, others much less so. And it's a risk, a big gamble. But I'm pretty certain I have no choice but to see it through: I'm sure that it's linked somehow to my 'original' poetry, though how exactly I have no way to know.

The Homeric Hymns felt to me like a turning point for my writing life, my poetry life. I think that having seen that through – which required a good deal of hard-nosed, head-down, solid labour – my old daydream of one day having a crack at the *Odyssey* had to be realised, somehow or other. Yet if I never in fact get further than the *Hymns*, I think I'll have left behind something pretty durable, and worthwhile. I like to imagine that my Greek translations are into a kind of Ulster English: and with Longley, Heaney, and MacNeice hanging around, that's no easy thing to make your own. They don't need to be 'relevant' to today, or to Ireland at all: the relevance is in the language, in the rhythms, in the diction and cadence. I really think that counts for everything.

Good translation, I want to opine, isn't much about spotting similarities between this language and that, this time and some other time, one place and another, and playing up to them. It's about making a real poem out of another real poem, when the distances and gaps of language, history, culture and all the rest of it are not to be denied or disguised. So, for me, that means inhabiting the forms of English poetry, and not trying to create a mock-up of classical form. Rhyme – which Greek and Latin didn't really have – is in an important sense *all* we have in English verse, the key to everything. (A great bugbear of mine is people who refer to rhyme as though it were no more than a tool, and who talk casually about 'using' it or not. They have missed the point about poetry *entirely*.) Well, I like writing rhymed translations of non-rhyming ancient poetry, because I like writing poems, and I think the originals deserve no less. If you want to really know that original ancient poetry in and for itself, you will just have to go away and learn the languages. You don't need me: get on with it.

Oh, but this will all sound so 'elitist', won't it? I wish I could find the words to express how wrong that interpretation of what I'm saying really is; but I can't, and it suits so many people to believe that they're being somehow hoodwinked by a culture designed to exclude them, that they won't or can't listen to what is really being said here. Can I tell you an anecdote instead?

I must be eleven years old, maybe twelve – so this is about 1973 or 1974. I am in the ground-floor council flat we lived in then, in a housing estate in east Belfast called the Braniel. It's a rough place: I've written about this in a good few poems since. As a family, we really have next to nothing, and prospects are bleak. But I've been very lucky, and have managed to get a place to go to a good grammar school on the other side of town. I'm not actually very clever, and am already falling behind. However, I've been allowed to start the Greek class: Greek! And of course I'm already finding it painfully difficult, so I'm at the bottom of this particular class, but I've never been so enthusiastic about anything. I keep gazing and gazing at the textbook, willing the squiggly letters to make sense, and fantasizing about becoming fluent. Anyhow, this culminates one afternoon in a vivid hallucination, where a single ancient Greek – cloak, helmet, crest and all – appears by my bedroom window. He just looks at me and looks at me, and his eyes are dark, alien, not unkindly. Then he goes, but I know what I have to do. I'm glad to say this is the only time I have ever had an hallucination: but it was so powerful that, in many ways, I'm still having it. If it was a vision, let me just say that I can't accept it was a vision of elitism, of cultural exclusivity, or social advantage. If only the Spirit of Property Law or Advanced Accountancy had appeared instead, I'd be a much more advantaged man now. But not a happier one, I would guess.

MC: Beware the Greek bearing the gift of poetry. You mention the scholarship of Dodds and the well-trained Longley, and certainly in the latter instance what can appear like classical translating exercises are exercises not so much in rhyming poetry, but poetry which has the voice of a contemporary speaking in English and speaking in metre, a regular rhythmic mutter, a haunting by something suddenly heard from the past from another (dead) language. In recent Longley this rhythm or metre engages with the fragment or the fragmentary, deliberately small-scale, up-close linguistic and botanical seeing in little fugitive tunes of partial loss, not so much last man standing as last man humming. But Longley has also used this for serious matter indeed – the hexameters in his versions of the Iliad *and* Odyssey, *in the 'Ceasefire' sonnet (a Greek sonnet if there could be such a thing) and 'The Butchers'. I agree with you about the awful locution – the poet uses rhyme – and we can blame well-meaning teachers or not-so-well-meaning exam setters when students reach for it, but if the matter of style starts off as just the way things turn out, poets like you or Stallings are also doing this deliberately, aren't you? That is, it's more than habit, there is stylistic deliberation and intent?*

P McD: In one way, certainly, everything's deliberate, and has been deliberated usually over long periods.. But yes, I do take your point: however a formal shape is arrived at, or wherever that decision to write in a particular form originates, once there are patterns they become parts of the thinking-up, the imagining, the shaping of things into cadenced sound. Experience in poetry means that you get better at working with rules – that includes, of course, working around them. Ideally, it becomes very hard to tell the 'rules' and your imagination apart. Or so I think. Hostile perspectives would depict this as a damning admission that I have no imagination, only a set of absurd 'rules'. But I don't want to start running on about Robert Frost and nets on tennis-courts: all I'm really saying is that these things are ultimately mysteries – not least that mystery of a poetic voice being, as Edward Thomas puts it, 'Fixed and free | In a rhyme'. I tried to explore that critically, and with a bit of historical specificity, in my book *Sound Intentions*. I don't suppose that now I can frame things any better than I did there.

I do like 'last man humming'! Michael might, too, as a matter of fact.

Not in any way, though, to underrate humming. Wordsworth and Yeats both composed with a lot of humming, apparently. A line of poetry makes a sound, and you can describe that sound in terms of patterning and all the rest of it, yes. But it is a human sound in origin, and therefore as various in its realisations as people are. The human hum. It's not just that, though, for it's a written thing, trying to imbed itself like a virus in other people's memories, by way of their voicings. The tension between these things is a poetic tension, sometimes even a source of inspiration I think. I'm doing no more here than reaffirming a central idea of the late Eric Griffiths: his book on *The Printed Voice of Victorian Poetry* is critically essential, but speaks also to what is artistically true.

This is really the kind of question I ask and ask myself, never being able to answer it: how far can that singular, geographically and historically specific thing that is Peter McDonald's 'voice' establish a real presence in the lines of poetry he makes into his poems? As I say, I can't come up with an answer, but I know it's the right question to be asking. I suspect, too, that measures of 'value' – which ideally shouldn't trouble a poet at all – reside in the answer to that 'how far?'

MC: It strikes me that in your most recent pamphlet, the Five Psalms *you are doing something akin to Longley, aware of the style of the past and setting a more fragmented poetry alongside it, but in this case not so much lyric as satiric. By that I mean that the controversy, rage, satire of the psalmist is sounded in your own fragmented accompanying poems – or 'Paraphrases' as you call them. It is as if you are working through a parallel text as in old translations, except adding in now a third parallel, as it were. That is immured in a tone I might call savage indignation directed at institutions – not just in any given controversy but also in places that go bad. (You say in another poem, 'Two Salmon', 'Know all the worst and see the worst thing whole'.) Regardless of the specifics, in your other poems about Dodds and Bowra and Spender in the 'Mud' poem, where in Dodds's case integrity was eventually rewarded, there is a turning in these Psalms / paraphrases on the bogus or the 'clever', a certain institutional bad faith, a place where power rhymes with PR, or stupid with putrid. I hear what you say about the shortcomings of Griffiths, but his book mounted a strong analytic attack on the cleverness of those theoretical positions which would relegate the poetic 'voice' to mere 'discourse'. You say in the 'Paraphrase on Psalm 94',*

> Words are real; meanings are real; words
> really have meanings. You are so old
> you can remember how you used to be told
> routinely this kind of attitude towards

'discourse' would surely mark you out as stupid
in the company of intellectuals: they
seemed harmless, but behind all that display
of brainy chic the pride was turning putrid,

If there is a question here, it is about the challenge for you in how the figure that the Psalmist strikes, like that of the Dean of St Patricks, can bear honest witness in the face of linguistic scepticism and the corporate meanings of the word 'disrepute'.

P McD: I'm pleased as Punch that you've heard 'disrepute' between 'stupid' and 'putrid'. 'Disrepute' was undoubtedly a word I kept hearing when I was writing the poems. Like all corporate or official language, it's dead: dead and dangerous. In that poem, it's simply unspeakable. The occasion for *Five Psalms* was an occasion of disrepute: toxic personal animosities – not primarily directed against me, I should stress – were being let rip. Of course there were – and are – rights and wrongs on both sides. But a poet is not the chair of a panel of judges, though the responsibility he has to right language is every bit as serious as a judge's responsibility to the law. There can be no 'honest witness' without honest language. No bearer of witness, especially one calling himself a poet, should ever be swayed by the fact that he is in a minority of one. *Five Psalms* says simply, about the institutional situation that provoked it, Well, not in my name. I really don't know where all that will end, and have no active role to play, but I do consider it wasteful and disgraceful, deserving of public attention and reproof.

So, *Five Psalms* is a private sequence that knows it's inevitably speaking in public, and that its language is subject to public testing and scrutiny. I hope there's not too much Swift in the mix (though I'll admit to finding Swift's poetry absorbing and energising); I did have Milton in mind, though, not least in tackling the Psalms themselves. That sounds absurdly self-important and arrogant! And of course, I shouldn't say such things. But he did feel like a contemporary when I was writing those poems.

As a brief coda, or a last word to ruminations like these, let me just say I'm fully aware of the dangers relating to mountains and molehills. It looks odd, I don't doubt, for a poet like me who has been (let's say) sceptical about the relations between poetry and the public realm in terms of political commitment to be writing a sequence about a squalid bust-up in one of the dustier corridors of largely forgotten power. I think it's important to take that one on the chin. Nobody cares, and I don't say they're at all wrong not to care; I also acknowledge readily that the world has larger and much more important evils to address. But as a poet, I have to react honestly to what is in front of my nose. In a way, it's as simple as that. I hope the poems, or something in the poems, will outlive their occasion.

MC: If I can just follow up in a more general way, can we think about the engagement of poets with public issues in their own personal ways. Geoffrey Hill and Seamus Heaney are figures about whom you have written much, and whose loss you mourn in recent poems. Hill's later poetry seemed fairly unequivocal in its gathering impatience with the idiocy that surrounded it, from Powellism to Thatcherism to Brexit. But Seamus Heaney ploughed another furrow – if I may be forgiven the cliché. He is more an example of someone working his way through to a balanced mode for addressing these issues – in his own even-handed way. The settling into balance and then working away from it in the later poems is something about which you have spoken beautifully in your criticism. And I find that the counterweight of the two salmon in the poem of that name, bears out the Heaneyesque mode: the beautiful effect of sonic involvement which is the ottava rima stanza. You too seem to be seeking a sort of spirit level as a tool for measuring what look like fairly difficult personal as well as social circumstances. Can you say something about how you resolve – or even don't resolve – those two recent influences on your work?

P McD: Hill and Heaney – yes. Great opposites, perhaps. I knew Geoffrey much better than I did Seamus, but both of them meant a great deal to me. I read both of them regularly; I'm always finding new things. I do have a sense, as a critic, that late Heaney still awaits his proper celebration. Seamus had a whole life full of *im*proper celebration as a poet, I think. But the white-hot core never dimmed (in the 1980s maybe it did come close to fading from time to time), and it flared out amazingly at the end. *Human Chain* is a great book, and will only become greater with time. Where Seamus was reconciliation personified, Geoffrey was in many ways the spirit of division. He didn't set out to be that, and the man was often every bit as humanly warm as Seamus, but that was part of the creative charge. It was Geoffrey, notice, who *did* go down the road of innovation, ever more fearlessly, right to almost the day of his death. It will take years – decades, centuries maybe – for people to take the whole measure of what he achieved. Needless to say – but I'll say it anyway – I can't take that measure. I know what I love, and what bewilders me. He was the last Modernist giant, and bigger in my view than many of those who came before him. But he contained hilarity as well as intense seriousness – the poetry, too, has that in its DNA, as too few of his acolytes seem to admit. In person, Geoffrey could always make me laugh.

I'm glad you've mentioned 'Two Salmon'. If I was forced to say – and I know you're too polite to force any such thing – which of my poems I feel proudest about, then that would be my candidate. Writing it broke me to pieces, almost: I felt the poem's disapproval for me, its accusatory payload if you like, as something quite final, more than just a punch in the gut. I really thought I wouldn't write another poem again – and perhaps I oughn't to have done. And in other senses it's so harmlessly literary – there's Yeats in the DNA there, and the whole thing is a kind of complicated homage to Heaney, which time quickly turned into an elegy – but I did feel I'd grabbed hold of a live cable, and the shock might finish me. If anything saves the day, it's the form – *ottava rima* to summon the ghost of Yeats, but actually *my ottava rima*, not his; and the poem takes care of itself, even if it is bearing only bad news for its own author. It left me wondering whether poetry might really be a kind of second soul, and... but the nonsense kicks in there, once you start to discuss this kind of thing: best not to. That poem, though, made the whole book (*Herne the Hunter*) 'click': I knew from it how to allow contraries to become formal, organisational forces, and I had a feeling that they needed to be given free rein, allowed to run riot, to do their worst. Insofar as I write with my ego (who doesn't?), that poem and its book left me shredded. 'The worst thing' tempts fate inevitably, doesn't it? Remember Lear: 'The worst is not/ So long as we can say "this is the worst".'

MC: 'Speaking with the accents of the dead', the Herne the Hunter *volume seemed to turn around a worst thing – the two mirrored sonnet sequences in the book both have the word in the second line. (If I were a keen grad student I'd run it through Literature Online.) Then the second sequence also says, 'I know that I should say the better thing'. Of course, talk about positioning of mirrored sonnet sequences and volume order and considerations of villanelle and ottava rima or whatever sound like the 'higher formalism'. And drawing attention to the shape and structure of books and individual lyric or sequence also suggests we think about things that are a little bigger than can be perceived in the reader's moment of understanding of word or line, or the localities of hearing a metrical or rhyming effect. It might even go back to numerological patterns in medieval and Renaissance long poems – though it's there in Yeats as well as Paul Muldoon's repeated patterns of rhyme over what are now decades of his writing. So, I can see why you say that setting up 'formal, organisational forces' are needed to let things 'run riot'. I suppose I would like to argue that what you are doing is in one way actually 'experimental', albeit working with the already-given periodic table of poetic elements. It was fascinating to see the typographical design of a sequence in your most recent book,* The Gifts of Fortune, *'Blindness', modelled, I guess, on the optician's test for field of sight, treating also, I guess, both with one's own memory and the witness of the memory dysfunction of dementia. One could argue that the sequence is mimetic, and of course Milton and Blake are in there, but nevertheless it doesn't look like a 'Peter McDonald' poem. To phrase this as a question, can you say something about that sequence and maybe about how innovation isn't wholly in the domain of the 'innovative'?*

P McD: We should probably acknowledge that poetic forms are actually these oddly hybrid things: they have an aural existence, and then a legible, visual one. They're rhythms and repeating sounds in air, and a series of shapes on a page. I think 'Blindness' tries to exploit that – definitely, the visual there is important. Or rather the visual in the act of decaying. I built the thing around squares: the component poems are ten-line tetrameter affairs, squares in themselves; but they start to crumble when gaps in the lines appear, and tiny squares, some wholly black and some empty white little boxes, start floating in from margins, getting in the way of the lines. In the middle, a ten-line space is occupied entirely by those black and white squares. The conceit – conceit is the word I want, in the 'metaphysical poet' sense – is to do with a particular kind of macular degeneration from which my mother suffered: eventually, the centre of her vision went away, and she saw all these little squares or grids where images should be. All she could see was what was on the edge, and she had to spend excruciating effort to read the shortest thing. She spent weeks making her way through the last book I was able to give her (*Herne*), line by line, word by word, from the edges in. She loved to read, and for the last ten years or more of her life, that was cruelly put almost completely beyond her. Anyway, that's the purely personal inspiration for 'Blindness': to some extent, its innovation is just mimetic.

May I say I'm bothered, though, as a matter of principle, by 'formalism'? In much the same way, in fact, as I'm troubled by 'innovation' or – that inevitable adjective that always tries to convey value – by 'innovative'. It brings out the Thomas Hardy in me! Basically, formal writing (which poetry is) can't help innovating; no need to make a fuss about it. Hardy barely wrote two poems in the same form, everything was always changing. Yet of course that's exactly what too many people do: they insist on labelling, pigeonholing. I'm very much averse to being called a 'formalist' – too many overtones of the poem as painting-by-numbers. As for the other end of the spectrum, I've little patience with 'experimental' either as a description or an aspiration. Scientists experiment. When I'm reading poetry, I don't want the experiments: I want results. And have you noticed how poetry claimed as 'experimental' is always so irritatingly intelligent? That's just bogus:

real poetry is a kind of intelligence in and of itself; it's never about *being* intelligent, and then showing off how intelligent it (or rather its author) is.

MC: The shattering of wood, the sense of personal crisis that was in Herne the Hunter *now seems to have resulted in a shattering of the printed page and syntax and perception. No matter that these recent poems are rooted in the everyday – the building up of pained experience into middle age, remorse, personal disappointment and disillusion, the deaths of friends and parents. These later books are filled with elegy and childhood memory, with dislocation and odd notions of home. I don't want to suggest that you are offering life lessons, exactly (I wouldn't recommend the poems for those seeking mindfulness), but do you feel that you have loosened an emotional persona or speaker, a figure moving between stoicism and anger, between resentment and acceptance?*

P McD: I'm more myself. Who else could I be? I've learned to become more open about that. When I was young I avoided the personal almost on principle; also, I buttoned up the anger. I don't regret that – actually, I'd say it was just as well: the angry young man was also a very stupid young man, as I see him now. He's visible (alas) in some of my critical writings from early on, for which basically I deserved a slap! But I suppose I think I've grown into a certain maturity: that means I can now be angry, or sad, or whatever, and have the confidence that the poetry can handle it, can expose itself to that, and that it can in turn expose itself to poetry. I hate poems saying just 'Look at me!' At the same time, I want to read (and write) poems that can say simply, and without dramatics, this is who I am. And any good poem says to its author – in the nicest possible way – Get over yourself.

MC: This is a conversation for an issue on Irish poetry, albeit taking place between two people originally from Northern Ireland writing to each other in an England which is moving out of Covid lockdown. And your childhood in the Troubles of the 70s and 80s returns in these recent poems, like the extraordinarily vivid poem addressed to a teenage child which remembers your own teenage self unhurt in an explosion ,'Club Bar'. So maybe I could end by throwing out a question on England, Ireland, and Northern Ireland. We are also conversing while Northern Ireland celebrates its first 100 years, a hundred years since the partition of Ireland, a centenary of much unsettled constitutional business. At the same time, the United Kingdom appears to have been provoked into its own constitutional questioning after a Brexit achieved by English and Welsh votes. These questions could take up all night in a suitably cosy hostelry – when they let finally us in (not, alas, the Club Bar). But I wonder do you think that all that old talk from the 1980s about culture as a Fifth Province might be recycled again for the Fifth Nation of these islands? Irish poetry alone is as likely to take place in Prague or Stanford as in Kinsale or Tubercurry. Then again, the much-mourned poet who never left Belfast, Ciaran Carson, wrote as well about Amsterdam or the Crimea as he did about the Antrim Road. (He too has a poem about another explosion in the Club Bar, published in his last book, Still Life, *though in his case it was about* not *being there.) As regards this Fifth Nation of poetry, is it perhaps an island somewhere beyond our current predicament of the Houyhnhnms ('listening to "the science"') and the Yahoos ('I think the people have had enough of experts')?*

P McD: Ah, the dear old Fifth Province. That dates us, you know! But I've always had a soft spot for it, and certainly I want to apply for citizenship. It's true that writers and people deeply into reading inhabit a special kind of place – big, baggy, permeable, hard to define. I – we – they – like it there. How well you can apply that (for it's a reality, not just a kind of metaphor) to the realities of a cultural and political set of places like Ireland and Britain is, let's say, open to debate. Fine with me, as long as debate is just that: airing and interchange of views; thinking, articulating, listening. It might be arrogant to say that the Irish are especially good at all that, but also maybe it's not untrue. We're also, alas, good at finding out what happens when debate fails: but as far as I'm concerned – and a lot of my generation, I think – never again. Period. I didn't know about Ciaran's Club Bar poem: now that I read it, I see it's about a separate incident in the same place – a much more serious one. But I hope nobody thinks I stole the idea from him. I did drink there with him long ago – with him and others. Longley and he – with Muldoon, most likely, for he used to haunt the pool table – got me horribly drunk there once one afternoon when I was mitching from school and they were all supposedly 'at work'. Oh, in a way we were all at work though, weren't we? It all seems a lifetime away, and of course that's exactly what it is.

As to the 'Irish' issue – the eternal question. I don't really know what 'Irish' is (thank God), but I suppose I know it when I feel it. I sense that at a very fundamental level it's much more than geographical. The big change in our lifetimes is that the other thing – Britain, Britishness – really did go into a tailspin. Kaput, finito. Surprisingly (well, to me anyway), Britishness sold its soul to nationalism, and in the process became a kind of Englishness Plus ('Plus' being Scotland, Wales, Northern Ireland: very disposable extra baggage, for an English nationalism). The result is Brexit and all the rest of it – too depressing to dwell on, so let's not. But I suppose it's fair to wonder what this means for the likes of me. The truth is, I don't know (and it doesn't much matter that I don't know). I'll follow my nose.

But the centenary, yes. I wonder how you remember 'Ulster 71', the fifty-year Stormont-sponsored jamboree? I recall it vividly. Well, it won't be like that. And it feels like marking the birthday of a fantastically old relative: you know that there won't be too many more. As a matter of fact – and I don't want to put the blink on what might turn out to be a creative thing for me – my father was born more or less on the day of the first elections to the new parliament of Northern Ireland, in 1921. He has his centenary in a couple of weeks: unlike Northern Ireland, of course, he's really dead and buried; but I'm turning over ideas of his life and the state's life: the times they went through, the ends they met or else now face. It may come to nothing, or it may come to a poem.

I'm so glad I'm not a politician (I was once asked by a party HQ to stand for an unwinnable seat, by the way: a nicely barbed compliment from the party concerned, I thought. The cheek of it!). My political instincts are useless, and whenever I have political opinions – not that often – they turn out to be useless too. Really, better not. But people who *are* political – young, intelligent and energetic people – will pretty soon find themselves re-imagining Ireland and Northern Ireland in the wake of what will have happened to Britain, and to the mind and will of nationalist England. There are new possibilities, maybe even good and exciting ones. You never know, and I don't accept that Irish history is some inevitable and over-determined narrative. I'd love to live long enough to see a freshly-imagined country occupying the island of Ireland. That would be an Irish country in the broadest sense, and would put away the twentieth century – and the centuries before – once and for all. The people I come from – the Protestant, Unionist people of the North – have a big role to play in that: they need to step up, and not fall backwards into the past. The past failed us: it failed all of us, on both sides of the sectarian divide. It doesn't deserve another chance. Like everybody else, my people have everything to gain, and nothing to lose. Also, of course, once we have a Fifth Nation, it can make me a Senator: I may affect a monocle and top-hat, and make absurd speeches for hours, much to everyone's amusement. Adding to the general gaiety of life; at least, as best I can.

MC: We might leave this to one who is not usually thought of as wise in this respect, Ezra Pound excusing Yeats's brief career in actual politics:

> If a man don't occasionally sit in a senate
> how can he pierce the darrk mind of a
> senator?

Hilary Davies

Michael Longley, *The Candlelight Master* (Cape Poetry, 2020)
Matthew Sweeney, *Shadow of the Owl* (Bloodaxe Books, 2020)

Why is the human eye so drawn to candlelight? And what does it do to the human psyche? The paintings of the so-called Maître de la Chandelle, who has been identified, though not definitively, with the Provençal painter Trophime Bigot (1579-1650), show us figures pooled with light in a surround of darkness; the style is reminiscent of Georges de la Tour or Caravaggio, his near-contemporaries. The intense and yet unstable luminescence cast by candles focuses us on the known by evoking the unknown, conjures up mystery by showing us light. Candles are both reassuring, and harbingers of death.

It is thus that we should understand Michael Longley's choice of title for his latest collection. The poems are all quite short, some only a few lines, but this serves like a candle to spotlight his subject matter. And, like Baroque masters who frequently treated the same theme in different ways and under different lights, so the collection approaches the theme of death and the passage of time from many varying angles. The opening poem, ' Matisse', seems superficially not to treat of these, but the artist's 'Memory replac[es] the outside world /And his imagination a lagoon/ Where, immobile, he swam every day/Contemplating his submarine kingdom'. We are already entering an underworld, and very soon we are in the landscapes of the First World War, associated in Longley's mind, not only with painters and poets, but also with his own father.

It is quite natural, especially for a poet as steeped in classical literature as Longley, that these events should lead to evocations of Homer, for the grief, the horror and the pity of war are universal and timeless. Glory ends in gore, and the chariots are always ghostly, whether they are of wood or metal, 'empty chariots clatter along/Down the lines of battle, in mourning/ For their irreplaceable charioteers/Who lay on the battlefield, far dearer/ To the vultures than to their wives.'

The intersection of the natural world with the world of human inhumanity (these ironies are not lost on Longley) allows him, obliquely, via the medium of insects and flowers, to talk to the 20th century ghosts of atrocity, the children of Terezin, without striking a false note (difficult to achieve). This in turn brings him back to his own children and grandchildren, and, seamlessly, to his own childhood. It is now that the alert reader begins to understand his prefatory quotation from Joan Miró, 'And what looks like a zig-zag is really a straight line'. Receiving the Yakamochi award becomes the occasion to fuse the vision of this 8th century Japanese poet, who also loved flowers and birds and the wild, with Longley's home landscape, 'We gaze on our soul-landscapes/ More intensely with every year --/Small boats passing Inishbofin,/ Small boats on the Nago Sea'.

Soul landscapes exert their flickering magic ever more powerfully as Longley ages. Just as individual, tiny things become invested with greater luminosity, so the language is pared back, spare yet capable of bearing a disproportionate load. Encounters with wild orchids become a narration of life, from many different memories of his Irish childhood through to later, loved, particular places in Greece and Italy, 'In my synapses early purples persevering/As in a muddy tractor track across the *duach*;/...Along the path to the waterfall at Cardoso,/... A blackcap singing (in Greece or Ireland?); just one/ Bedraggled fly orchid in a forgotten field,/ Its petals cobalt, chestnut-brown, as I recall.' The language is as delicate as the plant; the collection tender, full of the recollections which give the lived life its meaning.

Owls: birds of wisdom, portent, terror, beauty, death. They have haunted the human mind everywhere and in all ages because of their night hunting and silent, winged approach. One came to Matthew Sweeney as he awaited diagnosis for suspected motor neuron disease in 2017, 'that owl/ I heard outside last night might/ lead me to the terrain and call out/ the custodians so they/ can surround and welcome me'. This poem opens his last collection, written in the shadow of death, and is the first in a twelve-part sequence, 'The Owl', in which the omen bird visits him like a doppelgänger. He eavesdrops on Sweeney's conversations with his doctor; he leaves feathers in the kitchen; he is a shadow in the bedroom at night. The combination of hallucination and humdrum was very much a hallmark of Sweeney's poetry from the outset of his career and he always knew how to unsettle the imagination. Sweeney was a Germanophile and a Germanophone; his work often contained elements of the 'unheimlich', impossible to translate properly into English but akin to uncanny, eerie, something that makes your flesh tingle and your hair creep. One thinks of writers such as E.T.A Hoffmann, Ludwig Tieck, Kleist, or, later, Kafka. Now, in these poems written in his last year, the owl becomes both symbol and reality, the exact correlative of Sweeney's anguished situation as he faces the onrush of death. 'The Sequence', which follows, is the sequence of the illness, transformed into a series of ambushes from another world. A female archer takes aim at him as he lies pegged to the ground; a crocodile pursues him across a local bridge; he gets a mysterious phone call ordering him to a chess game that turns into a bomb scare; artisans arrive to carry out the crucifixion he has apparently commissioned; he climbs the stair of a haunted lighthouse. But gradually the poems also merge into the nightmare of his illness: to the invitation to an elaborate supper, he replies, 'Thank you, but I don't eat anymore'. At first the scenario is surreal, until one realizes later that one of the progressions of motor neuron disease is the inexorable loss of the ability to swallow.

'Other Poems' reads much more randomly; there are memories of different places he has visited, more weird encounters. The ghost of Valéry hovers over his visits to Sète, Dubrovnik, or was it all a dream, a projected trip down the Danube with the poet John Hartley Williams that never materialised? In 'Last Poems', the illness has stripped him of everything except itself. The owl has disappeared. And yet even here there is space for dreams, albeit, it seems, of the sort that Hamlet feared, 'For in that sleep of death what dreams may come'. Sweeney leaves us, leaves life, with a grotesque morphine-induced fantasy that may be only the beginning of something worse. Not so much a whimper, as Fuseli's 'The Nightmare'.

Patrick Lodge

Gerald Dawe, *The Last Peacock* (Gallery Press, 2019)

Writing to her aunt in 1874, Emily Dickinson noted that 'saying nothing…
sometimes says the most' and this provides a useful perspective on reading
this collection by the poet, editor and academic, Gerald Dawe. This beautifully
produced book from The Gallery Press may be considered slight inasmuch
as the poems tend to the short and often seem to be little more than single
observations on matters of small beer. However, these 'distilled, curious
little poems', as Roddy Lumsden described his own short 'ripple' poems,
require great control, deftness of poetic touch and unremitting focus if they
are to work. In *The Last Peacock* they generally do and the collection packs
a punch.

The book is in two halves with the first half offering poems focused on the
vicinity of Dún Laoghaire where Dawe, born in Belfast, currently lives. It
is a series of poems with a precise sense of place – 'Along Haigh Terrace',
'At the Coal Harbour', on the 'East Pier' – but a place where comings and
goings are plenty, as would befit a major ferry port. It is as if Dawe stays
still and the world in its oddity, and its poems, comes to him as the observer,
as if, like the bees in a lavender bed, in this town he can 'hop / and skip and
settle momentarily' ('Elegy'), the poet and his perception as the fixed point
around which the world flows.

E. B. White, the American writer, noted in his book on New York City
that 'a poem compresses much in a small space and adds music, thus
heightening its meaning'. He was, of course, describing that great city as
a poem but one feels that, for Dawe, Dún Laoghaire works equally as well
as a source as does that other metropolis. 'Rock Bottom' takes eight short
lines and twenty-nine words to say very little. A handful of trawlers are
moored up, some gulls fight over a crab shell – nothing happens, nothing
special but the final lines *'This is it. / This be all'* focus attention on what
one's expectations of life may be and capture succinctly the sense that the
view, the moment, are actually all. This may not be poetry of the big picture
– there is one poem which broadens perspective to bemoan the decline in
quality of American Presidents, another which covers refugees – but it is
none the less for that. Dawe might well agree with Blake's view that it is
possible 'to see a world in a grain of sand…and eternity in an hour' from
his adopted home town.

This first part is a set of gentle, musing poems in which careful selection
of language opens up the poem beyond the simple narrative. In 'Filling

the Tanks' nothing really happens again – a seal has a look around and goes away – but it is the choice of 'appears' in 'the seal appears / to be sunbathing' which gives it a sense of contingency, that something else might be occurring that we have not clocked. Maybe it's a philosopher's seal which would weave it firmly into the texture of the book. Thus, 'Keepsake' seems a meditation on the possibilities of the future though, if and when 'the going gets rough / and choppy seas / ever more perilous…', Dawe would say 'But let's not "go there' / quite yet"' and hope that 'the unequivocal heart,/ the righteous doubt' will be his keepsake to take with him into those rough seas.

The second part of the collection is preceded with a quotation from *Moby Dick* where the Mate, Stubb – cool in a crisis and happy-go-lucky enough to light up a pipe when everything around him is falling apart – wonders to Flask, 'whether the world is anchored anywhere'. This seems a suitable approach to a section which is ruminative, reflective and in which many poems are dedicated to friends, several of whom have died within the last few years. The Orcadian poet, George Mackay Brown, once wrote that 'as one gets older, one lives in a town of strangers' and Dawe may well share this view, 'are we all haunted / …(by) ghosts of one kind or another?' ('Early Days'). Like the last peacock of the title poem, living in the garden of Marlfield, you might barely spot him 'tucked-up / in a tangle of branches' but he still watches and records what he sees, 'blue eyes / in the darkness *blink, blink'*.

And though several poems – some of the best – are about passed friends, they are never mawkish nor maudlin. 'Swimmer' is a poem of celebration of a life lived by someone who 'lapped up the last sun on his face' though tragically dying at eighteen; a poem hinting only in the last telling phrase at the dedicatee who prompted it – '…olive trees whispering about / the silent hours, a shuttered house'. Of course, a problem with so many odes is that, if you don't know the person for whom they are written, it is difficult to fully appreciate them. It is Dawe's delicate touch and ability to thumbnail the person that redeems many; he always has a tight grip on the pencil. 'Elegy', about the Irish language campaigner, Aodán Mac Póilin, recognises life amidst death in juxtaposing comments on the dead in a graveyard 'as a bunch of foreign kids check messages / before their day begins' but captures perfectly the essence of Mac Póilin, singing *In Praise of the City of Mullingar*, 'head tilted, eyes closed, that's how it was'. Indeed.

These poems are a joy to read. Concise, never wasteful of word nor emotion, they have heft that belies their brevity. They are intense and are alive in their telling craft – a craft which manifests itself in the careful assembly of sounds and pace within the poems. 'East Pier' – the opening poem – reads mellifluously, especially out loud. Dawe, it seems, has an acute sense of the sound of things. Growing up myself within the sound of a pre-GPS foghorn, the poem 'Suddenly' with its foghorns 'in the house like a groundswell, / the sound of childhood in the dark / of early morning…' was marvellously redolent. The choice of words is meticulous and evocative. Often a poem contains colloquialisms – 'settle yourself', 'hither and yon' – which root them firmly. In 'House of Fiction' the use of 'scrim curtains' is masterly with its sense of the world as a stage and *'himself'* squinting behind them at times opaque, at times visible according to the lighting. The images are often perfect – a heron as 'a coat hanger caught in the riverbank's undergrowth' ('The Birds').

There is a valedictory feel to this collection – maybe unsurprising in a very well-published poet born in 1952. Dawe recalls himself as a child, as his mother dealt with a cut from a sardine tin, 'watch it all being / over and done with / in the blink of an eye' ('The Wound'). Like life maybe and this collection 'the last thing you'd ever think of / until you go looking // in the cubbyhole/ under the stairs'. But all that is found there is 'the splintered mirror' reflecting whatever comes its way', like memory, cluttered with 'candles / Camp coffee, waxed over paper, / little bottles of essence' ('Twine').

The closing poem, 'The Good Suit', offers a review of suits in a wardrobe, some having seen better days but the black one – suggestive of funerals perhaps – is still wearable: 'I can almost disappear / with it on, like a thief / in the night, a shadow / of my former self.' No need to worry about that – on the evidence of this very good collection Dawe is no shadow of his former self and we should look forward with anticipation to the next book.

Hilary Davies

Peter McDonald, *The Gifts of Fortune*, (Carcanet, 2020)
Five Psalms (Agenda Editions, 2021)

In his essay 'The End of Authority?' (*Serious Poetry, Form and Authority from Yeats to Hill,* 2002), Peter McDonald nails his poetic colours firmly to the mast: to have a serious purpose and to be taken seriously, poetry's essence lies always in language and form. The subject matter, the expression of individual emotions, the poet's personality or experience, the zeitgeist (one of McDonald's bugbears): all these are the contingent structures of a poem; they do not of themselves make a poem. The question to ask of a poem is not 'what is it *about*?' but rather, (my words) 'what does it *do*? And *how?*' Of course a poem has to have referents – concrete and pure sound poetry don't get you very far – but it is the welding of meaning to form that makes the hair stand up on the back of your neck. The poet's command of, and inwardness with, language is what makes this happen.

This implies both art and craft, an engagement with language that is conscious and subconscious, a knowledge of the materials the poet is using, and their resonances. For McDonald, an indispensable element of this is the grappling with what has been handed over, delivered, by past and contemporary exponents. In other words, tradition in its radical sense: not a stultifying straitjacket of rules, nor a slavish copying, but a soil that should nourish new growth.

Five Psalms comes out of such an understanding. McDonald has taken Psalms 98, 25, 94, 8 and 114, written his own metrical versions, and then, in his words, added five accompanying paraphrases. These are not in the normal sense paraphrases at all, but something more like poetic meditations, riffs that take off from the Biblical text.

The first of these two undertakings is an exercise with a distinguished history. One of the consequences of the late medieval and Reformation push to translate the Bible into the vernacular was the development of 'metricised' renditions of the psalms; these had the virtue, it was felt, of simplifying the message of the original and of making them easy for lay congregations to sing, now that the privilege of doing so was no longer reserved for clerics and monks. Luther's first edition in German of the Psalms (1524) led the way for the Genevan Psalter (French translation by Clément Marot: 1539-62 for all the psalms). The subsequent life of this new approach in the Anglican liturgy and in English poetry has been rich indeed, from early versions by Sir Philip Sidney and his sister, Mary Herbert, Countess of Pembroke (1599) through the poems of George Herbert, Henry Vaughan, and, of course, Milton; the hymns of Isaac Watts and Charles Wesley; and the visionary Christopher Smart, to name only some.

But there are potential disadvantages in such a wealth of precedent: that standards are high; that it is difficult to avoid pastiche; and that meaning risks being forced to fit the strictures of metre and rhyme with the result that the prosody ends up drawing far too much attention to itself. McDonald does not always skirt these pitfalls successfully, 'travail/Israel','danced/pranced', 'sprung/young', where he chooses an incorrect tense form for the rhyme, thereby making it stick out even more. The versions are at their best where they are simplest and unembellished with adjectives to fill out the beat, 'Play on strings of the harp for God; for him/ let your harp be the call of a psalm.// In the Lord's presence, with trumpet and shofar,/ again make joy split all the air'.

What the 'paraphrases' allow McDonald to do, though, is show the universal application of the psalms to the human condition, irrespective of historical period or linguistic convention. Herein, after all, lie this Old Testament book's strength and abiding appeal. Psalm 25 ('Make me to know your ways, O Lord; teach me your paths') is the occasion of an extended exploration of life as *a* way and *the* way. To what extent do we follow a law set by others? Does the law make us sinners? Or does the realisation of sin come anyway, in our recognition of our own failings? A sudden, half-sketched memory is all the more powerful for not being laboured: a desperate beggar in a train station long ago from whom he turned away, '... she could see// me shuffle my feet and look away./ Still broken, she moved on; and when/ God searches for my face on the last day/ it will be her face I see then.'

The famous phrases of Psalm 8 'Out of the mouths of babes and sucklings' and 'you have made man a little lower than the angels' produce several short meditations on that most ancient of mysteries, man's relationship to God and the cosmos. The sequence begins and ends with the image of an arm, enfolding both poem and universe, and the image of a breath, which cannot be seen or heard, but which is everywhere, paradoxically incantatory:

All of the sounds are one sound in the end
That can't be named, that is its own name,
And reaches into everything there is
Like an arm, or like a hand on an arm;
Like a hand, or like the fingers on a hand.

The Gifts of Fortune is less densely structured, more apparently conventional (for contemporary readers) in its format and themes, which are drawn for the most part directly from the poet's personal history. Yet there are underlying similarities: the collection is bookended by two poems with the same name 'Weaveley Furze'. Close reading reveals that the first begins with uncertainty and approaching death, the last with approaching life and the completion of the quotation only half-remembered in the first poem, 'Unawares morality expires'. In between, McDonald goes on a long search for what that morality might be. This is best understood in its senses of 'ethical wisdom', 'moral truth', even 'morality play', rather than in its commoner modern sense of 'system of moral principles'. He and we are to glean wisdom from the 'gifts of fortune' that life brings us, each accordingly. In the first half of the volume, McDonald re-travels the roads of his childhood and young manhood, where his modest Belfast upbringing and awareness of Northern Irish identity intersect, not always harmoniously, with his educational and literary ambitions. In 'Conundra' – the very title hints at the complex mesh of it all – the perplexed 16-year-old wrestles, 'balancing my cup/between the desk and the dark' with 'God and time/ and no-time and no-God', with visions of Dante's Paradise and Hell, while being simultaneously bombarded with the very real hell of domestic abuse happening next door, 'as next door shouted half the night, / every so often/ slamming some weight/ with big drunk screams, *Fuck UP, all right?/* always the woman's voice, */Fuck UP, you fuck UP!'* This poem is one of the best examples in the book of that fusion of discipline of form and tension of meaning so important to McDonald.

The hinge of the collection is the poem, 'Club Bar'. What starts as teenage daredevilry in a pub, 'the one big table with us all/round it, neatly stowed/ lifting underage pints like weights/ in a dark corner, not to be seen' turns in an instant into the visitation of death, 'everything/ stopped, and a wrong/ sound, solid as the wall,/lifted and covered us'. He has just survived the bomb planted by loyalists on 28th May, 1976, which, in a typically indiscriminate twist of fate, killed one Catholic and one Protestant. 'I walked out with my life/ in my hands, and carrying/ the gifts of fortune'. Now we understand what these are: the gift of life, and hope, of seriousness about what really matters. A long sequence, 'Blindness', in which the prosody incorporates gaps and the sorts of shapes ophthalmologists use to test acuity of vision, underlines the point by exploring different kinds of blindness and sight: the dazzling darkness of God, the difficulty of writing poetry, the increasing infirmity of parents, the closing door of death. 'Weaveley Furze' lifts it all up to the light of the unknown, and trust in it, 'the souls, *caro,/* the souls we loved are tiny and/ bright and everywhere; *the living God,* though, /imagine that: is it really so fearful/ to fall into those hands, when no/ sooner have we fallen than – look – he lets us go?'.

John Greening

Vona Groarke, *Double Negative* (The Gallery Press)
Kerry Hardie, *Where Now Begins* (Bloodaxe Books)
Shaun Traynor, Walking Away: *New & Selected Poems* (The High Window)

There are too many established Irish poets unfamiliar to British readers, and I fear that Vona Groarke is one of them, although she teaches at the Centre for New Writing in Manchester. Astonishingly, *Double Negative* is her eleventh collection with Gallery, her first since a 2016 *Selected* and a 'book-length personal essay' *Four Sides Full*. Groarke's is a very likeable and distinctive voice, with a light touch, never dull. Her poems incorporate all kinds of tonal and syntactical shifts and even about-turns, setting the colloquial and offhand against the yearning and philosophical. She likes to end with an understatement or throwaway remark ('which is something, as poems go', 'and that's the end of that', 'and no stone to speak of'). She likes questions, too. And we feel that she is willing to give the language a long leash, or let it off altogether, so there is always the feeling that we don't quite know where we will be taken. Formally, she achieves real variety: prose poems, regular stanzas in short lines or long lines, quatrain and quintain, couplet and tercet, list poems, anaphora, and a concluding set of epigrams. But most of the poetry is in a controlled free verse.

Double Negative is threaded by a series of twenty poems 'against': Against Anxiety, Despair, Boredom etc. but these prove to be not so very different from the others not obviously confronting negativity. And although there are passing clouds and shades of the prison-house ('Against Darkness'), it is certainly not a negative book. There is an energy and a lust for life, a willingness to accept its more bewildering aspects – sometimes by writing a little bewilderingly herself, as in the book's second poem, 'How Do We Get These Lives?', which begins:

> Being the question you'd strip to, if you could,
> if the words came clear over a night
> thinking itself a furnace
> to be stoked repeatedly.
>
> How riverly set it is on an answer
> while pretending not to be.

Most admirable is the poet's impulsiveness, her spirited defiance from the very start: if she wants to open her collection with a poem about doilies, then why not (Elizabeth Bishop hasn't cornered the market in doilies, after all). Like most such decisions, it's not quite what it appears. That first poem is really about language and change, so makes a fitting opener.

Admirable too is the way Groarke structures her poems, often starting off along an easy inviting path, but invariably encountering a rockfall or a diversion, or a moment of illumination, epiphany even. As one of her epigrams puts it: 'A day without a volta/is a day with nowhere to hide.' This usually involves bold metaphorical writing, as at the end of 'The way memory operates', which after some straightforward narrative of rose-planting, suddenly she takes us back (with a deft shift from 'hard' to 'hard to say'):

> to where we planted all those summers
> and tamped the months around them, hard
>
> and hard to say where the years have gone
> when we lay down, night on night,
>
> when the slipway sings so narrowly
> and the wind stoppers up the gap in the wall
> and the sky is civil in fits and starts
> and the boats play their moorings like spoons.

That slipway and its boats comes out of nowhere (we weren't obviously beside the water) but it concludes the poem perfectly. And it is indeed 'the way memory operates'. One of her 'Against' poems mentions 'whimsy' and there is that aspect to the writing, as in the rather Penelope Shuttlesque 'This Poem'. Just occasionally there's the sense that it's writing for writing's sake (and sometimes writing about writing). But there is never any doubt that this is the real thing. There's no big set piece here, only well crafted poems about travel and family and childhood (as well as about porcelain and the internet and self-storage and the Brontë Parsonage) each with certain little ornamentations and asides that mark them as the work of Vona Groarke.

Kerry Hardie is published in the UK by Bloodaxe, who in 2011 drew on her six earlier Gallery collections to make a very satisfying *Selected* and also brought out *The Zebra Stood in the Night* three years later. It's interesting to come to *Where Now Begins* from Vona Groarke's. Hardie's verse is less inclined to stay free, often seems to be lilting, veering to the anapestic ('on the glass of the window', 'of the black-and-white flash of a spaniel' 'the space in the ground which is ours') but she knows how to play this against other more sober rhythms, although she eschews the exciting shifts that Groarke enjoys. Both poets focus on the local (Hardie is from County Down), both confront emotions ('How She Disposes of Fear' as opposed to Groarke's 'Against Anxiety'), both, oddly enough, have poems about a yellow dress. Some of Hardie's poems are riskily laid back ('Shasta Daisies', 'Poem in a Circle'), or reveal a certain slackness (the line breaks in 'Piseog'). Consciously or not, she tends to repeat phrases, ('over and over' appears on pp.19, 20, 33 – twice, and 64, also twice) or to fall back on stock formulations ('the lattice of branch frames lakes of clear blue.//Only the grey-green furls of soft leaf/on the whippy stems of the woodbine have broken./The bark of the birches...'.

But it's easy to see why Hardie has a following, because these largely unironic, undramatic poems are sincere, full of longing ('American Pastoral'), gently thoughtful ('Inhabitants'), unindulgently nostalgic ('Last Swim'), often amusing ('Shopping') and generally go straight to the heart. 'Talking to My Stepson' puts into imagery what many step-parents must have felt, as does 'Permission' – in a bold litany of reassurance – for anyone bereaved. When she observes closely, it pays dividends. 'Taking the Weight' watches a son lower a father's coffin: 'A hard task, taking the weight/of those that have left before us./A hard thing to be facing into/the space in the ground which is ours.' (Note how 'task' prepares us for 'taking' and 'space' echoes 'facing', with that final assonance in 'ou'). 'Into Light' begins: 'All prayers are poems' and its single sentence concludes by calling them 'as brief and intense/as a coal-tit's fierce cling//to a coconut strung from an ash in the rainy air.' Not just a bird but a coal-tit; not just a tree but an ash – and 'cling' here is a noun, not a verb (a trick she pulls off elsewhere, e.g. 'banner the shield' in 'Bird Talk', 'a wanting' in 'The Emigrant's Letter'). Then, there is a good deal of interest in a more literary poem such as 'On Reading Michael Longley's *Snow Water*' or Hardie's ambitious take on a famous ballad in 'There's More Than One of Us in Here'; and particularly some of the plain short pieces such as 'Bolt the Shutter' and 'Civil War Aftermath'. There is a deepening sense of bleakness as the book progresses, of 'waiting for nothing' (and notice the line break here) 'to happen all over again'. Her credo appears to be in the brief unfinished five-line sentence of '...what I call god':

> there is nothing
> except nothing
> and everything
> is inside this nothing
>
> which is...

Shaun Traynor is also from Northern Ireland and his *New & Selected, Walking Away,* deserves to be mentioned here for its evocations of place and the natural world and for several touching poems such as 'Affirmation', about the poet's marriage, or the simple sentiment of 'Maureen's Cat'. 'The Cancered Tree', which shows him at his best, begins by telling us 'The tree outside the library window/was always skinny, bedraggled, too cloistered from the sun' and ends, strikingly, by remarking 'Maybe now it's a book; this one', and then foreshadowing his own death. Traynor has a good instinct for metaphor and there is some happy phrase-making: ('Lazy as the summer water,/three herons hang like grey mistakes/in Ripponden's green foliage' ('Herons')). The work is uneven, however, inclined to lecture us on politics, and rather too free with the ready-made phrase: 'battlefields in Europe vomit up their groaning dead/to witness this fresh sacrilege./A myth becomes reality'. Highlights include the plainspoken elegy 'Rough Music', the Ferlinghetti-like 'Vauxhall Cross' with its 'cacophony of activity [...] where Handel once composed' and a vision of exhausted labourers like 'great heads, hewn out of rock,/blind, staring bleakly out/at nothing' (though he's mistaken in relating this to the Valley of the Kings – more like Abu Simbel). The free verse ebbs and flows, easygoing, genial, but fallible. Traynor has a good ear, and there are pleasures to be found in his poetry.

* * *

Editor's Note:

Sadly, Shaun Traynor died as this issue of *Agenda* was being prepared. Requiescat in pace. Besides being a poet (reviewed above), children's novelist, storyteller and teacher, Sean was a dear friend. He lived and worked in London for many years. Our sympathies go to his wife, Ursula, and his family – for whom we print this poem of his:

Nocturne

As evening comes to meet your heavy trellis work of roses,
as darkness weaves them soft against the brickwork of a wall,
as the river splashes on behind the heavy backs of houses,
I know that we can call each rose and star by name.
But can we find a word to sing the sleepy dusk of parting,
a word to ease the journey that we know July will bring?

So, light a candle, many candles, there, beneath the necks of roses.
Let us wait until their wax begins to bleach upon the ground;
and I will speak of swans that always move like roses
cast upon my memory and this river's deepening sky.

Let us gather up your roses, carry them like swans
through this last word, 'Goodbye'.

Patricia McCarthy

Food for the Soul

Seán Hewitt, *Tongues of Fire* (Jonathan Cape, 2020)

Seán Hewitt is as exciting a find as John Burnside was when I first heard the latter reading while he was still unknown. Like Burnside's, Seán Hewitt's poems seem effortlessly exhaled in their perfect, fluent forms without the distraction of ornament and their admirable assurance makes it hard to believe that this is a first collection.

He is both a visionary and an earthy poet who embeds his narrative subtly in wonderfully observed lyrical images. Listen to the originality and accuracy of the images in, for example, the poem, 'I sit and Eavesdrop on the Trees':

> ...you can hear
> the voices caught in the earth, chattering,
>
> and the rain typing on puddles
> and the wind wiping them clean.

Another example of the original yet graphic image of the wind putting its hand 'over the forest's mouth' is typical of far too many to quote from this highly-charged book.

Many of the longer poems contain a succession of little scenes or chapters, usually terminating with the poet injecting his own presumably personal 'I' briefly, but with great resonance in order to draw together the disparate parts of the poem which is often summarised at the end.

Man is shown throughout this collection to be an intrinsic part of the natural world, occasionally as wild. In the dream-like poem 'Dryad', for example, each tree 'was like a man with his head bent' as the wood, and male sexual encounters coalesce until 'each woodland smells quietly of sex'. The trees and plants, even, seem to be part of the male sex act 'taking in the mouth/ the inner part of the world'. Hewitt is very subtle and delicate in describing his homoerotic experiences that are apparent only in snatches in these poems and retain a lyrical beauty so enmeshed are they in woodlands, with their safe 'dark chambers', heaths, gardens, in 'secret places' on the edges of day and the edges of night. In 'Dormancy', for example, after visiting a friend or relation in a ward full of death, he clings to life by masturbating: 'After seeing you// so sexless, unable, I sowed myself/ like a wych elm in a windless room'. His own body is part of the colourful touches of flowers such as the blossom of the 'Callery Pear' (in the poem of that name) whose 'acrid and sour-white' blossom causes a 'fist/ of longing, call of silvered// nights when I would make/ my body burst its bloom,/ then snug down, half-// sweated: the stain of myself/ (smelling almost of another man)/ held like blossom to my nose'.

This sense of depersonalisation occurs elsewhere. In 'October': 'And I saw myself/kneeling in the garden// from far away, caught between/ one man I no longer love,/ another I might never'. This poem demonstrates also Hewitt's tendency to repeat an image from the opening of a poem at the end, the image here being the 'marrow-flower'. This depersonalisation is pushed further when he articulates, not just his own, but perhaps everyone's wishes: 'Are we all/ just waiting to see ourselves/changed, made unearthly?'

This somehow recalls Heaney, when he makes the reader conscious of another world behind this one. Hewitt's barn owls in Suffolk have the 'sense of having slipped / through from another world' just as Heaney's boys, in the poem 'Markings', play football as if with a 'dream heaviness' on a makeshift pitch after dark: 'Some limit had been passed/... in time that was extra, unforeseen and free'. In the fog, there is the 'ghost' of the field behind the actual field as, all the way through *Tongues of Fire*, there is the sense of how we all try to transcend our limited bodies here on earth, 'the soul waiting/ at the door of the body, asking to be let out'. The poet and the flora and fauna experience an 'endless stretching upward' in an almost mystical manner, while at the same time much 'kneeling' takes place.

The kneeling perhaps links to a kind of pantheism, something both humans, trees and plants do. Hewitt does seem aware of a God, even of the God of the Christians, yet this God is not a personal one. Titles of poems bear religious names such as 'Psalm' in which the poet himself walks out with his lantern 'like the messenger// of God'; he says 'I confess a secret'; the trees themselves seem human with their 'long-suffering bodies'. In 'Kyrie' the parent, to a child, is 'a god/ who we weep to as we grow/ into the world, as we age into it'. In 'Petition', which is framed by night-fishermen and a pond, the miraculous is invoked as the poet recalls a visit to Lourdes and here 'to the deep chant// of a Latin rosary', his undressed body is wrapped in 'a sheet/ of cotton' and immersed in water. He experiences 'how the rhythm/ of the voices and the river seemed// to reassemble my life around me' and he feels miraculously 'remade' with the willow, 'its head laid down on the water... whispering something//in its sleep'.

Trees, with their 'leaf chartreuse' and circular time in their knots, are sacred, such as when carved in a church in the very moving poem, 'Tree of

Jesse' addressed to the poet's slowly dying father. Here are surely echoes of Geoffrey Hill:

> The body, clasped at the root,
> the tree lifting its blood
>
> in ropes through the trunk, feeding
> and at the top the Christ-child
> like the sun ringed
>
> in hammered gold in the arms
> of his mother.

He is haunted by the graphic picture of his corpse-like father lying in the hospice, reduced to 'a rhythmic, breathing body' – 'For so long/ your breathing has lived// beyond your body.' And it is this body Hewitt imagines being broken down into humus, or lifted up. In a separate little scene he imagines his father's chest and its 'constant rattling'in his own bedroom, after which the poem seems to become cathartic in its opening out and coming to terms with his father's decease, prefaced by the universal generalisation: 'Those who we love, and who die,/ become gods to us. Our speech,/ from that moment, is incantation'. In a few near-visions, he asks his father to place his hand on his shoulder, 'like a celebrant', he sings to him and, savouring his own life, he feels 'remade//beyond myself' – as if, more comfortingly, he finds himself being able to transcend the inevitability of his father's death. Already haunted by his father, he says 'I have become a living afterlife'. Finally, he merges the body of his father, 'the root/ of my branching', into the tree image from the beginning of the poem, and, like Webster in the *Duchess of Malfi*, he associates wedding images with funerals – with the silver birch and the mock orange's lyrical 'blowsy heads' – 'almost a wedding' close to the plot where his father will be buried. The poem culminates in a kind of prayer:

> ...May I always wake
>
> on that image – the eastern pyre,
> the bands of light and shadow ascending
> the trunk until the birch-leaves flash
>
> heaven-silvered on the underside
> like a thousand doors, and know
> that a soul is passing through.

As he admits in the following poem: 'Perhaps now, /father, only something old/ and impossible can save us' – Hewitt comes close to embracing the old Christian religion...

And even closer in the grand finale of the last poem, 'Tongues of Fire', which reaches a spiritual crescendo, a kind of prolonged epiphany, propelled by his dying father. Images and themes predominant in the collection are brought together here in a fine tapestry – the heath, uplands, the wood (personified again) – 'the branches rubbing their thin wrists// sore in the open'; the flora such as the 'fungus on the juniper' he sees as 'a bright, ancestral messenger// bursting through from one realm/ to another', the human body, lessons to learn, language, love, loss, immanence versus transcendence, a belief which hovers between the pagan and a non-denominational faith, the human father and a god 'like an intimacy that pressures/ and bends' that is needed to make sense, ultimately, of death. There is too much to quote here and indeed the whole poem, like a piece of music, needs to be imbibed at one sitting, so beautifully and passionately is it handled. Impossible not to compare it favourably with the conclusion to the last part of T S Eliot's 'Little Gidding' in *Four Quartets* which similarly brings all the themes and images together in a climax. Not only are there Pentecostal tongues in both works. Eliot has a resounding resolution when 'the fire and the rose are one' after the journey he has taken the reader on through the *Quartets*. Hewitt, however, is still on a quest. As a 'supplicant', he is still searching for speech – 'a tongue of fire/ lashing and nothing incorruptible', and for meaning. Love is the reprieve: he only asks 'when all is done' that we 'might/ listen, and hear love spoken back to us'.

Michael Longley sums up Hewitt's gift perfectly when he says: 'Seán Hewitt understands that poetic form is sacred and mysterious. In these godforsaken times his reverent procedures are food for the soul'.

Patrick Lodge

John McAuliffe, *The Kabul Olympics*, (Gallery Press, 2020)

It is said that you can't tell a book by the cover but I'm not sure about this old saw in relation to *The Kabul Olympics* from the well-published and prize-winning poet, John McAuliffe, originally from County Kerry and now residing in Manchester where he is a Professor of Poetry. The cover to this handsome production from The Gallery Press reproduces a vivid photograph – 'Foyer at Uday's Palace' – from the Irish photographer Richard Mosse where what look like US Marines stare out over the Iraqi landscape from a gross and ruined palace once owned by Uday, murderous son of Saddam Hussein.

It is difficult not to think of Shelley's hymn to the ephemera of power and fame and the lasting value of art and expression – his sonnet 'Ozymandias' where, as in the photograph, 'The lone and level sands stretch far away'. More relevant to this excellent collection is Mosse's approach to photography which was essentially to portray subjects prosaically, 'to allow the subject's poetry to emerge in its own right, through juxtaposition and detail'. I'm sure McAuliffe might consider this an apt description of his method.

The poetry has a strong sense of the moments a person occupied as organically linked to all others that have come before but also, with no less significance, to those ahead. McAuliffe's – a self-described 'student of uprootings and aftermath' ('City of Trees') – ideal position may well be 'To be / *here* and nowhere at all' ('The Coast of Nowhere') which, in a sense, means being everywhere, and the various subject matters of the collection support this. In the end all moments are unknowable except for the one a person occupies – and that is fleeting. In the aptly named 'A Minute to the Hour', with its sense of not quite being there but with a lot behind and possibly something to come, a hawk drops on a blackbird 'and with it the idea of speed / without purpose, / acceleration as an end in itself'. As a newspaper advises, 'Live in the moment' but this is too fey for McAuliffe who, in this distillation of time that is the minute to the hour, prefers to recognise being alive and with agency of a sort, by preparing the house for sleep and to 'call out the names / like a god whose time is not yet gone'.

Things are always passing; it is always later than you think. The opening poem, 'Germany', seems to revel in the possibilities of careering onward as reasons enough for life – the possibilities of recognising that, while there may be eight days of a rather unwelcome holiday ahead... 'now, wheel-spinning through / black German forests.../ is to be content for once / all in,

127

completely alone / and certain as an engine, / going for the exit, full tilt…'.

The emotional tone of this collection is perfectly pitched. Many poems deal with loss and tragic events but the gentle, insistent explication and the squint, the corner-of-the-eye, view which actually reveals more than the full-on stare, deliver up gems. The title poem of the collection, in memory of the novelist, Caroline Chisholm who died aged 43, explores almost with humour her decision to swim the English Channel and its role in the gestation of her debut novel, with lyrical recollection. A compelling, understated eulogy which, in typical fashion undercuts its own potential for seriousness by recognising how hard it is to express what the loss of someone close can mean, 'Something unspoken can be something known. / Saying it / would be another desperate matter" – and, in so doing, expresses it all.

Again, McAuliffe, as an adopted Mancunian, writes movingly about the events of the Arena bombing in 'City of Trees', though again the sideways view makes for a much more powerful poem. McAuliffe is cycling back 'under the candled chestnuts' along Oxford Road past the Whitworth Gallery, Rusholme's Curry Mile and the re-purposed pubs ('the Clarence / and the Whitworth refitted now as a Christian café / and a chrome-and-glass shisha bar' both of which, incidentally, I drank in as a student in Manchester – the former a renowned IRA pub and the latter a working man's pub in the late 1960s – promiscuous in his memories of Libyan uprisings, digging potatoes and Aguero's goal that gave City a long awaited title. The news of the bombing almost quietly filters in to the poem as a series of personal and historical vignettes and focuses on the bomber, not as a figure of hate and infamy but as

> this watchful ex-student, born here, ill at ease,
> walking through the May weeks of the trees'
>
> slow green explosions, the air
> thick with willow pollen and honeysuckle.

Of course these are TV images and the trees are 'all invisible in the greyscale's pixel / rendering of the place' but it is the poet whose role it is to see them and make art valedictory in so doing, the role made hugely more important when '…the information / which descends on us like summer rain, / the stories and images as much a distraction / as each attempt to make it all align…'.

The poems are full of an optimism that neither ignores the realities of the world observed nor sugarcoats it. 'Circumstance (Accession 8, Box

2)' is dedicated to Michael Schmidt and looks back to the IRA bombing of Manchester in 1996 in which the *PN Review* and Carcanet offices where Schmidt was an editor, were damaged. It is a gentle piece where 'There is ash and a smudged print / on the dry sheet when I move it a little, a dry scent in the air...' as he puts things back into the folder 'including the two pieces of elastic / which still hold all this paper together'. What survives is precarious and may need to be held together with whatever is available but, it survives. The unbroken Belleek vase in 'Two Vases' may have witnessed the breakage of its twin wedding present – which in turn is essentially an observer of a life lived '...flowers it has seen, / hands that moved it, the tables set / that set it off, the dressers and sideboards / travelled between, thirteen years / under the same roof...' – but the survivor, forgotten about on the dresser remains 'coolly at home', carrying on – 'a drink of air in its open mouth' – as we all must.

McAuliffe's heroes seem to be individuals or objects (like the Confessional box on the lawn, 'too awkwardly shaped and small for the lawn mower') whose main intent is to get on with their lives amidst the chaos and unpredictability outside. Their very ordinariness seems to provide a sustaining bulwark, a safe place against the dangerous, the volatile. They carry on with stuff going on off-stage, elsewhere. Until it becomes too much. 'Saloon' – another poem involving bombs – is dedicated to Mahdi Ziu, almost the epitome of ordinariness. A middle manager for an oil company with an ordinary life and an ordinary car (the detail is telling, 'a black Kia Sedan') in which he would take his family on excursions and which he drove loaded with gas canisters into an army base threatening the rebellion against Gaddafi. The ordinary becomes extraordinary in a cleverly, and typically, constructed poem where McAuliffe's car trip segues effortlessly into Ziu's story. McAuliffe has googled images of the wrecked car now 'beyond use' where 'The windowless door frame sticks out like a wire hanger aerial' – a perfect image which carries powerfully that sense of the crazily courageous, ramshackle response of an ordinary man who had to do something with what was at hand.

There are several poems in the collection which are rooted in a warm but never sentimental family life and others which capture well the activity of birds – notably the robin which, in a perfect image, 'flickers on and off the lawn'. McAuliffe is a close viewer of things – at home and abroad – but never a simple voyeur. He weaves the observed world into his own narrative effortlessly and draws out of both meanings universally relevant. By virtue of his craft, the writing of the poems, he becomes a part of the scene described and offers up its emotional heart for all to beat with. The aptly chosen final poem 'Blown Away' recalls a battle between tent and wind in which there is only going to be one winner. It becomes though a self-deprecating meditation on agency in life as the tent takes off in the wind: 'as if a life that had seemed to claw down on what came / within its grip.../was not so much gripping as 'in the grip of', / as if each old 'I am' and 'I do' was as useless as the mud floor / when it was engaged athwart...'

A marvellous close to a thoroughly engaging and engaged collection in which McAuliffe's philosophy of '...let's offer / something up, to living well and days / on which the axe won't fall' is sustaining enough for these times.

Jeremy Hooker

Seán Street and the poetry of radio

'Ears hear but a mind listens.' The words are Seán Street's from his poem 'Short Wave'.[1] It is a truth that Street, the poet , radio programme maker, and Emeritus Professor of Radio, has amply demonstrated in a series of books about radio, of which the first was *The Poetry of Radio*, subtitled 'The Colour of Sound' (2012),[2] and the most recent is *The Sound of a Room* (2020).[3]

During and between periods of hospitalization over the past fifteen months I have been absorbed in these books and have re-read Street's poetry. At the same time, I have returned to listening to radio at all times of the day and night, through headphones, while the life of the ward has gone on around me. The dual experience of reading Street and listening to the radio has enhanced my sense of the poetry of sound, and complemented the emphasis on visual experience, represented by my book *Art of Seeing*, in which I discuss poetry, landscape painting, and photography.

There is a curious duality to listening to radio through headphones in hospital, since one is at once isolated and in the presence of companionable voices, some of which, in my case, were the voices of friends. From this experience, it is not hard to understand why some of those involved with radio at the beginning, in the 1920s, felt there was something supernatural about the medium, in which disembodied voices came out of the dark. This sense of the uncanny is something that radio's more poetic features have never lost. As Street says in *The Poetry of Radio*: 'Voices and music coming through the air ... can hold a magic and a mystery partly borne of their very transitory nature'.[4] It is not surprising, therefore, that radio throughout its history has attracted poets as producers, writers, and makers of features. Certain names and titles of programmes come immediately to mind. One thinks of Louis MacNeice, for example, and of *Under Milk Wood,* produced by Douglas Cleverdon, who also produced dramatizations of David Jones's *In Parenthesis* and *The Anathemata*, and of David Gascoyne's 'radiophonic poem' *Night Thoughts*. Samuel Beckett's *All that Fall* stands out among

---

[1] Seán Street, *Camera Obscura* (Ware, Herts: Rockingham Press, 2016), p. 24.
[2] Seán Street, (Abingdon, Oxon: Routledge, 2012).
[3] Seán Street, (New York and Abingdon, 2020). The other books in the series are: *The Memory of Sound* (Routledge, 2015), *Sound Poetics* (Palgrave Macmillan, 2017), *Sound at the Edge of Perception* (Palgrave Macmillan, 2019), and *The Sound inside the Silence* (Palgrave Macmillan, 2019).
[4] *The Poetry of Radio*, p. xii.

many other notable examples. In more recent times the collaborative radio work of Tim Dee and Ken Smith, and of Julian May and Katrina Porteous, has produced memorable features.

Street himself has made radio features about a number of poets, including Edward Thomas and Keith Douglas, and David Gascoyne and Ezra Pound.

Street's books on sound following *The Poetry of Radio* have extended the subjects raised in that book, delving deeper into the relationship between sound and silence, and increasing understanding of what it means to listen. In some ways, his most recent book, *The Sound of a Room*, is the most haunting. This is an exploration of place involving specific examples drawn from personal experience 'as Covid – 19 altered the sound of the world'.[5] It is 'a journey into poetic acoustics' which begins with Street in the Picton Reading Room of the Central Library in Liverpool, and continues through case studies of numerous other locations, including Paris and the Metro, Lincoln Cathedral, a beach in North Wales, and Street's own garden. Recordings of these and other places reveal soundscapes with and without a human presence, and generate reflections on time and the timeless, past and present, the relationship between sound and silence, and personal identity.

Street quotes the architect, Juhani Pallasmaa: 'Sight isolates, whereas sound incorporates; vision is directional, whereas sound is omni-directional'(*SR*, p.5). This is essentially the key to Street's thinking, which helps to explain his habitual use of the word 'room' for the space of the sonic world, both in the mind and externally. 'Room' is 'a field of consciousness, a sonic energy field with ourselves at its centre' (SR, p. 3). This view has profound implications for the use of sound in poetry. As it appeals to all our senses, poetry works at the interface between the physical and the immaterial, the visible and the invisible, and sound and silence. 'We are touched by sound, one might say literally, as it enters us, vibrates through us, as we cover our ears to shut out its excesses, or lean forward to grasp its minutiae, always seeking for something to make a meaning' (*SR*, p. 8). Poetry 'touches' us physically as well as emotionally. 'With sound,' Street says of recordings, 'I am reimmersed in the moment, living it again through the time it took to happen in the first place' (*SR*, p. 2).

This idea of immersion relates closely to Street's principal themes of place, memory, and time.

In his own poetry, we find that it works in parallel ways to what we might call the metaphysics of radio. Rather than being mainly descriptive, it is immersive. This sense of immersion is reinforced by the fact that Street

---

[5] *The Sound of a Room*, Preface. Subsequent quotations from this book will be given in the text, and designated *SR*.

writes often of music and musicians. A short poem about Chet Baker[6] is a good example of the relation between sound and colour in Street's work. This elegy begins: 'The warm dark red wine flows/out of the mouth, the trumpet/smooth against the face's map./the cracked voice like broken stone'. The second verse of the three-verse poem continues:

> The trumpet wine rich and smooth,
> and the kind light glows warm
> on the gold of the horn,
> smooth against the cracked stone
> of the broken face. *Unphotographable ...*

The reality of Chet Baker, so closely involved with his trumpet, his voice and his bodily presence, would escape a photograph, but is realized here through images of blood and sound, and combined contraries (cracked and smooth). Instead of observing Baker, the poem immerses us in his presence, bringing out the extraordinary poignancy of the quoted words with which the poem concludes: *'Stay, little valentine, stay'*. The sense of music as feeling is strong in Street's poems about composers and singers. As he says in 'Hearing Buddy Bolden: 'There are some kind rooms in the blues, places/ to go we can walk and control our grief'.[7]

Street's poems, especially those about music, work with sound and imagery *inside* their subjects, as district from observing them from the outside. *Cello* is dedicated to the memory of Jonathan Harvey, composer and cellist, who is a presence in the verbal music of the book as a whole, in poems that push thought to the edge of the sayable. As Street says in a poem from *Camera Obscura*, 'I try to guess where matter/ends, where the spirit begins'.[8] In 'Cello Music', he addresses his dead friend:

> There's inner light founding the physical,
> spinning sound, evaporating sound
> back towards Spirit where it began.
> But you know that. You're there now in a space
> purer than silence. White light
> beyond the possibility of prisms,
> solo song moving towards starlight
> and the promise of angels kept.[9]

[6] 'Elegy for Chet Baker', *Time Between Tides: New and Selected Poems 1981-2009* (Rockingham Press, Ware, Herts, 2009), p. 54.

[7] *Camera Obscura*, p. 70.

[8] See 'Mass in e-flat major', *Camera Obscura*, pp. 58-61.

[9] 'Cello Music', *Cello*, p. 21-22.

Street's sense of place is closely associated with his sense of time. In his metaphor, places are 'rooms' of memory, sonic chambers in which the past is present, an audio experience in which pictures can be seen, and what they show can be almost touched. As he says in *The Poetry of* Radio:

> Points in a landscape have their own characteristics, be it a bright acoustic, a timbre, a rhythmic sound, passing animal noises or birds, and occasionally something unidentifiable. Making any sound recording and then playing it back at a later date, away from the original location, can have a powerful effect on the imaginative memory, often much more so than a photograph or a film. There is sometimes too, an intangible feeling, difficult to explain or quantify, a sense of being in a unique place with its own peculiar atmosphere, almost a spirit.[10]

One notable example of this sense of place within his features for radio is the series of location-based programmes he made with Michael Symmons Roberts about the metaphysical poet, Henry Vaughan. Here, use of sounds recorded in Vaughan's home country in Breconshire makes the poet present to us. The result is wholly appropriate to Vaughan's living poetry.

Street's imagination is often drawn to prehistoric sites, not in an antiquarian spirit, but in search of the timeless, and of living contact with the dead. One of his finest longer poems, 'The Calderstones', was inspired by stones that stand in a Liverpool park, 'profusely decorated with rock art symbols and believed to have been once part of a burial chamber used by a Neolithic community up to 3,000 years BC'. Like many of Street's poems, this is a meditation on time – indeed, a sounding of time in relation to timelessness. The poem begins with the sound of distant thunder and a baby asleep beside the poet, 'in a cupped stillness'. The image of prehistoric cup marks in stone becomes a metaphor for the 'room' of the burial chamber, which contains a sense of living continuity. The form the poem takes is that of a dialogue between the poet and a voice from the people who raised the stones. It is a complex meditation, but the following lines express the central idea of life in time forming 'cups of sound':

> All space holds echoes. A clearing
> in woodland, a circle of stones,
> shaped spirals into cups of sound,
> the tense of them always present,

---

[10] *The Poetry of Radio*, p. 26.

heard in stillness, spinning outwards
from the marks that a hand made then,
and here though muffled in thunder
murmuring across the city.

Street is a subtle thinker about the art of listening, who uses his poems to listen and to think with. He responds keenly to poets with a similar gift, such as John Clare, Thomas Hardy and Edward Thomas. These are among the writers whose work 'places them – and their reader – at one with the place and its time'. One luminous page in *The Sound of a Room* begins with Hardy's evocation of the 'voices' of trees at the start of *Under the Greenwood Tree,* and continues with a discussion of Clare's 'sonic observation' and the precision of Thomas's 'sound rooms'. This is Street's home ground, so to speak, but his books on radio are remarkable for their range of reference to thinkers, writers and programmes from many different countries.

Reading Street while I lay in a hospital bed both increased my understanding of radio, to which I was listening through headphones, and sensitized me to the soundscape of the ward. One effect of listening is to enlarge one's sense of physical inwardness. In stillness, as in some night hours of quiet in a hospital, 'we encounter the ultimate listening experience: ourselves, the beat of the heart, the soft whine of our nervous system, the low rumble of our blood stream'.[11] This may lead to a sense of isolation. But isolation is an illusion. Rather than being solipsistic, listening can open two-way portals – into the sense of self, and out into the world. Understood in this way, radio and poetry are both arts that exist on the boundary between the physical and the spiritual, and immerse us in a universe that is full of sounds.

From listening Street has developed 'an acute sense of being alive'. He is a metaphysical poet for whom audio experience takes him 'from the world of matter to the world of spirit'. Listening enhances the other senses, and works suggestively on the imagination, creating pictures in the mind. Reading Street in hospital made me realize how much the art of listening complements the art of seeing. Writing of Henry Beston's *The Outermost House*, Street places Beston's work 'in the company of a select band of natural world observers – Richard Jefferies, Tim Dee, Robert Macfarlane, Nan Shepherd and a few others – who blend knowledge with poetry in their writing'. In such writers, he says, "the word 'observer' becomes something of a misnomer, because the best of such work places them – and their reader – at one with the place and its time'. In his radio features and in his poetry, Seán Street is of this company.

---

[11] *The Sound inside the Silence*, pp. 191-192.

W S Milne

Lost Innocence

Frank Ormsby, *The Rain Barrel* (Bloodaxe Books, 2019)
Tim O'Leary, *Manganese Tears* (Poetry Salzburg, 2018)
Alan Gillis, *The Readiness* (Picador Poetry, 2020)
Seán Street, *The Sound Recordist* (Maytree Press, 2021)

Frank Ormsby's seventh collection of poems comprises a fine canvas of domestic scenes, recollections of his early life on a farm, beach holidays, schooldays, building snowmen, his childhood reading, noting 'the drowned field mouse/the dead wasp' in the rain barrel, 'the hopeless pecking at a plate of ice/by winter sparrows', the installation of running water on the farm:

> Somebody threw a switch and water bloomed
> in the new kitchen sink and the modest tap in the yard.
> The little pipes underground, veining the farms.
>
> Never again the walk from the well in the woods.
> Sensing the gift of its first stillness restored,
> it settles itself among ferns and floating leaves.

Domestic tenderness is evoked in an exact style, contrasting the rain barrel of the title with his ageing father:

> Two old warriors, the rain barrel and my father,
> sit with their backs to the wall,
> one receiving daily the gift of water,
> the other struggling to accept the gifts of air.

The rain barrel proves the image, or similitude, the young poet required to test his developing imagination:

> Idle imaginings of the life it might enjoy
> In another existence;
> Muscle-man, weight-lifter, bouncer,
> The strongman in a circus...

It is the central image recollected of his life on the farm. The eighteen poems of the titular sequence remind one a little of Wallace Stevens' technique in

'Thirteen Ways of Looking at a Blackbird', but the tone is all Ormsby's own. The theme of rural life is there in the poet's love of bees, butterflies and birds, and most of all in his love of flowers, their colours 'like the fabrics of African women' as he pictures it, his 'delight in small things' evident in a phrase such as 'the speckled throat/of the foxglove'.

The 'Troubles' are never far from his mind in this volume and such an ugly image as 'a lethal hook like a piece of dungeon furniture' is contrasted with his early memories when 'Our Woods Were Friendly' (the title of a poem) and 'nobody disappeared'. History's hinterland ('old battles') is always in his mind, and the realities of 'the Witness Protection Programme', the missing, the murdered, always replayed, but he pitches his own beauty against this brutality by evincing for the reader his love of second-hand bookshops, his digging out of family heirlooms, his revelling in the *craic*. His bright images always carry hope: the beekeeper who is 'a tiny astronaut' in his protective clothing is particularly memorable. 'The raw engine of the hive' (rural and industrial worlds meeting in a strange way), 'the bees that have sucked the juice/of the fallen apples, lie sozzled under the trees' summon visions of a loving harmony, and there is ardent humour in such an arresting image as starlings pretending 'to crash *en masse*/into the municipal trees', or when he remembers 'the scarecrow set... in Grandad Joe's old clothing'. At moments like these his poems 'quicken our sense of wonder' like the kingfisher he observes:

Was it pity or indifference kept him posed
half the afternoon, long enough for a neighbour
with a camera to whirr-and-flash
a dozen tasteful close-ups...
We too were fatigued by the speed of the arrow
into its jewelled future and the way evening
seemed to open as though it had held
for his expected message, the day's final highlights.

It is a wonderful moment of natural innocence closely rendered.

As in his earlier books, his gift for light humour is there in the cows' 'big grass-junkie eyes', 'The heron fluffs/his landing. A straight face/ from every fowl on the lake', and

Visitors stop to take photographs:
Colonel Armstrong's black stallion,
Parading his cock round the paddock.

His style has become more compact over the years (as it did in Ciaran Carson's poetry) as he worries about mortality (the 'manageable flux of time', 'time is thoughtless/and has no concept of loss'), his friends growing old or dying, his writing elegies for those friends who have died as the poet's own memory slips a little. He remains optimistic, however, believing in poetry's 'ageless echo', the poet as 'a custodian of language' committed to the 'artistries of colour and sound'. His one regret is that he believes 'the language of tenderness' is now 'suspect', and has resulted, as he sees it, in the demise of the love poem. He may have a point there, but his own verse reminds us that this may not be the case, and that innocence can still be redeemed through art.

The central concern of Tim O'Leary's pamphlet of twenty five poems is his dying mother, her fragile health and dementia: 'you sob yourself gently through lunacy/towards a sanguine dawn, agog at me/in the plenty of hornbeans, truffling for time' – and his dreams of her:

> She comes to me now
> on a phosphorescent raft
>
> laughing, with a message
> from another time
>
> and pledges in new accents
> to wake me as she used to do
>
> on mornings cold with air
> and warm with kin.

He worries about her health:

> Her life has moved downstairs
> with the vase of shrivelling daffodils
> and the empty pill dispenser
> on the side by the sink where
> expectorated cornflakes harden
> next to Colgate smears.

She is living now in an environment of 'kitchen reek' and 'sweaty breeze-block walls'. He tries to 'comprehend some new last end,/even in the faintest falling', and we see him at her wake, tidying up her things when she has gone, clearing shelves of her music and books, finding in this act 'the mystery' of

138

a 'new calm', 'with windows open to the street for air, beyond the traffic's taint... rain softly falling'. He contrasts his mother's faith with his lack of it:

> How long will her legs last,
> or the will to trust my care?
> Her thankyous mean as much as
> amens muttered during mass –
> religiously bare...
> not caring for herself.

She is 'a demonstrable believer', he tells us, whilst be states 'I give you up to a god I don't know', not understanding her 'notions of posthumous paradise'.

There is a dignified poise in the poet's tone, writing of death and suffering, which ennobles his mother, and a lyric strength to what he calls 'the civilising tongue' which he pitches against the 'new barbarities' as he sees them, seeking poetry in 'unlanguaged corners', defying 'the tortuous/ tick of the retirement clock'. He finds the exact metaphor for the moment of his mother's passing: 'Hugger-mugger with death, you cut out/like a Doodlebug descending in silence', the seemingly off-beat image just right for someone of her generation. We feel with him 'the scything loss' of his mother that turns his thoughts and feelings to 'mind-ice', and sympathise with the 'camouflages and aliases' he adopts to save himself from suffering, 'losing himself in dreams', seeking comfort in a world in which 'silence is always ambushed'. The pamphlet is an extended elegy, and is a very fine memorial to the poet's mother, and a fine addition to the Poetry Salzburg publication series.

The Readiness is Alan Gillis' debut volume from Picador, and opens early on with a touch of Marianne Moore spiced up with Paul Muldoon:

> The creepy wrinkled crawly schlong of the earth-
> worm squinches
> through soil to ooze in dew, only to be pincered
> in the beak of a crow...

This sets the earthy tone to the book, and is emblematic of a sense of place. That place is suburbia in the main (conveyed by the vivid gnome, supposed icon of the commuter belt, that adorns the cover of the book), the world of new estates and satellite towns, the domain of 'new appliances in narrow kitchens'. He envisions a suburbanite (himself possibly) facing the dull terror of each day, experiencing that feeling of blurriness between inner and outer reality on wakening like a trance or hypnosis, a sense of dissociation from self, a time when imagination comes into play, 'half of you still in the hall', 'the yin/and yang of this/lingering moment'. 'Is it yourself?' someone asks. He writes of 'alternate selves/from pasts that might have been', of the beginning of the daily round 'as the day undays itself', the tedium of the diurnal grind, 'A lifetime to own a house', 'the brazen lies of the day' stuck in 'the detention of our mind'. He writes in a Larkinesque fashion of dreaming on our 'solitary pillows', observing that 'the brutal demeans/and the night sends its demons' – our selves 'like clock faces on our rounds... ghosting everywhere and nowhere', facing 'another's day dolour' (with the obvious pun on 'dollar'), 'the furies of the night' as 'time splits to show/ the chinks in the chain'. He is very up-to-date with his terms, writing of 'encrypted chatrooms', 'A hybrid car ohms past', and of being dumped by a girlfriend for 'the deep feckin web' – virtual reality trumping the real thing!

The flux of time is an obsession with him as he writes of 'the whigmaleeries of the ticking clock', as 'time passes/by like steam vapours' under 'mood-mutable skies':

> the liquid night, curling its tail
> around you to slither
>
> and slide into your gaping
> mouth. And you know this,
> the oncoming day is nothing
> but the night's brief parenthesis.

We see the poet on hill-walks in the Mournes, on Tinder engagements, drinking fancy cocktails, going to the gym, watching Netflix, listening to the radio, feeling 'the air's brace' as he swims naked, delighting in the sensual, tactile pleasures of the body ('the voltage of your young/here-I-am' as he calls it), thrilling to daily gossip ('the usual crack'), shopping, thinking of his film idols (Charlize Theron, Emma Stone, Gwyneth Paltrow) and his favourite pubs and takeaways ('Kebabarama', for example).

The multifariousness (and treachery) of everyday life is expertly captured by Gillis in his poetry, where he always stresses (like William Carlos Williams and Wallace Stevens before him) what he terms 'This pristine now, this thisness of the air', 'the bedness about the bed' as he calls it, a world in which there is no transcendence, only this earth and nothing else:

> On a day like today you might lift
> your eyes to heaven, but better

to lower them, contemplate the yarrow,
the dog daisy, the angel flower...

We find the poet in hospital at one point, in 'the ward's dismal fluorescence'
with an 'intravenous feed snaked from his forearm', then see him back in
the world with 'the pile driver's graunch', 'the bulldozer's crunch', 'the
percussion of traffic', 'the pavements covered/ with unspeakable tissues
seeping to pulp'. In his poem 'Vespers' (I think based partly on James
Thomson's nightmarish poem, *The City of Dreadful Night*) he finds the
streets full of 'strays and waifs...lost friends, first lovers', 'the fallen, the
dropped, the broken,' 'the morphine-numbed', a vision far removed from
that of peace:

> If there is a holy war, let heaven
> assemble a nation army of pink
> deely bobbers and purple nail glitter,
> butterfly face paint, marching to a play-
>
> list of Beyoncé, Rhianna, Ariana:
> let each follow the steps, learn the moves
> of the dance with a gleam in her face
> and unclenched fists, free from fear.

It is a wonderful evocation of innocence in a world in which it is too often
threatened. *The Readiness* is a very fine debut, and a welcome addition to
Picador's poetry list. (There are a couple of typos in the book: 'buses' should
read 'bushes' on page 16, and 'unsnig' should be 'unsign', or 'unsung', on
page 51. Perhaps these can be emended in future printings of the poems.)

The title of Seán Street's latest collection (a pamphlet of twenty-four
poems) relates to his long career working in radio (see Jeremy Hooker's
essay on Seán Street's work, 'Seán Street and the poetry of radio', in this
issue of *Agenda*). The experience gained from working in radio has given
him acute insights into sound's various relationships with our world, and its
mysterious manifestations, particularly in poetry, music and the visual arts.
Sound's realisation within these disciplines is what grips his imagination in
The Sound Recordist, and it is its metaphysical nature which interests him
most. The epigraph to the collection gives us a clue to his thought: 'Music
always means more than its sound', taking us beyond the material to the
transcendental. The pamphlet reminded me in many ways of James Joyce's
Chamber Music, and made me think that the sequence is like 'a suite of
songs', a wave of verse creating 'a memorable phase of the mind itself', 'an

awakening of the mind' (Joyce's own words on the ethos behind *Chamber Music*). Street writes of the language of poetry 'quietly singing to itself', of 'the vibrating air,/the colour pulsing' it captures, of inspiration as 'a blank empty room filled with/possibility', 'a space waiting', 'blank paper's/white noise', 'the surround sound of enormous space'. He writes of 'the rain given voice by what it touches', of sea shanties 'chipped for deck, keel/and mizzen', their 'sense of salt in a cadence', and of the wonderful dissonances and disjunctions in the music of Miles Davis and George Melly. Writing of Louis Daguerre's painting 'The Ruins of Holyrood Chapel' he tells us here 'sound has turned now to mysteries of light', and the painter here 'saw light impersonate sound'. Of John Singer Sargent's 'Venetian Interior' he says silence here is 'a perfected brush stroke'. He takes joy in sound wherever he finds it, in quiet moments of contemplation, 'In the city I bathe in the voices of crowds', in hospital even when he is very ill taking stock of 'the singing of the morphine's/honey through the cannula'.

There is a poem about early memories of Belfast and Strabane, and a wonderful parable (as he calls it) in Irish vernacular about the ethics of putting down an ailing horse:

And Hughie Flynn says Willie, what'll you do,
will you shoot it? And says I to him shoot it?
What to do with it then, in the name of all?
No, we'll take it down to the beach where the sand's
alive and sinking. I've seen it swallow men
to the waist at a standing sure enough there,
I've seen it with my own eyes, him just stood there,
so we'll leave it there, let nature take its course...

That's not the end of the story, but it's certainly a memorable part of it! There is a fine poem on his intense interest in recording, and listening to, oral history, and one on 'learning new habits of stillness' (in 'Recording a Bell'). *The Sound Recordist* is a very memorable sequence of poems, and one that is excellently served by the wonderful painting by Paula Dunn on the cover. I'll end by quoting my favourite stanza from the sequence:

But I hear most in foreign places when I'm drenched
in the buoyancy of incomprehension, where
language rivers flow best, not being understood.
You can drown in meaning, so trust sounds' tidal song.

As Jeremy Hooker says, Seán Street's poetry helps us all to listen, and we can surely trust in the quality of its sound.

142

David Cooke

Nuala Ní Dhomhnaill, *Northern Lights* (The Gallery Press, 2018)
Catríona Ní Chléirchín, *The Talk of the Town* (The Gallery Press, 2020)

Northern Lights is the fifth Irish-English bilingual collection of Nuala Ní Dhomhnaill's poetry to be published by the Gallery Press. Appearing in the same year that Ní Dhomhnaill was awarded the Zbigniew Herbert International Literary Award, it may disappoint those already familiar with her work to discover that there are few poems here that they will not have read before, although the translations are all new. Nevertheless, with its judicious selection of some of Ní Dhomhnaill's best earlier poems, newly translated by Eiléan Ní Chuilleanáin, it is an ideal introduction for new readers. Alongside some of the classic poems that established her reputation, there are also some later poems and some unpublished work translated by Peter Fallon, Eamon Grennan, Bernard O'Donoghue and Dennis O'Driscoll. The publication of Irish-language poets in bilingual editions has sometimes been a contentious issue and for an informed discussion on this topic I would direct the interested reader to the Introduction to Liam de Paor's magisterial anthology, *Leabhar na hAthghabhála/Poems of Repossession* (Bloodaxe Books, 2016). Suffice it to say here that the Irish-language poet is in a uniquely invidious position. Irish is a minority language which has been in retreat for many decades. It has no monoglot speakers and is in daily competition with English, a global language. Bilingual publication is thus a double-edged sword. While it gives the poet access to a much wider audience, especially in versions by English-language poets who have major reputations, there is also the obvious danger that the original poetry is overshadowed by, and may even seem somehow subservient to, the translation.

The two poets under review here have a deep-rooted connection to the localities that have shaped both them and their poetry. Ní Dhomhnaill grew up in the Kerry Gaeltacht and Ní Chléirchín grew up in Gortmoney, a townland in Monaghan. Moreover, the poetry of both is steeped in dinnseanchas, the poetry of place and folk memories, a venerable tradition that Gaelic literature shares with Ancient Greece. Appropriately enough, the first poem in *Northern Lights* is 'The Shannon Mouth Welcomes the Fish'. Ní Chuilleanáin does a good job of capturing both the down-to-earth solidity of the fish: 'It's all food / this fish / not a scrap of bone / not a scrap of guts' and the sensuous allure of the river: 'And I play lullaby to my lover ... / ... my phosphorus glow a sheet under him.' However, in

'Leaba Shíoda', the poem which follows it, one senses immediately the challenge that faces the translator. The title is an Irish place name, which Ní Dhomhnaill herself anglicised and glossed in the title of her own earlier translation in the 1980s: 'Labysheedy (The Silken Bed)'. The meaning in the original Irish is of course transparent but that is not the only issue. Here is the first verse in Irish followed by the translation:

> Do chóireoinn leaba duit
> i Leaba Shíoda,
> sa bhféar ard,
> faoi iomrascáil na gcrann
> is bheadh do chroiceann ann
> mar shíoda ar shíoda
> sa doirecheacht
> am lonnaithe na leamhan.

> I'd fix a bed for you
> in Leaba Shíoda
> in the high grass,
> under the wrestling trees
> and your skin would be
> like silk on silk
> in the darkness, the hour
> when the moths are settling down.

It's impossible to convey the meaning of the place name while at the same time integrating it into the stanza with the repetition of 'leaba' in the first two lines and in the lovely phrase 'shíoda ar shíoda' in line six. It's difficult, also, to maintain the rhymes: 'gcrann' and 'ann', and then 'leamhan' in the final line, where there are also echoes of the 'l' in 'leaba'. 'In Baile an tSleibhe' is another onomastic poem in which Ní Dhomhnaill goes even further in her self-identification with local traditions and sees herself as a poet whose gift has been inherited:

> out of that house Seán the poet
> went to the Island
> and it's from him I get red hair
> and the gift of poetry
> Descending to me
> through four generations.

However, her Gaelic heritage is not the only influence at play in Ní Dhomhnaill's work. Her husband, to whose memory the collection is dedicated, was Turkish and for many years she lived in that country before returning with her family to Ireland. She is also fluent in its language and several others. In 'Venio Ex Oriente', she explores this dichotomy: 'I bear the spices of the East with me / and the secrets of the bazaar'. Nevertheless, in her concluding stanza she reminds us of her origins:

But there's another fragrance on my body,
the scent of honey from Imleacht Slat
that smells of turf and water-mint
and its colour is dark.

Still, lest anyone should think that Ní Dhomhnaill is a poet who wallows in the 'Celtic Twilight', it should be emphasised that from the outset there has been a streak of rebelliousness in her work, a sense of 'non serviam', like that of Stephen Dedalus in *Ulysses*. In 'Mother', the protagonist is a daughter who is unwilling to receive the gifts she has been offered with due deference and, in the end, has to accept that dialogue with her mother is impossible: 'With your medieval mind / you would write my death notice … / …you would set down the words: / ungrateful, schizophrenic.' In 'The News' she wryly subverts the doctrine of the Virgin Birth; while in 'The Visitor' her attitude towards religion seems ambiguous. The 'visitor' is at first welcomed: 'lay your Crown of Thorns and your Cross aside / move over to the fire and do sit down.' Yet by the end of the poem the tone is more ominous: 'I am not worthy that you should enter under my roof, / will you not let this chalice pass, O Lord?' In 'The Green Eyes', where the eyes are those of the serpent in the Garden of Eden, the prelapsarian vision is one of unabashed sexuality:

Before he came and got
a bite of the apple
there were buttons opening
one after another,
bodies revealed
under the shade of night.

In 'The Mermaid', she employs a folk image, which she was later to explore more extensively, in order to evoke the existential struggle that has to be faced by those determined to find their own way: 'Not without pain / I climbed up / on to the land. / I broke / the predetermined chain'.

Distinguished by their frankness and passion, some of Ní Dhomhnaill's most memorable work has been her love poems. 'The Race', in which a woman is desperately driving across Ireland to reach her 'beautiful man', is an extraordinary tour de force in which the poem's headlong momentum reminds one of Browning's 'How they Brought the Good News from Ghent to Aix'. In 'Blodeuwedd', the flower-faced goddess derives from the *Mabinogion*, but has the passion we associate with Neruda: 'Just the tip of your finger touches me / and I burst into flower, / the fragrant chemistry of my body / alters'.

From romantic love it is perhaps only a small step to parenthood, a theme which Ní Dhomhnaill has also explored memorably in poems such as 'Miscarriage Abroad', 'Poem for Melissa' and Feeding a Child'. In the latter, she imagines the child's journey through life in lines that might well have eluded translation but have been conveyed with great panache by Ní Chuilleanáin.

> go bhfuil do bháidín ag snámh
> óró ins an chuan
> leis na lupadáin lapadáin
> muranáin maranáin
> í go slim sleamhain
> ó thóin go ceann...

> that your little boat
> is out afloat
> with lapping and slipping
> and waving and diving,
> sleek and slippery
> stem to stern ...

The remaining poems in *Northern Lights* are more recent. They are either previously unpublished or taken from Ní Dhomhnaill's two out-of-print collections *The Water Horse* and *The Fifty Minute Mermaid*. 'Black' is a stark litany, a searing lament for the genocide that followed the Siege of Srebrenica. 'My Trojan Horse' revisits a similar theme by way of classical mythology, but with a glance perhaps at Ireland's own troubled past: 'ten years she stood up to a siege of arms, / keeping her courage, no notion of surrender'. The final poem included is 'In Memory of Seamus Heaney' and it is surely fitting, in the light of what the poet Thomas Kinsella referred to as Ireland's 'dual tradition', that one of Ireland's finest poets in Irish should memorialise one who wrote in English. It may be a truism, or perhaps a pious hope, to suggest that poetry should, ideally, be read in the language in which it was written. Translations, however, will always be necessary as no one can master every tongue. Nuala Ní Dhomhnaill has been fortunate in her translators and has much to offer the purely English reader. She deserves to be read by all who love poetry and, in particular the poetry of Ireland, for her glorious celebration of 'the fun and the pain / that are part of being alive.'

In 2018, the Gallery Press published *Calling Cards*, a bilingual anthology of ten younger Irish-language poets translated, as is now increasingly the norm, by an impressive array of well-established English-language poets. This is ample evidence that the literary tradition of the Irish language continues to thrive in spite of its declining fortunes as a means of everyday communication. One of the poets included in *Calling Cards* was Catríona Ní Chléirchín whose new book, *The Talk of the Town*, is a bilingual selection of poems – previously published in two monolingual Irish volumes – which have all been translated by Peter Fallon. Ní Chléirchín's work, like Ní Dhomhnaill's, has been indelibly stamped by the landscape and traditions of the area she grew up in, which, in her case, is Co. Monaghan. Behind her, also, one senses the figure of Patrick Kavanagh who, in his poem 'Epic', famously proclaimed his own brand of localism, that sense of identity which the Italians call *campanilismo*:

I have lived in important places, times
When great events were decided, who owned
That half a rood of rock, a no-man's-land
Surrounded by our pitchfork-armed claims.

Here, by way of homage to her distinguished predecessor, is Ní Chléirchín in her poem 'In the Middle of the Day':

And in the bracing air
we read your poems aloud
while a black hound strayed
as if your ghost in a shroud

were there among the graves …

Two poets, then, products of the same soil but with one important difference: the language in which they have chosen to write. Many of Ní Chléirchín's poems, like Ní Dhomhnaill's, are onomastic and, as we have seen above, this can be a challenge for the translator. The title of the Irish poem 'Droim Searc' is a place name whose meaning has to be glossed in the translation: 'Drumshark' (The Ridge of Love). This is of course the legacy of colonisation and one of the main themes of Brian Friel's classic play *Translations*. The poem itself has a wistful musicality which Fallon replicates with sure-footed assonance, rhymes and alliteration:

> Wind in the evening
>   kisses with honey
>   the mouth
>   of my memory

However, even though the original is only nine lines long, it is not without its challenges. Fallon's couplet: 'Once again with you, / *mon amour*, I lie' derives from one exquisite line in the original: 'Luím leat arís, a *lao* ghil', whose music depends upon the repetition of the consonant 'l' and the long vowel sound of 'í/ao'. Fallon also needs some ingenuity to find an equivalent for 'a lao ghil', an endearment which is virtually impossible to translate literally and means 'my bright calf'. Trickier still is another brief lyric, 'Coigeal na mBan Sí'. A good Irish-English dictionary will translate this as 'reed mace', 'cat's tail', which is the title of Fallon's English version. However, I'm sure I'm not the only reader who may not at first realise that both phrases refer to a family of bulrushes, while there is another meaning in the Irish which the translator is again forced to gloss. Even the word 'banshee', which in Irish is 'bean sí' has the more transparent meaning of 'fairy woman'. The upshot is that two compact lines in the original have to be expanded to convey their meaning:

Coigeal na mBan Sí

Tá coigeal ag an bhean sí
amuigh ar an abhainn in ndraíocht.

Reed Mace, Cat's Tail

Or bulrush
(and, literally,
the spindle
of the banshee)

adrift on the enchanted
river …

148

Of the various poems evoking places, it is perhaps 'Duskus, Gortmoney', with its understated cadences, that is the most affecting:

> And there's no saying
>   the home place's
> allure, from whatever window,
>   wherever one faces.

> *Gentle the trees,*
> *green, green, green.*

> The light at day's end
>   a silken light,
> silken and green.

Ní Chléirchín has no doubt learned much from the work and example of Ní Dhomhnaill. However, one finds in her poetry a quieter, more vulnerable voice. Here are the opening lines of 'There are Days that I Feel' in Fallon's elegant version:

> Not that I've taken to living
> in a souterrain by a freshwater well
> in the palace grounds, all on my own,
> or even that I'm steering clear of the world,
> but it's true, there are days that I feel –
> oh – as lonely as she, her highness,
> Queen of loneliness ...

Ní Chléirchín also has a sharp eye for detail as in 'Damsel Fly' where the insect, once spotted, seems an emissary sent 'from the other world' to bring her word of her dead mother. Many of her love poems, too, are understated, like 'Come Away with Me, Darling?, which has a timeless quality or 'Remembering', in which the memories of love are distilled to their essence:

> My mouth remembers your mouth,
> my hands remember the feel of your skin,
>   my eye recalls your eye...

However, in 'The Talk of the Town', there is a more assertive, dissatisfied tone:

From time to time I just
get tired of being a woman,
the cuts to the chase I've to put
up with, and the inattention.

I tire of constant
pretendings,
charades
and the concealment of things.

In 'Sting' she is more visceral and sexually explicit:

You prised open
my honey portal
and sucked all of the sweetness
from me. Now my body's

left spattered with purple stings ...

Although in 'A Moment, One Morning', an iron that 'smoothes every wrinkle' is employed as an effective image for domestic harmony, the three sections of 'Torc' are a harrowing portrayal of the physical and mental abuse that can occur when that harmony does not exist and concludes that the most enduring scars are the ones that cannot be seen: 'it's hard to be free / from the niggling fiend / that's buried in me.'

Finally, and unsurprisingly, given her upbringing in the North, some of Ní Chléirchín's poems are informed by the sectarian history of Ireland. Monaghan is one of the three counties of Ulster that were assigned to the Irish Free State in 1922, so that the poet grew up very close to the Border. The protagonist of her poem 'The Parting of the Ways' is Catherine O'Neill, the wife of the rebel Hugh O'Neill whose exile after the battle of Kinsale was the death knell of Gaelic culture in Ulster:

Just as smoke can be scattered,
so we'll be dispersed.
like wax by the hearthside
we'll come to our worst.

In 'Border Crossing', a sequence of six poems that brings *The Talk of the Town* to its conclusion, the poet explores the impact of this political divide upon herself and her family. In 'Sealed Lips, Ne'er a Word', Fallon cunningly incorporates an echo from Seamus Heaney: 'Whatever you say, say ...' – with 'nothing' being implied. 'Border (the Limit)' is a moving portrayal of the poet's mother being interrogated or, more euphemistically, being asked 'a few questions' while her children stare at the armed soldiers. In 'Border Crossing' there is an understanding, even amongst the children, that any manifestation of Gaelic culture, whether it be its music or its language, is likely to attract unwelcome attention: 'The sweetest sound was silence.'

Going back to the Dark Ages, that much vaunted age of 'Saints and Scholars,' the Irish language has had a long literary tradition but is currently clinging on in three isolated areas, each with its own dialect. It would be all too easy for it to lose itself in nostalgia, becoming increasingly irrelevant in a country whose social evolution in recent decades has been staggering. With poets of the calibre of Ní Dhomhnaill and Ní Chléirchín, and those younger urban poets who, even if it is their second language, have still opted to write in it, this is unlikely to be the case. Moreover, it is a temptation that Ní Chléirchin faces head on in 'Mowing (with Scythe)': 'There was a time / you'd hone / a scythe / with a sharping stone // that would be kept / stashed / under the dresser / for fear it be smashed'. Those days, however, she tells us are long gone so that now there is 'Nothing but these / smithereens in our memories.' To judge by the evidence of these clear-sighted, moving and memorably cadenced poems, the language is safe in her hands.

Gerald Dawe

Make-believe

Derek Mahon 1941-2020

You'll be peering through the binoculars
from your final look-out post, I guess,
covering all the exits and entrances
of that most illustrious harbour mouth,
for that's how it is this bright autumn
day in another coastal town you once
could call your own and on watch again
for what was happening beyond Howth Head.

Now your own dead have newly assembled
to welcome their prodigal son back home,
wherever that might be – under Cave Hill –
stepping out in full Hitchcockian mode,
pointing to this and that, a garden shed,
the vanished corner shop where all the pals
gathered seventy and more years ago
as the murky air settled on windowsill

and afternoons became dark before
you knew it and the chilly sky
broke to a grey-blue tinged with fire.
Oh yes, how easy it is to remember
what was left behind but not so good
when it comes to why. Why? Why? Why?
For there was no answer, and never is, so
let's make-believe a scenario for your safe return:

a seal perhaps, rolling on the shallow rocks,
in sea-surge – maybe not; what about
that urban fox disappearing back
into its own territory, unseen,
or more like a local bird, soaring high
enough to have a really good look
at what lies below us here amongst
our ordinary lives, the nooks and crannies.

('Make-Believe' was first published in *The Irish Times*, Dublin)

Only Son

Gordon Aubrey Dawe 1923-2015

How strange to learn
you kept an eye
on my unpredictable 'journey'.
Were the cuttings stored
safely away or kept to hand
in the living room
beside TV and fire?

Staged photographs from
the west, anonymous backdrops,
your only son awkward
as ever before the camera.
I have one of you in return,
looking the very best,
hands in embrace,
the sunlit beaming face.

Revenant

The other day, in 'recovery',
half-awake, drifty,
the bright sky sliced in two,
I was certainly not myself.

A door opened and out of the landing
you stepped in regimental army dress,
the creaturely plume of your beret
and all I heard whispered was –

'He's sleeping at long last'
before you left in the slanting
light of the closing door
as unexpected as it was before.

John McAuliffe

Church Music

"But all is cleansed when the marble weeps" – George Herbert

1. Lecture, *St Patrick's Chapel, Paris*
17.7. 2013

At a round table, the talk
starts to sound responsible, a *performance*,
as if the old piece being read
                is a bath
the sainted blackbird would take off from its airs
to dip into,
scattering water everywhere.

Later, the choir in the old seminarians' library
stands up to the notes; and suddenly
something unearthly:
the library *in* the choir.

2. Lectern, *All Saints' Braunston*
(after William Trevor Cox)

Copied across from the *Book of Kells*
his images hardly register
the history they preside over
but seem to know the wooden grain they're imposed on,
and made from.

                Each lined, knotted evangelist's face
is opaque and broad, so the lectern
shines flatly, its brown sloping panels
a pulpit where their author
reserves *judgment*
                for what would come later,
taking on board the possibility of forgiveness
but also how a place's four-cornered resonance
                    distorts.

3. An Impression, *Manchester Cathedral*
11.3.2012

It was not exactly
                     church music,
but 'Oileán' – on flute McGoldrick,
Sinéad Hayes conducting – reeled in
some crowd – a congregation.

At the interval
I was remembering the cassette version,
how the piece could shuffle
tune and orchestration
when the MC (now long gone)
pointed to this place's oldest part,
the 'angel stone', a Saxon fragment.

Going back to it,
I see the angel
who reads from a scroll, a sort of vertical banner,
which the text (roughly from the Latin –
'Into your hands I commend my spirit')
spills over,
                spilling over

                like how a tune will originate
in a certain place, a set form, or the soul alone,
making an impression, which can be re-shaped,
                           as it was that night,
by whatever course its players could unravel,
bending frail dotted lines into the cathedral's marble.

The Prospect

The wide quietness of the road, the seasonal
green in corner windows of the houses
spangled with lights left on overnight, and the tinsel
recovered from the furthest cobwebbed corner,
and earlier than ever this year, November
when it started to glitter in windows,
not just a distraction from our losses
but a beckoning at *hoped-for* returns... All's well
on a morning like this, dawn rain-bright,
dramatizing each home-made effort at light,
in one, a child in time to see a favourite show
drawing the curtain to better see right
what's banked, and stays ahead of her, even now.

Leontia Flynn

The small boat had turned

The small boat had turned
outward from the headland
into the grey field
of the Atlantic

when my phone buzzed
in my raincoat pocket:
another death
broke on the networks.

The main mast swung
like a metronome
as we swayed and turned
further into the wind.

The back white wall
was awash with emotion.
It rolled downward,
endlessly in slipstream.

One gull hung
in the uncrowded sky
as we kept on course
for the island – away

beyond the last beach
and the long reach
of call and response
and tumult, to go

where the word that breaks
on the steady prow
is ploughed down, back
to the undertow.

Niall McDevitt

John Dee

The name appears to derive from the Brythonic dēvā:
'River of the Goddess' or 'Holy River'

John Dee your name is talismanic
magic-mirroring friends
to your invisible house for consultation
on the shores of Mortlake

not progressing on a steed or a barque today
but by red bus
stopping off at St Mary's to divine your bones
feet shuffling from chancel
to a Christian plaque
remembering you as cleric
– oh man named after the holy delta -
as stained glass honeycombs
empty pews

in the green-brown Thames
there are red shrouds
a dust of ochre
Elizabethan wigs

one of your 21st century friends
steps into the water
to test the new soles of his leather boots
measuring
as if in Louvain
how fast it's rising

soon the bench he chewed and sipped on is swallowed
then the tow-path
as the river climbs to its apex
at four o'clock
in Beltane sun

flexing like a Chinese dragon
then magically, impossibly
stopping and about-turning
to flow east again

Lundrumguffa, called, isn't there
– oh man named after the holy delta –
but only an atmosphere
of DDD
a tree-trunk touching my forehead
whispering of seed-sown grounds,
a library of ciphers

Cernunnos

from the Gundestrup Cauldron

i

Cernunnos
floats in Shiva position
as irish as indian
               are gods

is he smoking a hookah
or fixing a band
to the nozzle of his hoover?
          no,
          he is friend
                    to the serpent

ii

Cernunnos
          here looking like Hughes
          clean-shaven with thin lips
          making a tiny O
hovers in relief on the cauldron
in a company
          a
          faber menagerie

iii

               the stag
               the pig
     are in love with him, very,
     exhaling into his ears
     their most urgent cares

     is that some cat
     or dog or boar
     who turns away from the handsomeness
     to a fairy darkness?

                              anyway,
                              the background goat
                              ogles

                    iv

academics quiz the silver

an earthenware pot on his head? a rose-tree?

                              no, they are horns
                              tacked off the stag
                              the exact stag's antlers
                              he
                    – antlered -
                              is more than man

                              but also isn't *he*
                              the highclass highfashion deity
                              in tunic belt and torc
                              of his forest court?

                              162

Seán Street

Journey Into Space

BBC Light Programme, 1953-1958

Unknown territory, one school after another,
moving day always a step into the void:
reinvention, beginning again, learning the rules
of the next exclusive club. The eternal new boy, ever
the incomer in the wake of a father's upward mobility.

Each promoted step meant a hostile dialect to unravel.
Children have no option but to follow, and to be seven
was to see migration from familiar worlds as bereavement,
every unaccustomed classroom's inquest betraying
my unacceptable accent, judgement by articulation.

As a sound can fall into silence, to speak was to become
solitary, until the home radio's primal light invented
alternative empires where everyone could be foreign
together once a week, and the aerial pulled Ariel
and all his quality out of the night, holding the literal at bay.

While the war of the world ignited round me,
there I was, tuning the Bush dial in to fellow aliens,
peopling galaxies with a mutual language,
my own wavelength listening for the companionship
at last of voices even stranger than my own.

Song for Mina

Foolhardy girl from bandit land,
they told you I was ill-advised,
and that my coming could kill you.
Tiny indomitable girl.

Just as if it wasn't enough
to marry His Majesty's Navy.
Then my coming, as if to prove
another stranger couldn't hurt you.

And there's the sound print of you now
deep in my head, the Irish girl,
the part they couldn't change, long gone
but embedded in DNA.

How many people does it take
to impose an identity,
to erase a past or deny
a name? And how to survive that?

Border girl with a fever-hurt
heart and broken lungs, no wonder,
biting a towel to swallow
your blood-letting screams, anything

to hide my birth murdering you,
to mock their mocking, the Irish
they watched and wanted to see fail,
flame of unbroken Monaghan girl.

No wonder your love could be fierce,
no wonder nothing was too good
for the child everyone feared for
but you and your emerald fire.

Well, you kept your voice for Ireland,
made the red stain that became me,
we came through it, right enough, so
I'll sing it for the two of us now.

An Old Violin

At first the strings creaked, then something came from deep
in it that must have been held for two lifetimes.
It was when he tried an air my father sang
that memory brought from the instinct of it
tides' full flow up past the estuary's end.
Who'd know the old thing had that much song in it,
part he said of time pent up and saved so long,
that would have learnt to sing itself anyway.

It was years later when I walked down the lane
to the water, and I was just past halfway
along, there where light seems to modulate, tense
with the river's closeness, that I was with him
again, and sound it did, just as he played it,
just as he said, singing in tides' flow, time's shift.

Stephen Sexton

An Act of Going

New geometries
of brilliant aluminium

a few pristine helmets
the boys of Christmas morning

pedal along the quay
a loose braid of dazzling oaths

big talk and cigarettes
for now the town is theirs

the universe for all they know
keeps the lights on for them.

No hands is elementary
but show-stopping

is two boys drawn parallel
uncrossing their arms

and by fingertip by palm
each taking the other's hand

however costly to balance
however alien the intimacy

and coming to grief
laughing on the cobblestones.

Across the river in which
teenagers drown themselves most months

the half-built Ferris wheel
is the nervous system of the moon;

wind shears off the water
through intricacies of spoke

and yes, boys, always yes,
someone should be watching

and I am your mothers,
but oh how the flag whips the flagpole.

Kathleen McPhilemy

Hand in hand

(for KFG)

Whisper of ash, finger of bone
hand that once I held in my own

sound of the sea sound of the wind
dune grass whip   damp sand

I've been here before let me come back
your ring on my finger your veins in my hand
your face in my mirror let me go back

escarpment, island, lights in the bay
shadow of Scotland furthest away

elegant swimmer you have swum from the shore
threading the breakers till I see you no more.

Imaginary Friend

Mine, of course, is male
and I'll never betray him
although I'm afraid of the truth drug
and what I may say on the table;
lately, however, I think
perhaps it's he who is leaving.

I have made up a code for his story:
scratched out hieroglyphics
no-one will ever decipher
etched on the inside of my head;
there like a comfort blanket
too tattered to be washed or aired.

He moves with the times and seasons,
though never much past forty
and he has no mobile phone;
he is unspecifically handsome
and that tiny twitch of the lips,
is a smile only I can imagine.

Gary Allen

Peace Wall

Meet me down by the Peace Wall
now there's a stretch in the evening
before the iron gate is slammed shut

before the quiet road littered with stone
broken glass, burning rubber

is cut in two.

Look love at this swift migration
the silver wings of aeroplanes
an aerial pattern above the mudflats
the cranes, corrugated workshop roofs

of the seeping lough.

And all the Kristallnacht windows of the high risers
open out upon the mountain tops
and tingle blindingly among the traffic on the bridges
the office workers going home

the last diesel fumed buses leaving the depot.

I remember your black hair
your crucifix snapping like bone –

someone played a piano on the Malone Road
that warm night we walked home afraid
and it seemed as if all the city was dancing in flames.

Ruth O'Callaghan

Challenge

On that beach in winter when the wind
took our words and hefted them into waves

and the wind and the words and the waves
were wild and the strand was laced with white

you turned away.

In that field of corn where flowers were deeper
blue than flowing ink, freedom held us in thrall

yet from the field and the flowers and the freedom
you turned away.

Under the willow you wept...

When and in which place will we ever admit the act
or will the throat always catch at the unsaid?

From what sunless distance does the mute watchman
wait and in the waiting worry each place, comb words

the way wind seeks answer in past seasons' harrow
or a droop of trees root toward soured earth.

Hayden Murphy

The Butterfly Key

For Craig and Eileen Henry

Protected by shadows the Grandfather
Clock in my Grandmother's drawingroom
Paced me from birth to childhood.

Now, in memory,
I reoccupy and re-install the remembered
Butterfly Key: winged and slender, flexible
As a conjurer's wand, hollow insert
To steel cobwebs rotating to order memory
To remember neighbouring memories
Of time. Ensuring I cannot forget that time,
Honoured by friendship, keeps time
By the daily, on the hour, up to the minute
Re-application of this life's imperative.

                              The Key,
Green bronzed by age, winds, rewinds,
Restores the yesterdays as todays.
                              Mirrors
The times of change but does not alter
Fidelities, reflecting on this our owntime
Healing love.

from
In Spain I came to my Senses

For John Liddy in Madrid:

In Spain I heard three cocks crow
Called the Destiny, Despair and History.
Deferring now to that fifty year old call
I halt its progress. Stay the moment.

> *Destiny:*
> In Spain I genuflected at the shadow cast by
> Limerick, my broken treaty with memory
> Earthed in sand, distant from flowers.

> *Despair:*
> In Spain I never dared to carry roses.
> The heated scent distracted from the thorns.
> Their absence hurt.

> *History:*
> In Spain I wandered to Madrid from Barcelona,
> And back, pretended I had had my gypsy moment
> As a balladeer, dashed at castles with Quixote,
> Followed the Wild Geese in order to refight
> The siege of Limerick, catch my breath and start
> A return journey.

In Spain my bestiary included snowfalls of gulls,
Peacocks dancing on poet's graves in Parc Guell,
A Lion Rampant carrying exiles to another's home.
Joining, off the bull's back, a dismounting Oisin.

Now in a City of Enlightenment
I draw the curtains. Drape the deserted streets with petals
That have no roots, watch the day grow flowers to decorate
The nights. Remember when in Spain I came
To my senses.

Brendan Cleary

Our Drive

before something
bad happens
let's drive
together again
head over
the Causeway
cross the bridge
at Ballycarry station
on the way
to Dada's grave
overlooking
the cement works
then homewards
past The Shoe Tree

Ghost House

growing up
I'm in the attic
deft guitar
licks & spins
of Jeff 'Skunk' Baxter
drifting down
& later Mama
at the rayburn
Martin with hair
playing Joe Walsh upstairs
& Dada settling down
in the backroom
to watch Benny Hill

Joseph Allen

Roll-call

After roll-call
the different coloured meal tickets
were handed out

those who had paid
were called out first
then half-price
free tickets last

at the back of the class we waited
always behind the kids
who were going to grammar school
the children of the doctors
the solicitors, the shop-keepers

we were destined for the factories
or the building-sites

everything was beyond us
and yet I saw
the streets illuminated
like a café at night.

The Hare

i

After two days
my father returned
bottles of Guinness, Babysham
and a dead hare

ii

my mother and aunt
feigned anger
giggled at the fizzing glasses
the hare hanging from his belt

iii

I was too young to care
playing with bottle-tops
for toy soldiers

iv

his beery breath upon my face
bristles rubbing my cheek
smell of nicotine stained fingers
the sound of a tongue
thickened with alcohol.

A. David Moody

Yeats, Pound, & Being Modern: A dialogue [1]

Yeats said of Pound in 1929, '[his] art is the opposite of mine, [his] criticism commends what I most condemn, a man with whom I should quarrel more than with anyone else if we were not united by affection'. That was in 'A Packet for Ezra Pound', his introduction to *A Vision*. The immediate causes of contention in that work would have been that Pound, as Yeats knew, would hate the generalities and abstractions of his (in Pound's view) 'spooks'-inspired system; while Yeats himself hated the modernist rejection of 'conventions of the intellect' in Pound's *Cantos*, 'a poem in which there is nothing that can be taken out and reasoned over'. Behind those differences was an apparent deep disagreement as to what it meant to be modern.

The story begins about 1906 or 1907, in one of the drafts towards the epic poem modelled on Dante's *Divine Comedy* which Pound was then projecting – he was 21 or 22 at the time. In the draft headed "Blake's Rainbow", which appears to have drawn on essays of Yeats collected in *Ideas of Good and Evil* (1903), Yeats is evoked, along with Dante, Ezekiel and Blake, in a passage summoning up the powers of the prophetic imagination –

> and here all lovliness
> yea and the palor of dreams
> And here his might that resang Oisin
> Yes that saught and set a whole land singing
> That Eire should be the soul of the nations he leader of the pack
> The celtic Eagle that singeth of dim stars
> And far out chanteth all that lived in thy youths May time
> Yea all such beauty of the dim blue cloths is here invivified
> And groweth might of might[2]

Notably, this 'celtic Eagle' doesn't renew its vision by gazing upon the divine sun, as Ezekiel's does, but is instead associated with 'the pallor of dreams', and sings of 'dim stars' and 'the dim blue cloths [of heaven]'. The

[1] A talk give at the W. B. Yeats 150th Anniversary Commemoration, 23 November 2015, Magdalene College, Cambridge.

[2] From 'Blake's Rainbow', ts. in Beinecke Rare Book and Manuscript Library, Yale University. Extract Copyright © 2020 Mary de Rachewiltz and the Estate of Omar S. Pound. Used by permission of New Directions Publishing Corp., Agents. See A. David Moody, 'Dante as the Young Pound's Virgil: Introduction to Some Early Drafts & Fragments', *Agenda* 34.3-4 (1997) 69-71.

passage owes nearly everything to Yeats' early poetry of the Celtic Twilight; but then it owes something more to the way Yeats was presenting himself in America in those years.

In November 1903 he had lectured at the University of Pennsylvania in Philadelphia, talking about a heroic Irish theatre rather than about his lyric poetry. A city paper, *The Pennsylvanian*, reported that he spoke of efforts to create a theatre 'for the expression of the genius of the Irish race', and of his part in the movement 'to reawaken a true national consciousness in Ireland'. There is some evidence that Pound was in the audience for that lecture, although at the time he was a student at Hamilton College in upper New York State. In any case, in 1906-07, as a graduate student at the University of Pennsylvania, he would have been hearing talk of Yeats and reading his work for Dr Cornelius Weygandt's course on Contemporary Poetry – Weygandt had been entertained by Yeats in Ireland in 1902 in connection with a book he was writing on contemporary poetry, and it was he who had arranged for Yeats to lecture at the university.

Pound can hardly have been unaware of Yeats' concern for a heroic Irish theatre, but evidently his interest at that time was in Yeats the poet, and as a poet, however paradoxically, of both the Celtic Twilight and the effort to reawaken a true national consciousness. In his early vision 'Eire' was to be founded upon its Celtic mythology, upon Oisin, and upon 'the dim stars' and 'the dim blue cloths' of the Celtic Twilight.

Pound determined that he must go to London and sit at the feet of Yeats, and when he managed to do that, in April 1909, he was not disappointed. Yeats was 'the greatest poet of our time', he told his father, and advised him to read 'Red Hanrahan's Song for Ireland'. At the end of the year he told his mother that Yeats was 'the only living man whose work has more than a most temporary interest'. He would refer to him familiarly as 'the Eagle'.

But now, in 1909, the Celtic Twilight aspect had lost its appeal. That April he published a poem under the title 'REVOLT / Against the Crepuscular Spirit in Modern Poetry' – it was a very direct rejection of dim dreams and mists, and a call rather for 'shapes of power' and mastery of the world. He had declared an ambition, in another draft towards an epic poem, to sing 'The Great Song of All the World'. Whitman had sung America, and he would do more – perhaps forge not just a national consciousness, as that of the Irish race, but the consciousness of the human race. 'The Great Song of All the World' might be a subtitle for *The Cantos* he would eventually write.

Yeats rather took to his young follower, and was reported as saying 'There is no younger generation [of poets]. E.P. is a solitary volcano'. That could have been on account of such eruptions as his 'Revolt', and his fiery persona Bertran de Born in 'Sestina: Altaforte'. Yeats also said of Pound, this was in early 1910, 'If he writes rhyme like an amateur / he writes rhythm like a master'. That was significant, because Pound was freeing his verse from the traditional iambics and pentameters, from fixed metres and regular verse forms –'To break the pentameter', he would write in the *Pisan Cantos*, 'that was the first heave', meaning the first heave in his effort to modernise himself. Yeats reflected that Pound was getting close 'to the right sort of music for poetry ... it is more definitely music with strongly marked time and yet it is effective speech'. But he would not himself 'break the pentameter', he would not modernise himself in that way, being convinced that his Irish poetic traditional metres and verse forms were right. 'Because I need a passionate syntax for passionate subject-matter', he would write in 'A General Introduction for my Work', 'I compel myself to accept those traditional metres that have developed with the language'.

But Yeats was emerging from his Celtic Twilight, to Pound's delight. 'Yeats has been doing some new things', he wrote to a friend later in 1910 – he had seen, along with other new poems, a version of 'No Second Troy' –

Why should I blame her that she filled my days
With misery, or that she would of late
Have taught to ignorant men most violent ways,
Or hurled the little streets upon the great ... .

Was there another Troy for her to burn?

What this meant to Pound was that Yeats 'has come out of the shadows and declared for life', and that gave him a tremendous 'uplift', 'for he and I are now as it were in one movement, with aims very nearly identical ... the movement of the 90s for drugs and shadows has worn itself out'. Pound's 1911 parody of Yeats' 'The Cap and Bells', 'Au Jardin' – '"The jester walked in the garden." Did he so?' – was perhaps more in sympathy than satire. In effect, Yeats had joined Pound's revolt – he had decided, as he put it in a 1937 broadcast, to write poems that would be 'not at all a dream ... but a criticism of life'. He had, in Pound's view, 'once and for all stripped English poetry of its perdamnable rhetoric', so that now twentieth century poetry would be 'harder and saner', 'austere, direct'. It would be in accord with Pound's primary Imagiste principle: 'Direct treatment of the "thing" whether subjective or objective'.

Yeats credited Pound with helping him 'get back to the definite and concrete, away from modern abstractions'. He might have said, to get back from the visionary to the actual. 'To talk over a poem with him', he told Lady

Gregory, was like getting her 'to put a sentence into dialect. All becomes clear and natural'. And he learned from Pound 'how much further the movement against abstraction had gone than [his] generation had thought possible'. 'Go in fear of abstractions', Pound had urged, 'Don't use such an expression as "Dim lands of peace".' When he reviewed the Cuala Press edition of Yeats' *Responsibilities* in 1914, under the heading 'The Later Yeats', Pound observed a further directness, hardness, and gauntness in his work, it had a grip on 'things as they are' and was 'no longer romantically Celtic'. He placed first in his *Catholic Anthology 1914-1915* Yeats' 'The Scholars' –

> Bald heads forgetful of their sins,
> Old, learned, respectable bald heads
> Edit and annotate the lines
> That young men, tossing on their beds,
> Rhymed out in love's despair
> To flatter beauty's ignorant ear.
>
> They'll cough in the ink to the world's end;
> Wear out the carpet with their shoes
> Earning respect; have no strange friend;
> If they have sinned nobody knows:
> Lord, what would they say
> Should their Catullus walk that way![3]

When he reprinted 'The Scholars' in his 1931 anthology *Profile*, Pound recalled that 'The anthology of 1915 appeared as it were under Yeats' *patronato*, at least it started with a poem in his then newer manner, which might be regarded as a turning point from the twilit to his more stony and later phase'.

In his 1914 review Pound had asked, 'Is Mr Yeats an Imagiste?', and had answered, 'No, Mr Yeats is a symbolist'. The discrimination was sharper in his review of the 1916 edition of *Responsibilities*. He still praised what he had praised before, but now he wrote that despite the 'occasional bits of realism, the tone of the new book is romantic', and he passed then what became his final judgment: 'Mr Yeats is a romanticist, symbolist, occultist, for better or worse, now and for always'. Behind that was what he knew of Yeats from their three winters together at Stone Cottage[4] in the Ashdown

---

[3] This is the version Pound gives. The second stanza was later considerably revised by Yeats.
[4] On their winters at Stone Cottage see A. David Moody, *Ezra Pound: Poet. I: The Young Genius*

Forest, East Sussex. The judgment was tempered by his adding, 'That does not matter. What does matter is that he is the only one left [of his decade] who has sufficient intensity of temperament to turn these modes into art'. That was a considerable concession, but it did not cancel the placing of Yeats' art as of the past, as not truly modern.

But then Yeats, in his Introduction to the Cuala Press edition of Pound's *Certain Noble Plays of Japan* (1916), was complaining that Pound's modern stuff in his *Lustra* 'gave him no asylum for his affections'; and as for 'realism' – here a side-glance perhaps at Pound's 'The Lake Isle', a take-off of his 'Innisfree' – well that was 'created for the common people', 'and it is the delight today of all those whose minds, educated alone by school-masters and newspapers, are without the memory of beauty and emotional subtlety'.

One can get some idea of what Pound meant by 'modernism' about this time from what he had to say about T. S. Eliot. When Eliot showed him 'The Love Song of J. Alfred Prufrock' in October 1914 he was instantly excited by it, and told the editor of *Poetry* (Chicago) that it was 'the best poem I have yet had or seen from an American'. Eliot had 'actually trained himself *and* modernised himself *on his own*'. Then when he reviewed the volume *Prufrock & Other Observations* in 1917 he declared, rather invidiously so far as Yeats was concerned, 'Mr Eliot's work interests me more than that of any other poet writing in English'; and he indicated that Eliot's modernity consisted in, primarily, his realism, in the completeness of his 'depiction of our contemporary condition'.

Pound appears to have been unimpressed by Yeats' 1919 collection, *The Wild Swans at Coole* – probably finding it still 'romanticist, symbolist, occultist'. It opens after all with those brilliant swans as romantic symbols, 'mysterious, beautiful', and it ends with the occult visions of Michael Robartes. 'W. B. still enveloped in celto-spiritist fog', he told his mother, and to his American friend William Carlos Williams he wrote, 'Yeats faded'. That was in 1920, and one wonders if Yeats had not yet shown him 'Easter, 1916', dated 'September 25, 1916', and privately printed in 1916 or 1917.

In January 1923 Yeats published in *The Dial*, his great poem about the condition of Ireland, 'Meditations in Time of Civil War'. Later that year he was awarded the Nobel Prize for Literature 'for his inspired poetry, which in a highly artistic form gives expression to the spirit of a whole nation'. Yeats accepted the prize as a recognition of Ireland as an independent nation with its own culture and literature. 'The work of my generation in Ireland', he said, has been 'the creation of a literature to express national character and feeling but with no deliberate political aim'.

Yeats was now coming to terms with the modernisms of Pound and Eliot and Joyce. In 1925, in the early version of *A Vision*, he observed in their work 'a hatred of the abstract' – they either eliminate the poet's phantasy and put in its place 'a strangeness discovered by historical or contemporary research', or 'they break up the logical processes of thought by flooding them with associated words or ideas that seem to drift into the mind by chance'. Though not actually named – *The Waste Land* and *Ulysses* are named – Pound's *Cantos* must have been in the line of fire. The attack became explicit in *A Packet for Ezra Pound* published in 1929, then included as front matter in the 1937 *A Vision*. 'You will hate these generalities, Ezra', Yeats warned, meaning that Pound would hate all that system of occult symbolism, of abstractions, revealed to him by his spirit-teachers through his wife's automatic writing. But before that he had expressed his own rejection of Pound's method of writing and structuring his cantos. He had talked for an hour with Pound in Rapallo, listening to his explanation of their system – at that date the first 27 had been published – and Yeats could not, or would not, see it. Think of a Bach fugue, Pound suggested, subject and response, counter-subject and so on, trying to get Yeats to grasp the idea of composing poetry on the model of music and musical forms. But Yeats could only see 'no plot, no chronicle of events, no logic of discourse', nothing but 'eternal flux'. That was how he summed up the *Cantos* in the introduction to his *Oxford Book of Modern Verse* (*OBMV*) in 1936. 'Ezra Pound has made flux his theme', he declared with extreme prejudice, 'plot, characterisation, logical discourse seem to him abstractions unsuitable to a man of his generation'. And that meant that to Yeats the *Cantos* presented 'merely exquisite or grotesque fragments'.

Yeats, deep once more in his 'abstractions', was clearing the modernist moderns out of his way. Eliot he dismissed in his introduction as 'an Alexander Pope working without apparent imagination', 'a satirist rather than a poet'. And he was putting down Pound not only directly but also in comparison with other poets. In the work of the now forgotten Walter James Turner he found 'a power of emotional construction, Pound has always lacked'. He also compared him unfavourably with the new generation of poets, 'Day Lewis, Madge, MacNeice', these being 'modern through the character of their intellectual passion', along with 'the modern vocabulary, the accurate record of the relevant facts learnt from Eliot'; but 'Pound with his descent into Hades, his Chinese classics, [is] too romantic to seem modern' – thus returning with interest Pound's word for Yeats.

Another word they were exchanging was 'nobility', a quality Yeats prized. In an article on Cocteau in January 1935 Pound had allowed that 'Yeats has a sort of nobility in his somewhat clouded way, in his language that is the speech of no man'. And in his introduction to the *OBMV*, dated

September 1936, Yeats wrote that in Pound's work he found 'at moments, more style, more deliberate nobility and the means to convey it than in any contemporary poet known to me', but then the turn, 'it is constantly interrupted, broken, twisted into nothing by its direct opposite, nervous obsession, nightmare, stammering confusion' – and so he went on, leaving little standing.

The sort of poem Yeats could appreciate was Pound's early, Imagiste poem, 'The Return', apparently finding in it something of his own 'abstract sky', and perhaps better words than his own. He quoted it in full in 'A Packet', and did so again in his introduction, though more guardedly: 'Even where the style is sustained throughout one gets an impression... that he has not got all the wine into the bowl, that he is a brilliant improvisator translating at sight from an unknown Greek masterpiece'. 'The Return' evokes the spirits of mythical heroes –

> See, they return, one and by one,
> With fear, as half-awakened;
> As if the snow should hesitate
> And murmur in the wind,
> and half turn back;
> These were the 'Wing'd-with-Awe',
> Inviolable.

It is a ghostly poem of psychic phenomena such as Yeats himself might have written, and he very clearly preferred it to Pound's major effort.

But then Pound had done much the same thing to Yeats, effectively putting him down as a poet while preserving an early poem which might have been one of his own in *Lustra*. 'The Scholars' was the only poem by Yeats in his 1931 anthology, *Profile*, 'a collection of poems which have stuck in my memory'. And Yeats did not figure at all in his next anthology, *Active Anthology* (1933), a collection of 'writers in whose work a development appears to be taking place, in contradistinction to authors in whose work no such activity has occurred or seems likely to occur'. There was simply this comment, that Yeats was 'now muddled, now profound, now merely celtic' or erroneously believing that a free Ireland or at least a more Oirish Ireland would lead towards 'a sacred book of the arts'.

Certainly Yeats was committed to an Irish 'national character and feeling' and to the work of his own generation. 'Even a long-lived man has the right to call his own contemporaries modern', he declared on the first page of his *Oxford Book of Modern Verse*. So Hardy, Bridges, Blunt, Henley and Wilde were all moderns for him, along with Dowson and Johnson, and Synge and Gogarty and Lady Gregory and Francis Thompson's 'The Hound of Heaven' was a modern poem. And in a BBC talk on 'Modern Poetry' coinciding with the publication of his *OBMV* he spoke at some length about the poets of the Rhymers Club, and about Sturge Moore, also as a modern poet, and about Binyon's 'noble poem' of Tristram and Isoult, and about Dorothy Wellesley, and about Turner again. Of Pound on that occasion he said not a word.

When he was making out the specific modernity of the Thirties poets in his introduction Yeats confessed to a 'moment of sympathy' for certain of their lyrics, and to preferring them to Eliot in that moment – and even preferring them 'to myself', he added, for 'I too have tried to be modern'. But he immediately distanced himself from them and from modernism –

> I have preferred, and shall again, constrained by a different nationality, a man so many years old, fixed to some one place, known to friends and enemies, full of mortal frailty, expressing all things not made mysterious by nature with impatient clarity...

The syntax is oddly obscure – is he saying that he is such a man, or that he has and will again prefer such a man? But in either case he is declaring the stance of the poet of *The Tower* (1928) and *The Winding Stair* (1933), as in such poems as 'Coole and Ballylee, 1931' (its title in *OBMV*) –

> We were the last romantics – chose for theme
> Traditional sanctity and loveliness;
> Whatever's written in what poet's name
> The book of the people; whatever most can bless
> The mind of man or elevate a rhyme

Yeats never meant to be modern if that meant being revolutionary in the manner of Eliot and Pound. What his poetry celebrates so magnificently is his chosen tradition and its romance – what could be more romantic than to declare 'We were the last romantics'? The war with Pound, from his side at least, was not about being modern, but about opposing his Irish traditionalism and his romanticism to the forces of modernism. And the better to do that he had learnt from his antagonists, from Pound and from Eliot, to ground his romanticism upon the relevant facts and to write it out in modern speech, to be at once romantic and a realist. In his *New Poems* of 1938, and in the last poems of 1938 and 1939, there is a sustained assertion, poem upon poem, of this romantic realism as his form of presence in the modern world. It is there from 'The Gyres' through to 'The Municipal Gallery Revisited' in the

1938 collection, and again from 'Under Ben Bulben' through to 'The Circus Animals' Desertion' at the end –

> Those masterful images because complete
> Grew in pure mind but out of what began?
> A mound of refuse or the sweepings of a street
> Old kettles, old bottles, and a broken can,
> Old iron, old bones, old rags, that raving slut
> Who keeps the till. Now that my ladder's gone
> I must lie down where all the ladders start
> In the foul rag and bone shop of the heart.

Yeats was cheered in 1938 when his old antagonist told him that his recent poems were 'rather good' – he felt that, coming from Pound, that was 'rapturous applause'. Pound happened to be in London and Yeats had him to dinner at the Athenaeum – that was their last meeting and the end of their contending against each other.

When Yeats died in January 1939, Pound wrote that his death 'closes the great era of the Irish literary revival', thus honouring Yeats in the way he would have appreciated. In his *Pisan Cantos* he named Yeats among 'the lordly men', his former companions, recalling him as 'William who dreamed of nobility'; and in another of the *Pisan Cantos* he recalled 'Uncle William dawdling around Notre Dame', admiring the symbol of the great cathedral in its rose window, ever the symbolist; and he recalled how what sounded like the wind in the chimney at Stone Cottage was actually 'Uncle William downstairs composing', making 'a great peacock .... For the pride of his eye'. There was real affection in these memories. Then in 1965, in his 80th year, Pound attended the memorial service for Eliot in Westminster Abbey, and afterwards, instead of flying straight back to Venice, he flew to Dublin to sit with Yeats' widow and commune with his spirit.

Martin Caseley

Birmingham Trams in the Poetry of Louis MacNeice

Arriving in 1930 to lecture in Classics at Birmingham University, Louis MacNeice called the city 'a sprawling ink-blot of nineteenth-century industry'[1]. Altogether he was to spend the following five years there, newly married to Mary Ezra, writing poems reflective of his urban environment such as 'Sunday Morning', 'Museums' and commemorating it more explicitly in 'Birmingham'.

In MacNeice's *Collected Poems*, 'Birmingham' is placed next to 'Belfast', suggesting a striking contrast, despite the two years between the composition of the poems. The autobiographical slant of much of his work ensured that a childhood in Ireland travelled with him: in 'Perdita', this becomes 'a green/ flag...waving under an iron vault'[2], but whether in an old attic, or locked in a vault, it still summons him. In a fragmentary, foundational description of his early life included in *The Strings are False*, MacNeice lists the 'human elements' of his world: 'guilt, hell fire, Good Friday, the doctor's cough... melancholia...violent sectarian voices'.[3]

'Belfast' itself mentions elements of Irish culture such as the Orange marches, the nearby lough and the harsh colours of the Virgin Mary but, like 'Birmingham', it reserves a special, forensic eye for mass production and the life of the factory. Factory hooters were also part of MacNeice's creation myth and in the two poems, there are elements of continuity as, in the former, the hunted faces of those who pass in the street, guilty, religious and murderous, become those called to the factory-gates in the latter poem, helpless victims of all that is severely workful. This, more distanced recognition of their exploitation and victimhood, to me, indicates a slight softening in MacNeice's stance, and the latter poem is better for it.

This vision is nothing if not democratic and urban: all is movement as 'Birmingham' begins at a road junction, a traffic policeman exerting all his authority like an Egyptian ruler, while drivers race their car engines impatiently. The city as a temple to throbbing consumers is indicated by the vistas of shops stretching away, MacNeice listing examples of the goods available, denoting their aspirational, domesticated sexuality in a

---

[1] Louis MacNeice, *The Strings are False*, Faber, 1965, p. 130.

[2] MacNeice, *Collected Poems*, p. 188. Edna Longley *(Louis MacNeice: A Critical Study,* Faber, 1988, p. 3) notes this.

[3] MacNeice, *Strings*, p. 216.

way Larkin was later to utilise in 'The Large Cool Store' and several other poems. The diagrammatic layout of the city streets allows MacNeice to guide us past the radiating slums and suburbs full of half-timbered, half-understood desires, erected on 'jerry-built beauty'[4], before coming to rest at lunchtime, with shopgirls described as empty, incoherent fairgoers, looking forward to cheap, weekend thrills. Again, the cheap slogans recall the 'cut-price crowd' of Larkin's 'Here'[5], although parallels with the leaded Burne-Jones windows in Birmingham Cathedral endow them with a brief aura of spirituality. Even so, 'crawling leads' seems rather harsh on Burne-Jones: the actual womens' faces are enhaloed and the 'diaphanous...green glass' is mostly used for clothing and robes, rather than empty expressions. As they were manufactured by William Morris & Co., however, MacNeice may wish to damn them as just another mass industrial product (despite the Pre-Raphaelite associations) rather than allowing them any individualised religious allure.

MacNeice's political stance may be reflected in the representative straw figures he creates in the second and third stanzas: the aspirant middle-class suburban man and the female retail slave. Both are implicated in exploitation – 'sweated labour'– and his view of the lures of immediate gratification returns in the later 'Sunday Morning' where the deadening effect of religion shuts off their roads to art and improvement: 'the church spire...will not tire/ to tell how there is no music or movement which secures/ escape from the weekday time.'[6] In *The Strings are False* he does, in passing, mention those taking night classes in Plato, but confesses his unease: 'My snobbery was at this stage willing to accept a clean-cut working man, but it could not accept these hybrids.'[7]

It is in the fourth and final stanza of 'Birmingham' that a grander, spiritual palette really intervenes, at first in the unlikely shape of the humble corporation tramcar. At this time, Birmingham had an extensive network of tramways, over 80 miles of route stretching from Erdington in the North to stops at Rednal in the south. Major arterial roads like the Bristol Road, now the A38, had trams running down the middle of them, whilst other routes penetrated deep into Dudley and the Black Country – the very places where 'Vulcan's forges', as MacNeice describes the local industry, were located, key to its dark prosperity. The tramway system was deeply embedded in

---

[4] 'Birmingham', line 16, MacNeice, *Collected Poems*, Faber, 1966, p.18. Unless otherwise noted, all subsequent MacNeice quotations come from this poem.

[5] 'Here', Philip Larkin, *Collected Poems*, Faber, 1988, p. 136.

[6] MacNeice, *Collected Poems*, p. 23.

[7] MacNeice, p. 131, *Strings* op cit.

Birmingham's infrastructure (and psyche) and MacNeice presents these as the 'shining lines' ascending away from the city into symbolic grandeur, towards some unrealised burial, taking precedence over the stilled cars kept at bay, 'gently breathing'. In his essay, 'Experiences with Images'[8] he makes the point that the lyric poem is dramatic, ironic and 'above all', symbolic. Longley sees this as a rhetorical technique which might stand in the way of some readers.

However, 'Birmingham' does not just end with symbolism: having criticised the shopgirls' faces (and, by extension, the Burne-Jones stained-glass windows) as 'insipid', MacNeice substitutes what Roy Fisher later called a 'Birmingham industrial sunset'[9], a decadent, grand guignol vista of plum, mauve and traffic lights splashed with cocktail-hour colours 'creme-de-menthe or bull's blood', interspersed with the Pentecostal fire of headlights flaming out from horizontal side-roads. This deliberate, polyglot of chattering tongues may be particularly apposite to the place as a multicultural city. Concerning landscape itself, the most famous depiction of an industrial sunset is J.M.W.Turner's 'An Industrial Town at Sunset', a watercolour of the Black Country, painted around 1830, showing a mellower, diaphanous cityscape, bathed in veils of mauve and orange, a colour range much subtler than the melodramatic flares in the poem.

In 'Morning Sun', written eighteen months later, MacNeice was to return to the tramline image: trains are shuttles on a loom, weaving through the urban haze, cars offer vigorously discordant rough music, but 'the shining of the lights of trams like swords'[10] is once again, destructive. The colour tones here, however, are closer to Turner's vision: 'chromium yellows', white sun filleting a 'purple mist' unnaturally. In the final lines of 'Birmingham', the lurid procession to death takes workers 'through the daily gate', an oppressive, routine appointment. The chimneys are like blackened organ-pipes (again, images of religious decay and oppression) and the 'frayed and fading zone' suggests a Western, sacrificial destination, rather than any Isles of the Blest, provisioned with elysium. The house of the dead transporting these lost souls is the tramway car; MacNeice the classicist offers no further comment, beyond narrating the journey to this destination, the poem ending with the mighty chord ushering 'sleep-stupid faces through the daily gate.'

In his later poetry, post-'Autumn Journal', there is less of this journalistic scenery, but many of these earlier 1930s poems retain a distinct, gritty tang of

[8] Quoted in Longley, op cit, p. xi.
[9] Roy Fisher, interviewed by Robert Sheppard and quoted, p. 79, *Interviews through Time*, Shearsman, 2000.
[10] MacNeice, *Collected Poems*, p. 26.

the documentary about them. The final stanza of 'Birmingham' in particular, could be a set-piece from a Humphrey Jennings film. Of the poems written at about this time, there is almost a consensual landscape: urban life is full of traffic ('Birmingham'), suburban repression ('Spring voices'), railway epiphanies ('A contact') and all the miscellany of varied lives ('Sunday morning'), sometimes closing in on what he called, in another context, 'an inventory of the dreary world of habit'.[11] Biographically, however, he admitted an initial period of isolation from the city. In *The Strings are False*, MacNeice describes how he eventually began to explore it, stumbling upon existing cliques of writers, many of them working class. He comments sniffily how local novelists such as Walter Allen 'wrote about the People with a knowledge available to very few Londoners'[12], but he himself was soon on the move again, to Hampstead, to mingle with London men of letters such as Robert Lynd and J.B.Priestley.

Leaving aside his political views, there is much in MacNeice's writing of this period that we encounter again in Larkin, not least his feeling for consumer detail. MacNeice notes the cinemas sprayed with cheap perfume, Larkin notes the latest racks of nylon nightwear. The consumers Larkin sees as typically resident 'Here' travel 'from raw estates, brought down/ the dead straight miles by stealing flat-faced trollies', and the 'grim head-scarved wives' are surely MacNeice's shopgirls, grown older and coarsened by life. Structurally, too, MacNeice and Larkin share an occasional taste for the neo-symbolist 'lift' at the conclusion of a poem: compare the glass windows in 'Snow' with Larkin's dazzling, puzzling high windows in the poem of the same name. Many of Larkin's conclusions, when not undercut by the bathetic, are straining for exactly this sort of ironic, symbolist detachment.

Unlocking the precise meaning of these symbols is fraught with danger: they belong to a symbolic order, but what exactly do they signify – nihilistic freedom, airless, guilt-free knowledge, some unspecified transcendent understanding? MacNeice's vessel transports the dead-in-life on their way, beyond the impatient breathing of paused cars, to a zone beyond complete explication which is, like the ending of 'Here', somehow out of reach.

---

[11] MacNeice, *The Poetry of W.B.Yeats*, Faber, 1967, p. 189.
[12] MacNeice, *The Strings are False*, pp. 133, 154.

Patrick Lodge

Ethna MacCarthy, (Lilliput Press, 2019)

The academic, Anne Mulhall, writing in the *Irish University Review* a few years ago, noted that the work of past Irish women poets still tended to languish in obscurity. This can certainly be considered the case for Ethna MacCarthy who published in her lifetime very occasionally – though having work in the influential 1948 American anthology, *New Irish Poets* – and waited sixty years after her death for this first collection. The answer to a query as to whether the wait was worth it must be an unequivocal 'yes'.

Ethna MacCarthy was a very talented, self-determining and achieving woman. Born in 1903 into an upper middle-class Dublin family steeped in medicine, writing and poetry, she taught languages at Trinity College, Dublin until studying medicine which she practiced in the 1940s and 1950s in Dublin and London. She had many well-connected friends, not least Samuel Beckett to whom she was very close and who seems to have based the character Bianca, in *Krapp's Last Tape,* upon her. It appears also that she had several relationships with married men including a long-standing affair with Beckett's close friend, Con Leventhal, which was formalised in 1956 with their marriage following the death of his wife. Tragically, MacCarthy herself died of throat cancer in 1959.

This collection, which includes an extended verse drama, has been put together under the editorship of Eoin O'Brien and Gerald Dawe who have provided excellent introductory essays to place MacCarthy in context. The actual poems – both translations and original poems – derive from several sources including those published in Irish and English magazines and newspapers. Interestingly there are many so-called 'archive' poems which were unpublished and discovered in the papers of Leventhal following his death in 1979. The poems are arranged as far as possible in a chronological order which is helpful in highlighting the development of her work – notably after her graduation in medicine in the 1940s.

The poems give the impression of someone who was very much in love with life but who was entirely unsentimental about it. Her translations are from several European languages and she seemed particularly drawn to the German-Jewish poet Else Lasker-Schüler – the 1935 translation of 'Weltende' with its couplet 'In every heart the life-urge sleeps / underneath the coffin lid' giving a hint why. MacCarthy's poems frequently contain variations on the idea that, in the midst of life we are in death. Again, her translation of Calderón de la Barca, speaks of men 'whose very day of birth is day of doom'. Such a sense that life is transitory suffuses her own work too – *Advent,* published in *The Irish Times* on an Easter Saturday, concludes rather pessimistically for the celebration of the Resurrection, that '...All things stiffen from this same disease / we only die of being born'. Yet there is little sense of pessimism and gloom in this collection. As Eoin O'Brien notes, she simply has a 'deep acceptance of what existence is'.

The early poems in the collection are deft, neat and technically sound with clever imagery and alliterations. They are an interesting read but rather conventional. A ballad sequence cleaves too much towards a cold European romanticism with a few too many 'damozels' and 'brindled serpents'. They are slick and a little glossy but lack heft. However, MacCarthy gains her voice and a harder edge to the poetry as the collection progresses and, one imagines, as her life pans out. Thus, she reworks early translations several years on – such as 'The Prisoner's Song' and 'Nächtliches Bild' – and evidences a much stronger sense of trying to capture an essence rather than simply translate a work – there is a lighter, more confident touch and the expression is more sparse, more direct.

Though it is conjecturing, the poetry seems to shift – in subject matter, in voice and in her acute sense of place, notably her city of Dublin – following her graduation in medicine in 1942. That change of career is 'celebrated' in *MB, BCh, BAO* where she finds herself 'Ferreted from a five-year cave, / expelled from his earth womb confused, / my eyes assaulted by the light, / I am at bay in feeble fear'. Indeed, some of the best writing in the collection derives from her work as a doctor. The no-nonsense realism, the unsentimentality, is still there but it is now drawing its source from the realities of life met head-on. 'Viaticum' is a powerful reflection on being awake in a night-time hospital where sleep takes some but others '...it leaves marooned / Who cannot sleep'. Others will not make it through the night; they '...watch the shadows with unfocused eyes, / Dull and indifferent, ears attuned / To soundless music of the Boatman's oar / And rhythmic singing of the rowlocks' strain / As the dark ferry swings to shore'. Such strong imagery here and it is no surprise that this poem, and the similarly excellent 'Insomnia' and 'Ghosts', were selected for the 1948 American anthology.

There is not too much of the overtly personal in the later poems – these are not in the 'confessional' mode though one feels that the archive poems were, to some extent, at least a conversation with herself. Indeed, one wonders what she might have achieved in perfecting her craft and developing her voice had she not died so young and, had she been part of a vibrant public poetry scene such as that of today.

However, the later poems are not entirely dispassionate and may hint at the complexities and joys of MacCarthy's relationships. 'Harlequin' speaks lyrically of her love as 'of the moon' with a hint that the 'fearful maturation of the light' necessitates acceptance that the relationship lives on scraps – 'And so he goes, / to skim the scattered sequins from the pools". There is disillusion with the empty gypsy promises that true love would wait in a shower of petals under a tree 'on the moonlit grass, / with a fairy coach / of sparkling glass' but the reality is that the 'strange lover in a black cockade, / of pine that trysting tree was made; / and dark the road we must traverse, / that crystal coach a lamplit hearse' ('Song'). Humour and optimism is never too far away and MacCarthy's close observation of the natural world allows her hope – in 'The Chestnut Tree' she writes, 'The snow will wind her / shroud in vain, / for she through love / will live again'. The marvellous 'Untitled' with its images associated with Aphrodite is almost post-coital in its sensuous warmth.

This is a fine collection – and a beautiful production by Lilliput Press – which restores to the readers of poetry a neglected female poet of some grace and charm. Ethna MacCarthy was, as the editors note, 'a very special, multi-talented and humane Irish woman' and all one would want to add to that is the descriptor 'and poet'.

Ben Keatinge

'Far from at home': Richard Murphy

Richard Murphy, who died at his home in Sri Lanka on 30th January 2018, experienced the acute dilemma of being perceived as Irish in the UK and English, or Anglo-Irish, in Ireland. Speaking of his historical poem *The Battle of Aughrim* (1968), he explained that: 'I was trying to get clear a division in my mind between England and Ireland – between an almost entirely English education, an English mind and Irish feeling' (as quoted in *Richard Murphy: Poet of Two Traditions*, ed. Maurice Harmon. By presenting both sides of the 1691 battle, the poet hoped to disentangle his own heritage while also obliquely expressing his 'guilt in not having served in the war that was brought to an end by the bomb on Hiroshima on my eighteenth birthday' (Murphy, *The Kick*). Murphy would later adopt the sonnet form to express his sense of hybrid identity in a series of 'sonnet-houses' which ventriloquise his mixed identities through the voices of different buildings connected with his life. 'Nelson's Pillar' conveys the poet's sense of dividedness in a changing Ireland where he was both at home and 'Far from at home':

> My duty done, I rose as a Doric column
> Far from at home, planted to reach the sky;
> A huge stake in the crossed heart of a glum
> Garrison city overlooked by my blind eye.

This erstwhile Dublin monument was blown up by Irish republicans on 3rd March 1966, an event noted in the sonnet as a 'blast' which 'wore / Red, white and blue in a flash of puerile skill'. The tricolour and the Union Jack are thus superimposed in 'Nelson's Pillar' on the demise of a former Dublin landmark.

Murphy's fascinating memoir *The Kick* (2002/2017) takes its title partly from his schooldays where 'a monitor's "kick"' was 'a boy that the monitor fancied'. The ambition to be a poet took root first at Canterbury Cathedral School and then at Wellington College where early readings of 'Shakespeare's sonnets and the poetry of Donne, Herbert, Marvell, Milton and Wordsworth' shaped his lifelong belief in poetic form. But it was the juxtaposition of music and architecture in his early education which gave Murphy his sense of 'poems as buildings and as music', and a sense of their 'architecture', as he later told John Haffenden in a 1981 interview. The poet and his older brother Christopher were from 'dissolute Ireland' ('Choir School'), and one may speculate that the displacements of their upbringing set against the formality of an English education, early on tuned the younger Murphy's 'ear for poetry' ('Canterbury Cathedral'). This peripatetic life (the Murphys' father worked in colonial Ceylon / Sri Lanka), left its imprint, and is implicit in the title of *The Price of Stone* (1985) suggesting, I think, the price of stability and the costs of being cast adrift, living between the social orbits of the UK, Ireland and outposts of the then British Empire. One need hardly add that life in boarding schools was not conducive to the poet's happiness and a telling anecdote is related in *The Kick* about 'an elderly gentleman standing alone, looking up at one of the dormitory windows' in Wellington College apparently lost in thought. When asked by a 'senior boy' if he 'might need guidance', the man replied '"Oh no, thank you very much . . . I am just looking up at the room where I spent the most unhappy years of my life"'. It transpires that the visitor was 'Field-Marshal Sir Gerald Templer, Chief of the Imperial General Staff' who departs in a chauffeur-driven Rolls-Royce. Not surprisingly, as the sonnet 'Suntrap' tells us, it was only during 'One year at home under our flagging roof' at the family demesne of Milford, Co. Mayo where Richard and Christopher enjoyed private tuition 'During the war', that 'learning and love made peace'. Milford, and more generally Connemara and the west of Ireland would become the 'unfenced romantic pleasure ground' of Murphy's mature poetic imagination.

The poet completed his formal education at Magdalen College, Oxford where C.S. Lewis was one of his tutors. He would later admit that he 'attended few' lectures and that he became distracted from the official English Literature curriculum by his 'Celtic passion to write poetry' temporarily abandoning his studies for a remote 'cottage' at Lecknavarna, 'near Screebe' in Connemara where his 'verse began to flow'. However, he was prevailed upon to complete his degree and in 'Oxford Staircase', another of the 'sonnet-houses', the older poet is admonished by the staircase of his youth, 'You slipped up, going down'. The curriculum did leave its mark, however, and the lineaments of Oxford are evident, for example, in signature poems like 'The Cleggan Disaster' with its *ubi sunt* motif, from Anglo-Saxon, and in the heavily alliterative and narrative style of 'Sailing to an Island' and 'The Last Galway Hooker'. He also made important friendships, notably with Charles Monteith who would later be his editor at Faber and Faber. Monteith would subsequently visit Murphy and sail with him off the coast at Cleggan and Inishbofin, north Connemara after Murphy moved to live there from 1959 until the late 1970s. Indeed, so many UK poets, writers and actors joined Murphy in the west of Ireland in the summer season – including Philip Larkin, J.R. Ackerley, Ted Hughes, Mary Ure and Tony White – that Monteith would write, in a letter of 30 November

1960: 'If things go on like this, Days Hotel will turn into the Garsington of the '60s!'. The main hotel on Inishbofin island is thus viewed as a hub of contemporary intellectual ferment akin to Lady Ottoline Morrell's country house, Garsington.

After Oxford, Murphy lived in London, sharing a flat near Harrods, Knightsbridge with his sisters Mary and Liz. Working briefly for Lloyd's insurance, he soon abandoned 'clerking' and found work as a reviewer for the *Spectator* via the good offices of Harold Nicolson who was an influential mentor. The Irish poet would later write that he 'received from the *Spectator* an education in modern poetry that Oxford never gave me' and he would publish almost fifty reviews between 1950 and 1956 including pieces on American authors like Robert Frost and Robert Lowell and emerging UK poets like W.S. Graham. Further formative encounters included his friendship with J.R. Ackerley who was a 'generous' critic and published several of Murphy's early poems in the *Listener* where he was poetry editor. Even after Murphy moved back to live in Ireland, having won the AE Memorial Award in 1951, his career crossed the Irish Sea continuously. For example, *The Battle of Aughrim* was commissioned by Douglas Cleverdon for the BBC Third Programme and broadcast in September 1968 with simultaneous publication by Faber and Faber. Although 'written in Connemara between 1962 and 1967', Murphy's effort to examine 'colonial war and its consequence in Ireland' was sponsored by UK cultural institutions.

Murphy's poetic legacy leaves many traces of what he called his 'split-level life'. His remarkable poems from *High Island* (1974) have some of the raw energy of Ted Hughes' early work:

> The calamity of seals begins with jaws.
> Born in caverns that reverberate
> With endless malice of the sea's tongue
> Clacking on shingle, they learn to bark back
> In fear and sadness and celebration.
>
> ('Seals at High Island')

Later poems, scarcely remarked on in the Ireland of the 1980s, have a 'queer' confessionalism which Thom Gunn would have recognised:

> The powers that be, served covertly by AIDS,
> Strip to the bone your skin-deep masquerades.
>
> ('Gym')

Meanwhile, his powerful elegies to Tony White, the London-born actor who was Richard Murphy's closest friend and collaborator while writing *Aughrim* and the *High Island* poems, adopt a plangent authority to speak of White's rebellious lifestyle, the actor's unheralded returns from London to Connemara and equally unannounced departures:

> He lived at the hub and not the rim
>   Of time. Within himself he moved
> Deeper toward dangerous ideas he loved
>   To moot with bodily risk:
>   Flying too close to the sun's disk,
> [...]
> Because his kind of love taught me to live
>   His dying I forgive.
>
> ('Tony White')

Richard Murphy was, perhaps, more of 'A Conventional Rebel' than White, as his sister Mary suggests at the conclusion of *The Kick*. Nevertheless, Murphy's poetry has all the 'tension, ambiguity, defensiveness and advantages' of being 'Irish in England and English in Ireland', a predicament he understood but moved beyond.

W S Milne

The Poetry of Ciaran Carson

Ciaran Carson was a member of the Belfast group of poets organised originally by Philip Hobsbaum at Queen's University (other writers from that same 'school' included Seamus Heaney, James Simmons, Frank Ormsby, Paul Muldoon and Edna and Michael Longley). He published fifteen collections of poetry from 1976 until his death in 2019. Irish was his first language, but he chose to write in English (the language of the coloniser as he saw it), suffering from guilt in not writing in Gaelic, calling himself at one point in a poem 'a turncoat interpreter'. In his verse he praises Irish place names such Ballinliss, Aughaduff, Slievenacapall and Carnvaddy, writing of those who named them:

> To hard hills of stone they will give
> The words for breast; to meadowland,
> The soft gutturals of rivers,
>
> Tongues of water; to form plains, flesh…
> For this was the land
> That they fought for, loved, and killed
>
> Each other for…
>
> (from 'The Insular Celts')

The title of the poem is, of course, ironic, voiced by a coloniser. The poet's work is particularly influenced by the intricate formalism associated with Gaelic art and poetry, describing the 'Words, whorls and braid and skein and spiral helices' of the illuminated manuscripts, 'the spirals of their brooches is seen in the flight/Of one thing into another', 'Their bronze swords took the shape of leaves,/How their gold spears are found in cornfields,/Their arrows are found in trees'. So it is this Gaelic heritage that grips his imagination, but it is a tradition overlaid with the glories of the English language. Like Austin Clarke before him he is very interested in Irish poetic forms, especially that of the *aisling* (see, for example, 'The Display Case') which he terms 'a labyrinthine dream in which the imagination can wander and find delight', a metaphor as he calls it in his notes 'for musical and poetic inspiration'. He translates poems from Middle Irish (see especially his fine version of a poem by Colm Cille, which serves as the opening to his *Selected Poems and Translations*) and he likes to play around with words ('Catestants and Protholics') with a Joycean sense of humour (see especially his 'The Ballad of *HMS Belfast*'), the fireworks of *piazza, pizza, putz, paparazzi* in 'Oscar' and 'a tangled tagliatelle linguini Veronese' in 'Romeo'. He revels in language, telling us of his joy in 'rummaging through the OED's delights', exploring what he terms 'the dark forest of language', contrasting cultures along the way ('the prison that we call Long Kesh is to the Powers-that-/Be *The Maze*', 'You ask what's in a name? Where I come from it tells you where/ you're from, I said, whether this allegiance or the other'), 'adapting new methods for new situations' as he calls it, maintaining metrical strength and order in his poems, particularly in his tightly framed sonnet sequence of 1998, *The Twelfth Of Never*. His is a poetry in which craft and thought coalesce, meld and integrate, with formal risks taken and new departures made, with never a hint of grandstanding or pomposity in the tone. His work is also very learned, with references, for example, to Colm Cille (St Columba, patron saint of Derry, mentioned above), Douglas Hyde, W.B. Yeats, Richard Murphy, Seamus Heaney, Derek Mahon and Séan Ó Ríordáin, amongst others, acknowledging the 'deep draught of wisdom... enriching those who like to read' (in 'Colm Cille Recited').

The lovely place names mentioned above become poisoned through Empire and internecine warfare, reduced to 'Chlorine Gardens', 'Raglan Street', 'Balaklava Street', 'Crimea Street', (see 'Belfast Confetti', perhaps his most famous poem), legacies of occupation by a foreign power and its inevitable condescension towards Irish culture ('They drink and talk too much. Not all of it is gibberish' – see 'Spenser's Ireland') which forces the occupied to 'guard their tongue' in order to survive, to protect their language, and forcing them to lead 'double' lives as he puts it in 'On The Contrary'.

From his second volume, *The Irish For No*, onwards, Carson's poems became more and more concentrated on the 'Troubles' ('The city is a map of the city,/Its forbidden areas changing daily') and war generally, employing a longer line to tell a more expanded tale, especially in 'Dresden' and 'Hamlet', a style I think he inherited from poets such as Louis MacNeice, Patrick Kavanagh, Thomas Kinsella and John Montague. He likes to think, however, of the city's confidence, defiance and resilience in restoring what has been destroyed (referencing at one point the god Shiva's capacity for destruction and renewal) evident in a line such as 'Belfast tore itself and pulled itself up again', bomb after bomb. But he is equally aware of the terror:

Suddenly as the riot squad moved in it was raining exclamation marks,
Nuts, bolts, nails, car-keys. A fount of broken type. And the explosion
Itself – an asterisk on the map. This hyphenated line, a burst of rapid fire…
I was trying to complete a sentence in my head, but it kept stuttering,
All the alleyways and streets blocked with stops and colons…

(from 'Belfast Confetti')

The public explosion intrudes on his private thoughts, as later when the train he
is on is blown up whilst he is reading poetry:

I'm about to quote from Bashō's *The Narrow Road to the Deep North* –
Blossoming mushroom: from some unknown tree a leaf has stuck to it –
When it [the bomb] goes off and we're thrown out of kilter. My mouth is full
Of broken glass and quinine as everything reverses South.

(from 'Yes')

'South' of course implies a reference to the Republic, and a possible clue as to
where the poet's sympathies lie. This shocking alliance of peace and war, of the
public and private, occurs often in Carson's work, where opposing spheres fuse
in the strangest and often most bizarre and brutal fashion. A world of innocence
is lost and betrayed in a travesty of domestic peace, for example, in the poem
'Fragment':

From a piece of
the Tupperware
lunchbox that held

the wiring

they could tell
the bombmaker wore
Marigold rubber gloves

Could horror be more concisely portrayed than that? It is also there in a single,
terse line like 'His hand had been clamped in a G-clamp to the Black & Decker
workbench'. Brutality spills over into the streets for no apparent reason, as
when a landlord of a pub is wrongly suspected:

They had questioned him for hours. Who exactly was he? And when
he told them, they questioned him again. When they accepted who he was, as
someone not involved, they pulled out his fingernails. Then

they took him to a waste-ground somewhere near The Horseshoe Bend, and
    told him
what he was. They shot him nine times.

(from 'Campaign')

Such brutality and violence contrasts with the comfort of the pub lounge familiar to Carson, and makes him wonder how peace and conflict can coalesce in this way, but somehow connections are made in the strangest fashion as when he writes of the paradox, the irony, of 'Poppy the emblem of Peace and the Opium Wars', for example, the contradictions, comparisons and contrasts building up day by day as the Troubles continue. This observation he calls a 'sfumato air', an ambience in which one thing shades into another and where connections are made from disparate areas of experience. This becomes his chosen narrative technique (sometimes described by critics as postmodern). As in his novel *Shamrock Tea* (2001), characters' names in his poetry (I'm thinking especially of his masterpiece 'Dresden') such as Horse Boyle, Mule Boyle, Quigley, Carrick McCloud, Young Flynn, Mister McGinty, and so on, take on a life of their own, as they do in Beckett's novels, the poet demonstrating his ability to sustain a strong narrative full of rumour, gossip, fantasy, tall tales, spinning yarns, the whole realm of what he calls 'The Groves of Blarney'. The openings to his poems give an indication of his skill:

Horse Boyle was called Horse Boyle because of his brother Mule;
Though why Mule was called Mule is anybody's guess. I stayed there once,
Or rather, I nearly stayed there once. But that's another story...

('Dresden')

As usual, the clock in The Clock Bar was a good few minutes fast:
A fiction no one really bothered to maintain, unlike the story
The comrade on my left was telling, which no one knew for certain truth:
Back in 1922, a sergeant, I forget his name, was shot outside the National Bank...

('Hamlet')

The reader is immediately drawn in, and wants to know more. The language is energetic and colloquial, and is not in the least bit forced. It has the stamp of similitude about it.

The epigraph to Carson's *From There to Here: Selected Poems and Translations* (2019) is translated from the Irish *Aistrigh liom siar sa ród* as 'Journey back with me along the road', an invitation for the reader to walk with him through his poetic career, to recollect with him in the first instance the warmth and brutality of his childhood ('There was twine to tie the turkey's

legs./There was the taws behind the kitchen door'), to rub shoulders with
him as he remembers adolescent flirtations and dances, the clash of English
and demotic in his home ('a power of *poitín*', 'that *poitín* is quare stuff')
and fine domestic scenes recalled (the first quotation reminds me a little of
a Vermeer interior):

> The wrought-iron flowers
> Of the gate breathe open to
> Sooty alcoves, the withered shelves
> Of books. There is a light
> That glints off tin and earthenware
> Reminding me of touch, the beaded moulding
> Of a picture frame –
>
>   (from 'Smithfield')

> Hearing that soot was good for the soil
> She threw it on the flowerbeds. She would watch
> It crumble, dissolving in the rain,
> Finding its way to lightless crevices,
> Sleeping, till in spring it would emerge softly
> As the ink-bruise in the pansy's heart.
>
>   (from 'Soot')

He remembers his postman father playing the melodeon (its 'nicotine-
stained bone buttons'), has fond memories of his mother 'darning, mending',
his father on his rounds, recalling (and relishing) his father's sayings and
how he aged, shops full of 'A musk/Of soap and turf and sweets'. These
homely scenes are embedded in (and sometimes contrasted with) the wider
context of new estates (the title of his first volume of poems was *The
New Estate*), demolition, clearances ('Zigzag stairwells, chimney flues.../
suddenly more sky/than there used to be'), the industrial landscape of 'the
dark city' of Belfast's 'gantry-clank and rivet-ranks...Brackets, bulkheads,
girders, beams, and stanchions...Sheaves of brick-built mill-stacks...
cranks and link-pins, cross-roods, hook blocks, cleats... the smell of docks
and ropeworks', 'Eggshells. Bricks. A broken hypodermic', the whole
complex grid of the 'monstrous city', its 'endless night'.

That city is now one of 'bulletproof glass', balaclavas, bombs, 'the armed
wing' (an oxymoron, surely) of this and that faction, redolent of fear and
uncertainty: 'They stopped me inadvertently and asked for my identity. I
did not know/until the mouth of a gun was pressed against my forehead, and
I felt its *O*'. The poet finds himself living in a world of prejudice, hatred and

difference (see 'Birthright'), a place never free of 'ancient wars'. He lives in a locus of 'the 'disappeared' ('The faces of the disappeared in blown-up, blurred wedding-photographs' – 'blown-up' is a very apposite pun), a domain of absurd borders ('Here, it cut clean across the plastic/Lounge of The Half-Way House; my heart lay in the Republic//While my head was in the Six' – the irony of 'The Half-Way House' is very apparent), a setting where 'the vast expansiveness of things' has become 'awry and slant'. His poems record the constant need for caution, circumspection and suspicion, in order to survive, and of domesticity regularly compromised where 'the searchlight trawls across the bedroom window', 'the helicopter trawls the murk with its wand of light' and daily movements are observed from 'the blind conning tower'. He portrays a world of shadows and secrets, of deceptive appearances and 'disappearances', of 'demarcated roads', of armoured cars and tanks, of the innocent 'caught in crossfire', of the parades and marches of the Orange Order and the Ancient Order of Hibernians – 'everything is slightly out of sync', he notes, 'Tell no one,' someone says to him, 'I mean no one, what you're up to. Never./Never. Never' (a mood, or warning, akin to Seamus Heaney's 'Whatever you say, say nothing'), an atmosphere of silence, claustrophobia, fear and anxiety, a world in which 'every dawn is desperate'.

The gloom of this urbanscape is relieved often by Carson's liking for the entertaining, sometimes crazy detail, such as 'the gate that was a broken bed', 'the applause of pigeons//Bursting from a loft', 'desultory handclaps turn to rain', 'Above the roof, she saw the frayed sunflower/Bloom triumphantly' (he is writing here of a chimney sweep's brush). He takes a Joycean delight in sights, sounds and smells, always trying to catch the right sensuous detail. In the following example he is trying to capture the colour of a ping pong ball: 'its neither ivory /Nor milk. Chalk is better; and there's a hint of pearl, translucent/Lurking just behind opaque'. He is a master of the startling image, the wayward observation. We have 'guzzling trumpeters' with 'tilted trumpets to their lips', 'the adenoidal honking of wild geese', 'A fabled swan the image of an ampersand', 'the rallentando of a roulette wheel', 'the red-and-white guillotine of the checkpoint', 'the crazy map of a dried-up reservoir'. Here above all, perhaps, lies that 'freshness and surprise' David Wheatley finds in his poetry, a freshness of newly minted metaphors and similes.

Carson turned more to translation in his later books. He was a distinguished translator of Dante's *Inferno*, and translated many of Rimbaud's visionary poems, as well as those of Baudelaire, Follain and Ponge. He also translated poems from the Middle Irish and from the Romanian of Stefan Doinas. These poems are often pastoral in theme, and perhaps served as a relief from the ubiquitous urban terrors of Belfast. The vivid contrast between war and peace is still there in his very fine translation from the eighth century Irish poem, 'Immran Brain' ('The Voyage of Brian'), which sums up, I believe, his own poetic endeavour. The style is economical, precise and delicate, with a numinous sense of the natural world, and also evinces a sense of peace and war being fused, as in Homer's image of Achilles' shield in the *Iliad* (or perhaps Auden's reworking of that image):

> a huge army shimmers on the plain
> > brimming with every colour
> banners of silver and cloths of gold
> > in jubilant array

> shaded by the spreading trees
> > men and women freely play
> a game of such delight and ease
> > they know no sin or wrong

Innocence always seems to be compromised in this world, and in his poetry Ciaran Carson explores not only the illimitable possibilities of language but the unfathomable depths of the human heart. Like the very best of his contemporaries his work stands in an intimate relationship with the social and political realities which surrounded him, and his poems have a dignity which is rightfully respected and listened to. His work sits securely in the heritage of those Irish authors who have chosen to write in the English language, and his poems shine out clearly and strongly.

John O'Donoghue

Seamus Heaney: Poet of the Irish Diaspora

i

I'm sure there was something of the same pride my mother and father took in seeing JFK elected President that I had when I heard Seamus Heaney had won the Nobel Prize for Literature. When I lost touch with my family in Ireland it was those collections of Heaney's from the mid-70s to the mid-80s that kept me informed about what was going on. I read them with all the affection – and not a little trepidation – of letters from home.

In Heaney's tones and cadences I recognised a fellow Ulsterman. I was only an Ulsterman by descent, but those collections of his starting with *North* in 1975, followed by *Field Work* in 1979, *Sweeney Astray* in 1983, and ending with *Station Island* in 1984, came like vivid reports from the frontline in a voice I recognised as surely as I recognised my mother's voice.

But it's not the Irish Heaney I wish to recognise here. No. It's the Heaney who represents the Diaspora I wish to focus on.

ii

If I seem to be making a special case, bear with me. For one of my favourite poems of Heaney's has nothing to do with turf cutting, or frog spawn, or blackberrying, or armed patrols, or penitential islands. It's a poem that celebrates Harvard Yard, from his last collection, *Human Chain*, yet is still a typical Heaney poem in that Heaney 'sanctifies' (the word is Blake Morrison's) a stretch of ground that is actually a workplace, albeit a very privileged one. 'Canopy' is in quatrains, in lines of various lengths, and starts very plainly:

It was the month of May.
Trees in Harvard Yard
Were turning a young green.
There was whispering everywhere.

But then a strange turn: 'David Ward had installed/Voice-boxes in the branches…'. Next comes lines that sound like the Heaney we've grown accustomed to. The 'voice-boxes' amplify the whispering until there's: '… sibilant ebb and flow,/Speech gutterings, desultory//Hush and backwash and echo.' And then these lines, which read more like Dylan Thomas:

'It was like a recording/Of antiphonal responses/In the congregation of leaves.' Later on in the poem we get a typical Heaney reference: '…Dante's whispering wood –/The wood of the suicides –/Had been magicked to lover's lane.' Heaney ends the poem on a further note of magical transformation:

> If a twig had been broken off there
> It would have curled itself like a finger
> Around the fingers that broke it
> And then refused to let go
>
> As if it were mistletoe
> Taking tightening hold.
> Or so I thought as the fairy
> Lights in the boughs came on.

Here Heaney turns Harvard Yard into an enchanted grove, that reference to 'mistletoe' reminding us of the ancient Druidic associations of poetry in Ireland. And notice what he does with all those long O sounds:

> If a twig had been brOken off there
> It would have curled itself like a finger
> Around the fingers that brOke it
> And then refused to let gO
>
> As if it were mistletOe
> Taking tightening hOld.
> Or sO I thought as the fairy
> Lights in the boughs came on.

Those echoing Os ring through the lines like the whisperings coming through the trees, and also evoke the poet's O that indicates the mouth opening to speak inspired words. And that note at the end: 'Or so I thought as the fairy/ Lights in the boughs came on' brings us into the realm of *A Midsummer Night's Dream*, those 'boughs' acting like a pun as Heaney takes his leave of us – makes his bow amongst the trees' boughs. Notice the line break between fairy and Lights and that buried rhyme of tightening and Lights. It's as if suddenly, by placing Lights at the start of the line and rhyming it with tightening, the Lights are turned on, the surprise of them accentuated by placement and sound, for this poem all about sound gives way in the end to light, a common movement in Heaney's poems.

His insouciance in those last two lines, though, is I think what delights me most about the poem. Harvard Yard becomes the complete antithesis of Station Island, a place of enchantment as opposed to self-accusation, a place Heaney's poetry and career has taken him to. But this is not just the privileged place of an Ivy League university; it's an arcadia the poet has constructed through his resistance first of all to oppression from the State in Northern Ireland, and second his resistance to partisanship during the Troubles. Heaney carves out a new space, and Harvard Yard is a kind of paradise after the purgatory of Lough Derg and *Station Island*.

iii

It was towards the end of his time in Philip Hobsbaum's Belfast Group that Heaney started sending his poems to Charles Monteith at Faber, and went on to a more public, less provincial career as a poet. I should mention here Heaney's relationship to Britain at this stage. It was, ostensibly, a benevolent one if looked at from the British point of view. For Britain was where Heaney was born at Mossbawn, near Castledawson, Co. Derry; where he was able to avail of the 11+ and gain a scholarship to St Columb's; where he entered University thanks to the Butler Education Act; where he was published.

He was as much a son of the Empire, in other words, as Ted Hughes, who had a fairly similar country upbringing and gilded Grammar School education. What complicated matters was Heaney's Catholicism, his sense that – no matter how editors of anthologies might characterise him – he was Irish not British. To be sure, he was aware of being brought up not just 'in a different physical location but in a different cultural location as well.' In a BBC Northern Ireland broadcast of 1998 he delineates the boundaries of this location:

> Castledawson was a far more official place altogether, more modern, more a part of the main drag. The very name of the place is from the orderly English world of the eighteenth century, whereas Bellaghy is from an older, more obscure origin in Irish. So, as I once said in a poem – a poem called 'Terminus' – I grew up in between.

This sense of duality is typical of members of the Irish Diaspora who must often negotiate between 'where they're from' and 'where they're at'. After several inclusions in anthologies of British poetry in 1983 Heaney finally chose where he was from over where he was at. He makes clear his objection to over-simple categorisation in his verse letter to Andrew Motion and Blake Morrison (editors of the *Penguin Anthology of British Poetry* that came out in 1982), which includes the famous, ringing lines: '...My passport's green/No glass of ours was ever raised/To toast the Queen.'

A word about the stanza Heaney uses for 'Open Letter'. This is Standard Habbie, a form popularised by Robert Burns, and taken up again by John Fuller in his *Epistles To Several Persons* (Martin Secker & Warburg Ltd, 1973), a series of witty verse letters to correspondents such as James Fenton and Ian Hamilton. Fuller's title echoes Alexander Pope's volume of the same name published between 1731 to 1735, and by allusion aligns itself the Augustan wits. Here's a sample stanza in Standard Habbie, Heaney signing off:

> Need I go on? I hate to bite
> Hands that led me to the limelight
> In the Penguin book, I regret
>   The awkwardness.
> But British, no, the name's not right.
>   Yours truly, Seamus.

So Heaney is borrowing a form used by a polished Oxonian English poet – John Fuller – to chide, seriously and with high literary playfulness, Motion and Morrison, a way perhaps of saying to Fuller and by extension his English peers, 'Anything you can do, I can do different.' The poem is addressed at once to Motion and Morrison as Editors, but also to Motion and Morrison as cultural arbiters, who would recognise the use of Standard Habbie not just as a tip of the hat to the Fuller volume of a decade previously, but as the reclamation of it from eighteenth century metropolitan condescension in an act of cultural re-appropriation or perhaps more accurately, cultural re-placing.

iv

Heaney, of course, had written a much more sombre poem reckoning with his relationship with Britain some ten years or so before *Open Letter*. 'Act of Union', collected in *North*, first published in 1975, takes the form of two sonnets, and uses the extended metaphor of rape to speak of the conquest of Ireland:

> And I am still imperially
> Male, leaving you with the pain,
> The rending process in the colony,
> The battering ram, the boom burst from within.

The conqueror is here personified, those plosive p's and b's encoding the violence of domination. The 'act of union' leaves a product of this conquest: 'His parasitical/And ignorant little fists already/Beat at your borders and I know they're cocked/At me across the water.' After the polysyllables of 'parasitical/And ignorant' we get again a pair of plosives 'His... little fists/ Beat at your borders' which are 'cocked/At me.' The word 'cocked' works on a number of levels: like the conqueror the 'child' of this union is phallic and male, as if to say those conceived in violence are doomed to perpetrate and perpetuate violence themselves. There's also the Freudian antagonism rather than filial piety to this child's father. And finally, there's a sense of the child being likened to a cock in a cockfight, a desperate foundling who can only resent its absent parent.

v

Heaney's excursions abroad then, fulfilled two functions for his personal and creative development. Like so many of his countrymen he was going abroad to work. But he was also travelling away from home to arrive at a perspective on what home meant to him. He was not 'diluted' by travelling abroad to work, but enriched, encountering poets in print and in person such as William Carlos Williams, Czeslaw Milosz, and Derek Walcott who inspired him and enhanced his work. If in the end home meant poetry as much it meant Mossbawn, or Glanmore, or Sandymount, that should not come as any great surprise. Heaney made over, 're-placed', the various locations of his life until as Anthony Smith, President of Magdalen College Oxford, observed:

> It was as if he was at the top of a well of Irish Literature and Irishness
> of all kinds but that well led down to the whole of world literature
> and he could as it were let bucket down into it and pull out through
> his Irish culture all the cultures of the world... It's no accident that his
> great friend was Brodsky; he knew a lot of Polish and Russian poetry;
> he was at home in the world of poetry and could hear the echoes of all
> that poetry through his Irish identity.

And so Seamus Heaney is not just a poet who belongs to Ireland, or to the world; Seamus Heaney ultimately transcends nationality, finding through poetry a depth of community internationally that his predecessors such as Kavanagh had only just begun to encounter.

Heaney's rootedness in Ireland did not confine him but nor did his voyages abroad etiolate his poetry. Like his fellow Nobel Laureates Brodsky and

Walcott he embraced the opportunities of exile. As such we should see him as first and foremost an Irish poet, but secondly as a poet who looks beyond Ireland, casting his gaze backwards to the Classics, and on to horizons that are much wider than his reputation as an Irish poet allows. When I think back over his life and career, I am reminded of all those other places he invoked in his work: Berkeley, Aarhus, Harvard, Oxford, London, Stockholm. And so he is in the end, a citizen not just of Northern Ireland, or the Irish Republic, but of the much wider Irish Diaspora.

Gerard Smyth

Derek Mahon: *Against the Clock* (Gallery Press, 2018)
Washing Up (Gallery Press, 2020)

In the first poem of his valedictory book, *Washing Up*, Derek Mahon presents us with a lovely image of contentment, of himself as 'the old author'

> framed in the window at his writing table
> who was at peace here in a world ill-at-ease
> with itself, its past, a future yours to know…
>
> ('The Old Place')

Acceptance of old age and its inevitabilities is contained not only in the titles of both these collections but with candour in several of the poems. Other poets might be downbeat and humourless on the subject of death but not Mahon whose wit was always as good as Auden's. The opening title poem in *Against the Clock* is honest and forthright in acknowledging that he is now writing 'not to a regular but final deadline' and 'An Old Theme' has him echoing the Spanish poet Vallejo: 'I shall die in due course on a day of rain', but looking ahead to that day as one on which he would be

> …in an armchair at the twilight hour
> reading something favoured by old crocks:
> gossip, philosophy, maybe Schopenhauer

In the extraordinarily fruitful late resurgence of creativity that, after a long hiatus in the flow of poetry, began with *Harbour Lights* in 2005, a recharged Mahon followed the example of those 'poets of old age' who 'wrestled with language' even as their lights were dimming: 'Dante and Coleridge, Hugo, Whitman, Yeats'. Implicit in both collections, rounding off his gold-mine body of work, is the need to keep continuous the process of testing the limits of language and turning life into art, and while Mahon's perfection of his art was long ago achieved, he continued to believe, and with great avidity, that the poet should 'stick it out until the pen falls from the trembling hand'.

His pen here is drawn both to the personal and the universal, the private and public, still showing its stylistic panache and exceptional metrical and rhyming skills, still master of formal technique and its muscular poetic forms and structures. In 'Arts Poetique' he reminds us that 'The music is the important thing' adding the injunction that there should be 'no rhetoric and no posturing'. The poem as an instrument of clear and direct communication has always been an imperative in Mahon's work and one of its chief virtues. In another poem, 'Working Conditions', he outlines the ideal situation in which to 'sit down and write', suggesting that a theme that 'troubles your sleep' might always be best, but with this warning:

As for your contemporaries, stay abreast
to avoid things already there in their pages.

What troubles Mahon, igniting the concerns of many of the late-period poems, is the world as we have been experiencing it in recent times, what one title calls 'Trump Time'. Despite casting the shadow of his own mortality across these pages, he remains very much aware and critically observant, as well as disdainful, of aspects of modern life: the 'online scene', 'the star wars crowd', the world's *faux* democracies' and its consumer culture. The poet of 'tormented insights' expresses his existential anxiety for earthly life and the planet, its own struggle against the clock as time runs out with governments and citizens turning a blind eye to the threat of ecological disaster and potential 'extinction of the species', as he puts it in 'A Line of Moore'. The meteorological aberrations of recent years is powerfully evoked in a poem about the local effects of this century's recurring storms, with the poet sitting it out in 'excited reverie / listening to climate change doing its work' ('Ophelia').

But there is also a joyful note to some of his insights and perceptions: 'I am noticing once again the singular things / I noticed as a boy', he tells us in 'Data', a poem in which he goes through a litany of those things catching his attention: the sound of silence, scent of clothes as well as migrating swifts and the hawthorn in leaf. There is a homely feel to many of these poems, the poet well settled in his surroundings (as indeed he was in the Cork town of Kinsale, the final stop on his geographical odyssey). Those surroundings gave rise to poems that focus on the natural and elemental world and a realisation that 'salvation lies in love of the simple thing' as he tells us in 'Rising Late'.

When he does take a backward glance it is fleeting; getting back to the present moment is what matters. In the delicately compact 'Salisbury Avenue', he begins:

I used to live here once...
climbing trees and running races
in the immediate post-war years.

But he then swiftly comes out of that reverie to notice that a young couple nearby, 'beside the latest four-by-four' (his method of reminding the reader that the poem has moved on from past to present) are looking through him 'as if I don't exist /even as a shadow or a ghost'. Moments of self-regard in Mahon's poetry tend to be mocking or witty. In 'Olympia', an amusing and good-humoured paean to his typewriter, he sees himself and the machine as a performing duo:

> two crotchety relics of a previous age
> jazzing it up again as
> in the great days.

The cinematic fluidity of cherished keynote poems such as 'A Disused Shed in County Wexford' or 'A Garage in County Cork' is in evidence, but on a smaller scale in poems such as 'Rising Late', 'Ophelia', 'A Dove in the House' (from *Against the Clock*); 'The Old Place', 'Alone in the Dark', 'Another Cold Spring' and the title poem from *Washing Up*. The intensity and flintiness of earlier Mahon gives way in much of the newer work to a more relaxed – perhaps even sanguine – mindset, but one showing no default from the standards of the greatly esteemed Mahon poems of his inaugural books, no relinquishing of his disciplined aesthetic.

Whatever about that old-fashioned adherences to a manual typewriter instead of a computer, he knew what a modern readership could identify with and was always up-to-date in the ways of the world, noting its 'real values on the blink'. The catholicity of what Mahon admitted into his poetry, its wide range of vision and subject material brings to mind the comment by Randall Jarrell about his fellow American poet Conrad Aiken – 'a kind of Midas, everything he touches turns to verse'.

He keeps to his habit of referencing other writers and artists, his select touchstones: Graves, Victor Hugo, Jean Rhys, Swift, Moore (both Tom and Brian), Chekhov, Montaigne, Crane, Bishop and Anne Brontë, as well as the inclusion of poems rooted in other texts (Brecht, Verlaine, Neruda) and in communion with a number of classical Chinese lyric poets.

His antennae have also been alert to popular culture and its idols, specifically Paul McCartney (in the almost wistful reminiscence of hearing a blackbird in a Dublin park), Paul Simon ('the voice of an age') and Shane MacGowan whose 'Fairy Tale of New York' and 'Rainy Night in Soho' lyrics inform the imagery and mood of his 'Triad for Shane MacGowan', one of those surprises that Mahon delivered from time to time. His vivacious imagination even extends to a homage to Ireland's national vegetable, the potato ('Spuds in Space'), with its sly allusions to Patrick Kavanagh and his

'Spraying the Potatoes': 'Paddy's spud has pride of place' and 'stony soil stuck to the outer spud'.

In 'Quarantine', one of two up-to-the-minute poems set in pandemic lockdown, the author of the popular and consolatory 'Everything is Going to be All Right', sees and seizes, the 'silver lining' in the crisis, taking consolation in the fact that 'the vague / threat represented by the tourist plague / recedes and the place is dozing once again / in its narcotic haze of drizzling rain'.

In the last poem of his last collection, he returns to the epistolary form in an address to Ireland's President, Michael D Higgins. The poem is both a song of praise for the president and a hymn of invective against 'the venal and obtuse' who hold political and economic power. To the president, he says:

What we admire most about your performance
is its high-spirited independent stance
on the inflated 'neo-liberal' programme
that makes no secret of its global scam.

An independent stance – but perhaps more stately than high-spirited – could also be used to describe Mahon's own place in artistic life over the past sixty years as one of poetry's heavyweights. In one of his earlier great poems, 'The Sea in Winter', he speaks of words leaving a 'brief glow in the dark'. His work, including many of these final poems written as he approached his eightieth year, will leave its own inextinguishable glow.

Vona Groarke

New York, Hell's Kitchen: Snow

Last year, in the dip of the usual bad sleep,
I opened the shutters on an Eighth Avenue
freshly snowed-on, vacated both directions,
Columbus Circle down to 50th, even Rumour's Bar
in darkness; not a sinner. Not a peep.
And not a window lit, not even mine
even though it was my city then, on loan
or on approval or on tick.

And I had learned the run of it,
the underground shortcut to the library,
where to buy cheap fruit, coffee with taste,
thrift stores; $20 haircuts, dive bars,
a Moorish movie theatre,
the best free views of itself.

I gathered words chalked on curbs
in an Empire State notebook
bought for this purpose alone:
'Hey Pretty'. 'Trump stole my weed.'
'Jin, John's @ 9'. 'Help me, I'm hungry'.
'You will die too.' And so forth.

I was slipping my hand in the city's hand
and it did not pull away.

The panhandler on 50th and Seventh
would say, 'Good morning, Young Lady'
every morning, and sometimes add, 'Nice coat!'.
(It didn't matter what coat I had on.)

Weekends were films and lattes sitting
in Elizabeth Street or community gardens
with gates you had to close by hand,
maybe a pond with an ancient,
much-loved frog no one has seen.

Weekends were eavesdropping
on the kind of things a city tells itself
when it wants to believe in a future, even so.
Couples in cafes playing with each other's hair.
Students dancing round a fountain to music
on headphones only they could hear.
A small girl in front of a Barnett Newman
saying, Hey, That line's not straight.

I'd save quarters for the laundromat
that was Dublin, down at heel, circa 1982,
except I'd be slipping over the road
to sip pricey cheap winebar Sancerre
while the clothes were in the dryer.

Home again, home again, night after night,
to a lime green room of notionate height,
a marble fireplace and a four-poster bed
I fancied myself Edith Wharton in
and then, Edith Wharton's servant.

Four brown floors with a brick façade
and a fire escape that used put me in mind
of climbing out some unstrung night
to knock on a door, to knock on a door,
to step over into love.

Well. I put all that in a purple suitcase
with my clam-tight heart and my scratched-at words
to be hauled back down those same four floors
to the taxi's threadbare airport run,
to the up and out and never come back,
to all the struts of the Queensboro Bridge
strumming as I passed, *What if, what if?*

I left when I had to leave, when my time was up.
Brought with me a tin, thrift-store candlestick,
swanky New York shoes, a book I'd written,
a brace of friendships dear to me,
and an aftertaste of hope.

I was young there, it felt like, almost,
on furlough from my life.
And it was kind to me, that unkind city,
taught me lessons worth the learning
about alone and not alone.

Not lessons to be forgotten exactly,
but still, I'm a diligent student nightly,
practising them in the crook of a mountain
in my converted byre.

Where I too have shutters to fold back
on a dirty night, attending to the weather.
Not snowfall here but wind and rain,
a fire in the stove to countermand them.

And me, wakeful as ever I was,
with rain stabbing the skylight
and not even cars out on the road
but a mountain lording it over the house,
wishful and sullen by turns.

I think myself back to that snow-still street,
my fourth floor window facing west
(the same west as here, can that be true?)
my breath on the glass, blooming and withering
so it looks like I'm part of what happens,
so it looks like I'm part of it all.

David Cooke

The Tale of the Talents

He likes it best when the house
is quiet and the windows
are shuttered against the dark –

its scattered stars like silver
lying beyond his grasp.
A plain table, a sturdy chair,

are all the comfort he allows
when 'foolishness' and 'waste'
are the words he keeps by him,

the rubbed coins he places
in importuning palms. In his own
he weighs the pouches.

Loosening their strings,
he lays out his hoard.
Lit up by a candle-stub,

his profits glow. The sum
of his days, they're counted,
increased and totted up again.

When the house awakens,
those he feeds, knowing
his due, tiptoe around him.

My Grandson writes his name

for Ziyad

The first letter he has known for months
in zig-zag lines getting nowhere.

Turned on its side and crayoned blue
he can stretch it out like a river;

or if he changes colour can make
a mountain, some grass, a fire.

Cut back to its simplest form
and laid out in rows like ghosts,

he follows the dots over and over
before he does it on his own.

When he learns its sound is a buzz
he likes, he hears it and sees it again

in the stripes of *zebra*,
in the bars of a place called *zoo*.

He has five shapes to master.
They stand above or hang below

a line that's always there –
even if you think it's vanished.

But when it all comes together
in a final downward stroke

– staunch and straight as he will be –
it tells him who he is,

this name he has always heard
ever since he's been here.

Maurice Riordan

Questions for the Oracle

for Nadine Brummer

Will it rain? Will the hibiscus be in flower?
Will the boats arrive from Naros safe and on time?
Will Phillip come? With his new bride, Alcmene?
Will everything go according to plan
and everyone get along? No sulks or quarrels,
no tasteless jokes about the Christians?
And Penny, my dear friend who cannot come
– will this be the very night she gives birth?
Will it be a boy or a girl? Will it be born
without mishap, I pray, or too much pain?

Will Bella come? And Quintus behave
and not jump in the fish pond? Will everyone
get along? Will my husband frown at the sweetmeats,
the sauces, the wine? Will the food taste good anyway?
Will I be at ease with the wives, and avoid
nervously finishing their sentences?
Will Quintus give me a drunken kiss,
like he did a year ago? And those who've died since
be here? Saul, and my mother? And Simonides Rufus,
who teased me when we were children,
crucified six weeks ago in Smyrna?

Will the rain keep off, at least till night falls
when people come indoors? And Quintus play
the old tunes from the islands? My husband then
be full of fellowship and army gossip,
and this become one of those nights
the islanders talk of, recalling a time blest
by Demeter and by your kind light, Lord Apollo?

Katherine Gallagher

Margaret, dancing

When Margaret penned her proposal
to Eastville's most eligible bachelor –
farmer Tommy Robb, Esq – the district knew
the season had started fortuitously.

Margaret brought flowers and light
to his dry patch of terrain,
marked out the farm into airy spaces, weaving
around stumps of ringbarked trees,

and she and Tom, virginal, fiftyish, danced
like young things, throwing off their years
in moon-spurred reels and bagpipe skirls
as piper Alex, kilted and medallioned,

brought *The Banks of Lock Lomond*
to the lowlands of Eastville, giving the nod
to promises, and lift-off for all who loved
and danced, danced and loved.

In the Faith

(i.m. Mary Phelan)

My grandmother couldn't
sing in tune. Music-lover,
she walked tall, wanting
everyone to join in.

So the family sang from habit
the way birds might – popular songs,
memories, *The Sunshine
of Your Smile*.

We learnt the importance
of being ready to sing at will.
In my ten-year-old maze,
I imagined that was how the saints

and martyrs managed, even
if walking on hot coals.
When we trumpeted *Faith of Our Fathers,*
the words entered our hearts, gusting belief,

How it held us together, despite
ourselves, in spite of everything outside –
illnesses, deaths, droughts –
that threatened, kept edging in.

Retrospect

She crawls across India, bus-slow –
weeks alone have made her anxious,
looking forward, looking back.
She hunts wide blanks of sky,
sees him everywhere: the weight of it
burning through her days.

In this country's vastness
villages and people are mindful, steady.
She sees palaces, walks in time
with painted elephants, watches people bathe
in the Ganges, pray, burn their dead.
Jaipur, Agra, Benares: cities wake her whole.

At each hotel, the smell of laurel
lifts a clear cerulean sky.
The soft night air slides over
a day of cameos: heavy-shouldered vultures
picking bones, cloudless skies,
the faces of people who love their gods:
Brahma, Vishnu, Shiva – the spirit
of this place. Slowly she is learning to accept
his absence, an ocean away now –
this being alone, being herself.

John O'Donoghue

The Gift

i.m. Seamus Heaney

That I have come in wedding clothes
To Ireland on the day you died –
Does that make me a pilgrim here,
A figure gaunt, alone, austere,
Or should I pass as one of those
Who raise their glass to toast the bride?

Strange calling that has brought us here,
Not knowing what response to make,
Stunned as much by death as love,
Uncertain what's ahead, above,
And moon now suddenly a tear
Dissolving in the starfilled lake.

And so on wedding's eve I shape
These feelings into forms we share
And tie them into bows of rhyme.
Tomorrow when we wake and I'm
Aware that opened ground might gape
I'll bear my gift with extra care.

First

For years he'd been baptizing my cool white
Lemonade with the seeping blackness of
Stout, a broad man, somehow summery – sight
For sore eyes – in his gentle gangster suit, love
Double-breasted and shy, me stood outside
On the pavement, freckling in the sunshine.
And after, when he had drunk his last, died
On Saturday, buried and gone, I'd pine
For pints with him, remembering the first
I'd had, a Guinness by the Ha'penny Bridge,
A man then with a man's desperate thirst,
Him smiling, us sat in by the passage,
Watch me sup in the pub's boozey shade,
That stout sweeter than any lemonade.

Twenty-five

My mother first taught me Twenty-five,
That intricate game of sixpenny tricks,
Dealing quick hands in a sneaky skive
From milking the goat, stooking the ricks.

She taught me how to rob and renege, saving
The Knave 'til the Fingers had fallen,
To play Ace of Hearts when battle was raving,
To not be at home when court cards came calling.

'The lowest in black, the highest in red'.
Dark colour of mourning, bright colour of blood.
Deal in the angels, the quick and the dead:
None of her cards will ever be dud.

Naomi Foyle

How it feels sometimes, surviving breast cancer

The light has been off for hours. Outside, the rain
bubbles like a pot of black rice. My mushroom belly
grumbles, squashed inside my folded bones, and I wonder again
why love is so difficult. If yesterday's cool breeze
on my breast as I lay alone on the beach
is the only kiss this summer will bestow. If the hormone
treatment is lowering my libido. If that's a good thing.
The rain falls harder now, popping like popcorn, and

*

For years I bathed in a golden ocean,
swam in gleam and chime,
spent the wealth of youth as if
cavorting in warm cascades of coin,
limbs gilded by the sun,
never noticing the tide, until
I washed up on a rocky shore
thumbing a worn doubloon —
rare and alluring, but not legal tender
in this strange land where women
in their prime are sent to live
with the butterflies and donkeys,
and the exchange of glittering glances
is a pleasure neither love
nor burnished chests can lay in store.

*

So let love be an unknown, and
the unknown a kind of love
                        Mahmoud Darwish

let a walk in the rain
                break into a run
beneath shivering oaks

and a book on a shelf in a rented room
reignite the soft flames
of your nerves

        let it not matter
                        if or when
        the erotic correspondence
                between man and woman
                        resumes

for the world pens love letters
in lemon juice tears

and the future
                is a candle
no storm or breath

(not even death)
can snuff out

Wrong End of the Telescope

i.m. Mairtín Crawford

Little details always gave you pleasure.
Snails on the cliffs at Whitehead,
crawling up.
Signature phrases:
Easy peasy lemon squeezy.
Okey doke.
Bok choi in the fridge. Toto:
'She's a Pomeranian, you know.'
That Muldoon poem about trees
you read to me three times,
perched on the edge of the bed.

Small things also enraged you.
Perceived slights.
Accidental brushes with indignity.
Dog shit
on your coat
before the Ulster-Scots debate.

I learned not to laugh.

If you had tunnel vision,
it was a mountain shaft on fire.

Joseph Horgan

The Rural Electrification Scheme to delay Emigration

I don't want us
to waste our time
putting up
these electricity pylons
when we have
such little time left,
even though this is the past
and you are not yet dead,
so let them settle there
at the side of this field,
these tarred and dressed giants,
we can lie down
in the long grass,
you can hide
from anything there.

An Inexact Paper Map of the City

Down by the canal
I would,
if it was possible,
show you an otter,

watch you imagine
the impossible pelt,
the wordless
liquid skin,

we would let
the last bus pass,
think about
never going back.

Steven O'Brien

Mist on the Curragh

My grandfather as a boy
Combed his hair to be good
And tidy
For his mother's burial.

Mirror above the hearth,
Dim as a bog pool.
His reflection moved under the smoky glass
But over his shoulder, much deeper within
His mother walked down the stairs behind him,
Formal and pale
And went out silently
Into the mist on the Curragh.

A story repeated surely as Sunday tea
With the clock ticking at his back,
To my sister, my brother and me
Sitting along the sofa.

Each time his grey eyes shifted between ours,
The same troubled look,
And his open mouth
Asking us to go with him, that long ago morning
On the gravel path towards the grave –

To see what he had seen
But scarcely could believe himself.

Nick Burbridge

Retreat

Here I find peace.
From exiled strands
in retraced steps
along thin high-hedged lanes

past Enniskean, to a smallholding
of strawberries and courgettes,
I come to sit
alone with my grand-uncle.

Porter, and a peat fire
flickering on his cheeks,
this eager white-haired figure
leans back into memories

through songs and scars
to distant hours as prisoner
and vigorous young farmer
harvesting lost fields.

Around the glimmering cottage
dark hills of Cork grow silent.
I kiss his brow, take his tilted glass
as he falls asleep, and stoke the flames.

Pratibha Castle

Octopus Ride

The cage dangles upside down
on the tip of a tentacle flung,
like a baby's arm in sleep,
to its steepest sprawl.

It idles in the breeze,
quivers, my knuckles white,
tight with clutching the metal bar.
A singe of sugar rises from the candy

floss stand, axle grease, *Woolworth's*
cheap scent, shouts, laughter, hurdy
gurdy grizzle of the fair. I breathe
like sipping water in a

drought, barely enough
to keep me conscious lest,
falling into a belly bloating wail,
I loose my grip. How might it be to

slip, soar, a swift inscribing secrets,
or the blood clot that might
have been you slipping
out from between
my legs,

to slump, limbs
akimbo, a crooked star
glinting in the churned up
mud, essence seeping through
jelly fish skin. My fingers tire, begin

to fail, open, but the engine judders,
grunts back to life. Cogs, once
smooth, stutter me back
to the start. I

clamber out,
stagger through
quicksand crowds,
my face a clown's mask,

and though my lips curve upwards
as if all this has been nothing
more than a lark, my heart
weeps clotted tears.

Paul Jeffcutt

Moving House

I dug a kidney-shaped pond
where I settled and gave it to nature.
Scooping my net into a clogged mat
of speckled duckweed, I tip the spoil
in a dripping heap at the water's edge
and knelt to observe.

Sniffing the half-warm April air,
the serrated crest on your back glistening,
you clamber over tangled strands
with four sets of delicate fingers,
skirt tadpoles and water boatmen,
and sinuously slip into the water.

A lifetime ago, I'd picked you up,
orange belly with black spots,
put you in a jam-jar held with string
and carried you from that scruffy pond
filled with green algae and half-bricks,
through the estate to our new house.

You'd rested beside my bed –
head of a miniature dragon,
tail as long as your body;
despite the clumps of weed I'd included,
you stared forlorn as I tried to sleep.
At daybreak, I took you home.

CHOSEN BROADSHEET POET

Tristram Fane Saunders, 27, lives in London and works as a

journalist. He has reviewed poetry for *The Telegraph* and Radio 4's *Front Row*, and has performed at Latitude Festival. His 2019 pamphlet *Woodsong* (Smith|Doorstop) won the New Poets Prize.

from The Unauthorised Biography, Vol IV: 1730-1960

He spent twelve decades polishing his craft,
studiously darkening the floorboards
in dens of moderate iniquity,

or decorating red-light district windows
with his gaunt reflection; hand-in-hand
with syphilis and debt, he whiled away

ten years in private, plain or padded cells,
then out again into the brittle evening,
pockets rich with laudanum, neglected

correspondence, old French letters, borrowed
neckerchief and snuff-box, borrowed pearls.
The latest melancholy smile perfected

daily in his little shaving-mirror.
After a lifetime of these skits and turns,
playing to the gallery each morning

and to the private boxes every night,
like a slow, malignant growth around him,
unnoticed, the world began to change.

Years pass. He lurches up the gilded stair
from *cad* to *rogue* to *fiend* to *devil*, till
tripping on *national treasure* he alights,

breathless, on the upper landing: *myth*.
And like all myths, not quite the thing it was,
elevated now to something less

than truth, he grows familiar: a click,
a whirr, the tired back-and-forward whip
of drying polaroid, and in no time

to speak of, his name dissolves: a sugarcube,
relaxing into absinthe. All politeness,
the Rake agrees to sign his photograph,

tousling the ringlets of the youngest fan,
kissing the ringless fingers of the eldest,
and all the while remembering the tale

of how the pampered fox became the dog,
and Narcissus in winter, how he watched
his own reflection as it turned to ice.

2nd Edition

A week before my twenty-first,
it arrived. Your gift for every occasion:

The Oxford Book of English Verse
(Sir Arthur Quiller-Couch Edition)

Wide for First Class, its green weight forced
through the letterbox tore the wrapping open.

I'd half expected it. Of course
the same book. The same dedication.

You gave it to my mother first,
for some anniversary, now forgotten.

I found it after the divorce,
and would read it often,

skipping the first page every time.
with love, from me to you

in your thin scrawl, a snagged line
of her favourite Beatles tune,

your first dance, above a rhyme
for an eight-centuries-dead cuckoo.

Early bird and earworm tied
like a joke, or something true.

Foolish, inseparable. Why
not, for a gift, forgive you?

It's April 1st. I crack the spine
and watch the words spring new:

Sumer is icumen in
lhude sing cuccu

Monkfish

It'd always be late. High on Red Bull and *Blue Planet*,
Attenborough levelling her mind, she'd call
up again, still up at four in the morning,
not tearful, just earnest and wired, calling
for no reason, no better reason than to share

her latest newly memorised litany of names.
Lophius, or monkfish, or fishing frog, or
sea devil. Revision. Of course she was fine.
One time, she told me that she empathised
with its teeth. *The teeth will become temporarily*

depressed, so as to offer no impediment
to an object gliding towards the gut.
God knows why I'd pick up. Pity, or pride
in my own selfless patience? She the seashell
held to my ear, I'd listen then half-listen

like the line I pictured in the air between us;
neutral, intermittent, static. Cagey about being,
but reluctantly talked into it, *the body,*
given time and a stable bed, will change
and blend with its surroundings.

Given time, I thought she'd learn to fit
in, tone down the strangeness,
or even occasionally sleep, to call
someone else, anyone – Samaritans, Nightline,
the talking clock... *standard network rate. Your call*

is a low, keening sound. Your call
is inaudible to divers. Your call
is inaudible to all the undrowned.

How The Raven Ate The Moon

She couldn't tell me past the lump in her throat, but something
was broken, or breaking. It had been four weeks exactly
since she'd stopped taking whatever it was that she'd been taking.

The last white pill was gone and nothing else was working,
so I gave her *How The Raven Ate The Moon*
filled with hot milk, and wrapped her palms around the hollow

eye of it and kept on talking. *In the story,*
Raven has been flying for (I told her) *twenty*
eight long nights and days without a crumb of sleep

or wink of meat. He makes a wager with a sockeye
salmon over which is stronger: human love or...
By the time I'd finished talking, she'd stopped shaking.

Crazed with hairline cracks and chipped, it still holds water
even now. Although it's years since we two split,
I just can't let it go, this tacky mug I bought

in Canada – I've filled it with the warm and bitter
nettle tea, handpicked, each leaf plucked like a feather
from the black-and-white-and-red unfaded picture

printed across it, of a photo of a painting
by a famous local artist, of a myth
I never learnt. She needed something she could handle,

so I made it up and meant it, every word.
A white lie, like a desperate last-minute gift
picked up before a flight. I brewed it from the floating

scraps that fill my head like weeds, like *lunary
is honesty, unless it's only mugwort*. Like
love, or the other thing. And like a starving bird

she swallowed it. Or made me think she'd swallowed it.

CHOSEN BROADSHEET REVIEWER

Elizabeth Ridout, 32, is a writer originally from Yorkshire, based in London and Kent. Her poems and reviews have featured in a variety of magazines and she has done readings and interviews at festivals and on BBC Radio. She won a Creative Future Writers Award in 2017 and her debut poetry collection, *Summon*, was released by Myriad Editions as part of their Spotlight Series. The collection was shortlisted for a Poetry Book Award and received a special mention in the Saboteur Awards. She was recently selected for the Next Up programme in support of her first novel, *The Samothrace Project*.

Colette Bryce, *The M Pages* (Picador Poetry, 2020)

Aoife Lydall, *Mother, Nature* (Bloodaxe, 2021)

Aibhe Darcy, *Insistence* (Bloodaxe, 2018)

Róisín Kelly, *Mercy* (Bloodaxe, 2020)

Miriam Gamble, *What Planet* (Bloodaxe, 2019)

Cathy Galvin, *Black and Blue* (The Melos Press, 2018)

We are currently experiencing a collective grief for our old lives, for our 'normality'; the processing of this loss is a collective as well as an individual experience. The best poetry acts as a kind of trail for humanity to follow and recognise, a path out of the forests – and Colette Bryce's new collection, *The M Pages*, fulfils this wonderful task wholeheartedly.

The collection is structured in a V shape – beginning with euphemism and concluding on a plateau. The central, titular sequence is addressed to a named 'M' who has unexpectedly passed away, and acts as the vacuum at the centre of the book, sucking all prior and following pieces into its path. Bryce writes with a grace which is derailed by the unexpectedness of loss into viscerality. Before 'The M Pages', the pieces are collections of images, 'morning' poems which turn into mourning poems, deliberately like photographs or a build up of memory, 'like an early photographer rising from the cloak/ of her machine to a world devoid of colour''. Memories of travel – 'skinny old timers in the Plaza/soft shoe salsa for a couple of cucs/and the rattle of maracas or begging cup/ guaranteed bona fide/ Buena Vista Social Club' – are seen through the lens of mortality and the constant underlying awareness, soon to become flagrant, of decay, as in the wonderful, Plathian 'Fungi':

Always, fungi
is feasting,
working
its quick
saprotrophic
magic on all
matter, even
this seasonal
litter I've just
finished clearing
from your grave.

This piece launches us into 'The M Pages', the fourteen-part poem sequence
which lurches, like grief itself, from terrifying unacceptability – 'And that's
that' – to the spiritual questions raised by absence – 'The whereabouts of M,
I'm afraid/are simply unknown./ She must have gone out someplace./ She
has not come home.' These poems address death as it is lived, combining
the horror of death with the boredom of pain:

Unopened packages from Bradley's Pharmacy,
unfilled prescriptions, scattered blister packs.
bottles of Chardonnay, full, and empty,
oil paint tubes, dishevelled costumed dolls

The pieces are richly intertextual, combining references to Dickinson, Plath
and Mantel with MacNeice and Pink Floyd. Indeed, the concept of voice is
crucial here – what is spoken remains alive: 'you, dear M,/plus all of us, will
become unspoken.' These poems act as a kind of Ouija board, keeping M very
much alive amongst her own words, her own belongings and her own reality:

It isn't as if
I have anyone to answer to
I live on my own
I am not beaten yet
I am paying respect to my past
which over the last
three years has been
drink drink drink
I will hang on
to this sobriety for dear life
it is very much living in the day.

The voice outlasts the body for Bryce – the body is here, but a problem to be discarded 'like a winter's coat'. It is 'leftover', 'cumbersome', and 'difficult', a grotesquery: 'A small perforation/ in the skin near her jaw,/ where the elasticity/ has snapped. The size of a little fingernail./ We all notice.'

The M Pages succeeds, ultimately, in fighting the unreliability of language to hold down the intensity of experiences such as loss – although 'the language/strains – *for ever and ay,/ forever and a day* – and ultimately/ fails: *for a very long time.*' The collection is admirable, and succeeds in trail-laying; it does, as Bryce writes in her closing poem, 'A Last Post', 'track those trails/ of human spoor to the point/ at which they always disappear.'

The capacity of language to convey the intensity of the most human moments is explored with an unusual combination of directness and gentleness in Aoife Lyall's startling debut, *Mother, Nature*. An intimate look at the pain of miscarriage and loss, bolstered by the blessedness of healthy pregnancy, this debut is assured and has the strength to be vulnerable. The collection begins with devastation – 'When a silence came/it was your heart not beating.' The emotional issues around physicality which are so emphatic in pregnancy and miscarriage are tenderly examined: 'A wake/ for weeks I am the grave they send the lilies to.' The black biro mentioned several times becomes a totem for the cruel bright violence of the bureaucracy of loss. The 'empty home' of the non-pregnant body becomes a map of pain: 'your name is the folded treasure map/ I hide in my throat: when I am lost/ it will lead me back to you.'

As the collection moves forward, the potentiality of new life and the joy of the birth cycle becomes the focal point. A range of beautiful reflections on new motherhood are present, using the newborn as object to pivot around, whilst never forgetting or driving away memories of the unborn baby, such as in the lovely 'Conditions of Sale':

> Only if cancelled due to miscarriage
> or similar circumstances
> will you receive a full refund.
> I lay you down in your new cot.
> Twelve weeks old, you stretch your limbs
> into the oblivion of space and sleep.
> Downstairs, your father swaddles
> the Moses basket in plastic sheets.
> Careful not to tear them, he tucks
> the price tags in.

The potential of the new baby is as much of a void as the lost baby, but a positive one: 'the space around the words/ the breath   between   the turning pages'. The titular poem, 'Mother, Nature' captures the potential of the egg and the newborn and compares the animal experience of birth and motherhood with that of the natural world: 'In the pause of nine million swallowed breaths I see the nine-month / journey that brings you to a place where bystanders call for help/and start to mourn but she flies through Special Care until she finds you.'

The collection closes with the reminder that laws policing women's bodies are a tragedy on a par with lost pregnancy, with the haunting 'Acrania': 'by law she carries you.' This is a strong first collection, rich as a newborn with promise.

The capacity of a new child for hope is turned on its head by Ailbhe Darcy's new work, *Insistence*. The juxtaposition of global crisis and personal fulfilment makes for an interesting consideration of responsibility – readerly, writerly and individual. Darcy writes as a commentator on and participant in the world, simultaneously engaged and outside, as the poet so often is: 'When the future was annihilated by the future's arrival,/ I was only the father of my son, as if no one were anything but small.' The climate crisis and the political landscape is seen through the eyes of the small, the object. The object, the capacity for consumption, is the site where the personal and the public intersect in these poems, they become Platonic forms of themselves: 'it's not an umbrella, it's a silken manifestation/of something they've talked over and over.' These poems form a space where 'buses looked more like buses than buses I'd seen', where every object, every choice is a responsibility: 'To be honest I usually care quite a lot about the reader but today/ I just want to get the whole thing down on paper'. The car becomes a hearse, which becomes a metaphor for climate change: 'they died of us and we sang out./ We drove the baby home in that black car.' The intersection between the personal and the political object peaks in the wonderful 'Jellyfish', an exploration of the Syrian refugee crisis set against the play of a parent and child on the beach: 'where ice – far away but you can't help/knowing about it-/calves and crashes-/Where comb jellies-far away but you can't help/knowing about it-/spawn deliriously-/where plastics- far away but you can't help/knowing about it-make an island'

The unseen but omnipresent nature of the jellyfish echoes the tragic overlooking of the refugee crisis: 'Once you saw a photograph/of a child – lifeless – /on a beach-/ so did everybody'

The blind eyes we comfortably turn to human and environmental crisis are at length opened through the long piece, 'Alphabet', a revisited Inger Christensen piece addressing the Hiroshima tragedy, a lullaby for the world. Playing with letters of the alphabet, the pieces stretch to extinction and doom via the family unit:

> We are not doomed yet
> juggle the numbers
> some are doomed
> but not the three of us
> just yet

The personal and the public collide spectacularly in part eleven, with the hope of the child and environmental loss placed at extreme odds and yet together:

> Kin insists, kin insists;
> your pink cheek tucked up
> with mine, not thinking
> of solitude or extinction,
> of the whale in your book.

The collection is a fine example of Darcy's skill to spur and to play with narrative – to make the language of her work reflect the urgency of the issues it portrays.

The intersection of the personal and the political comes to the fore in *Mercy*, the first collection from Róisín Kelly. The collection merges a range of mythologies to explore Kelly's sense of identity and heritage – ranging from the poet as Christlike to personae poems from Penelope and Eve. The trying on of and embracing of identities is key to this work, and is very effective when used to explore the unique combination of pagan rawness and Catholic sensibility and belief that speaks of Irish poetry. The religious imagery in this collection plays well against images of cyclical decay and rebirth – for instance, the role of fruit in 'Oranges' to represent lush fertility and the counterpoint of rot:

> You'll feel warm
> between my palms
> and I'll cup you like
> a handful of holy water

In a similar vein, 'Easter' works to juxtapose the egg as aforementioned pagan symbol of potentiality and rebirth with the images of the poet as Christ:

I'd tap at you like an egg,
cracking your thin chocolate shell.
If I were made of chocolate too, I'd break
off parts of myself to give to you and your girl.

The piece closes with the assertion, the prideful combination of identities of pagan and Catholic: 'The words are everything. With them,/ I'll turn water to wine at your wedding.' Astrology and Greek mythology are given equal play – pieces such as 'Mercury in Retrograde' and 'Ithaca' elegantly merge the mythic with the everyday. This poet says she has 'seen the future and am not afraid' whilst 'listening/ to the rush of gold in my veins/to the oven's hum in the kitchen.' Kelly speaks of a capacity to take elements of various traditions and weave them together into a new identity which is at once deeply empowering and deeply feminine:

Amongst women, I wait on the shore
of our twilight world, with its threat of storms always.
stripped naked, we shield little candles
with our hands: prayers for salvation, or a funeral offering.

Kelly's closing poem is a testament to the pirate queen of Ireland, Granuaile, a voyager who takes and amalgamates her identity like treasure, one who knows her 'way in the dark'. Kelly's collection is a stirring call to the power of the transubstantiation of culture to create a shifting but also strong sense of self.

Miriam Gamble's third collection, *What Planet,* instead of pulling together strands, celebrate in their diffusion. The surrealism of this collection is matched only by its humour – and its capacity to investigate the concept of perception in a post-truth world. The instability of these poems draws your attention to the poems as objects, as experiments – the concrete piece 'Time Ball' forces us to reconsider an inconcrete concept: 'the clocks still ticking in the centre/ with the neat hands and the mark of the maker/ will tick for no one'; the piece 'Urn' becomes an urn for the poet's own voice and that of others: 'I was anorexic who/ wants to hear it here is world made metaphor/ words like a hummingbird's bill siphoning the inner nectar.' These poems occupy a dystopian world, a scorched world: 'They say I have the look/ of a fragment but display no seam./ No one is more confused than me/as to what is meant by it.'

These pieces have a bareness which highlights their capacity to shock; 'instead of greenery you have stripped-/ backery.' Objects are destabilised, often in a comedic way: 'On this shoe you have centred all your hopes/ of becoming a finished person.' Scissors feature in several pieces, a method of cutting up and detaching the truth. In 'In Memoriam Your Stuff', objects both represent loss and represent nothingness:

> But you
> did not seem to want your history told
> and in the end it went en masse
> down to the dump. You engineered it so,
> who snuck warmth from the whisky of chaos
> who prized without hierarchy every thing.

The wonderful 'Girl with Book and Rubber Bands' plays with the concept of book as object, which can too be destabilised by the perceptions of others: 'She has a book and she's attached it/ to a string of rubber bands.' This girl, this poet, is 'sending out and reeling in a book on a rubber leash' who 'sends the book cantering through the air'. Our perception of it, and of her, will make it ours, but it will in the end always come back to her, her voice.

Some of Gamble's best work in this collection comes from the prose pieces, with 'Wonderland' a particular highlight:

> It came to me of a sudden that my neighbour was a threat to peace, security, the nation. Previously I had had no sense of this but I knew it to be true so I set about letting the people know who should know and I must say it was a source of pride when, on the basis of my information, he was carried away for questioning, his face blank as a moon.

Gamble plays with the battle for truth in an increasingly individualistic world, particularly in relation to social media and the constant undermining of any sense of reliability, in spite of a growing sense of being monitored. In spite of the strangeness of Gamble's work, there seems a sense that new connections and new metaphor is fruitless: 'nothing makes the news/ and no one follows up my call.' Many of the poems occupy a space of liminality, which works well as a place in which to explore political issues, such as 'IndyRef, 2014' – the ballot is a place of both 'Yes' and 'No' until the box is ticked. Similarly, the following piece, 'Samhain', occupies that place between, when 'the veil of existences' is blurred, the 'once-strong evidence is fading to a hiss'. Ultimately, we bring ourselves to all perception, we are 'stamped/ on the image like a pale moth on a pale tree,/ a white crow on a field of white, or nearly.'

To come full circle, Cathy Galvin's new pamphlet from The Melos Press is a moving sequence meditating on loss. The sonnet sequence allows Galvin to investigate with a turn, to move through the poems as one moves through grief. The pieces are arranged cyclically, with the phrase *'It's blacker than blue. Your hand is going black'* opening and closing the collection. The process of grief, grief as a 'doing', is drawn attention to – 'trees roar to me. When your names are invoked,/ herons stand sentinel. Still I cannot cry.' The power of faith is strong in these poems – faith not just invoked from a Catholic childhood, but 'Faith in the perfection of single moments,/ in resurrection, epiphany.'

The blurring of the moment and the memory works well here, as Galvin brings us to and fro, the here and back again of the griever:

> Knowing the lessons
> we must learn don't come from what's seen or said
> but the song of who we are, living and dead.

The elegance of the sequence allows Galvin to explore the capacity for memory to crystallise and transform grief. The words spoken may be forgotten, but the memory of a moment, a smell or a piece of clothing can be forever: 'All she said has been forgotten. Anything/ of wisdom, maternal advice, simple kindness/hidden in a medicated fug; narratives, begun in chaos,/ needed reordering; dresses they had thrown away,/ I wanted to caress and keep.'

Galvin writes of the story of grief in human, yet sophisticated constructs. She succeeds in pinning down the flighty nature of intensity, in spite of the fact that, in her words: 'Nothing that we see and hear can be owned./ Only kissed, held, let go of./ Stories told.'

NOTES FOR BROADSHEET POETS

Selected quotations on writing poetry by Michael Longley (from *Sidelines: Selected Prose 1962-2015*, Enitharmon Press, 2017 (compiled by the editor):

Like Samuel Beckett, I prefer the word 'shape' to 'form'... I write out of a jumble of emotions and vague notions and scraps of knowledge. At some stage a form, or, rather, a shape mysteriously emerges.

Like George Herbert, Edward Thomas possesses the poetic equivalent of perfect pitch. I have revisited 'Tall Nettles' hundreds of times. Like all true poems it is always brand new – 'Worn new/ Again and again' as Thomas himself says in his poem 'Words'.

Poems are aware of each other. No poem is a solo flight.

I think being a poet is different from being a writer. Some poets are writers as well but they are usually protecting a core. Poetry can't be created to order. You can't write your way out of a poetic block.

Much contemporary writing sounds to my ears syntactically flabby, linguistically impoverished. In losing touch with Latin (and Greek) it has lost its backbone.

Looking back at my passionate desire to share the landscape, I think I can recognise the incipient poet – someone for whom no experience is complete until he or she has written about it, someone who would hope to share the experience with others.

I have tried to sing about everything.

I test the line in my mouth and in my ear.

Surely one writes simply because one has to.

This may go straight into 'Pseuds' Corner', but poetry, the effort to write it, reading it and living it is, if you like, my religion.

When I sit down I don't know what I am going to write. There's some frisson, the nexus of an idea, a word, an emotion, a rhythm, and then the writing of the poem is an inner exploration that takes me to where I haven't been before, to unknown territory… I'm using the shapes, the forms of the poem as an explorer would use a compass.

… gradually you think you might have a book – a book rather than a miscellany of poems. If you're lucky, you'll discern some pattern in it that your subconscious has been bringing about.

New poems respond to old ones.

Most poets write and publish far too much.

So much contemporary verse lacks propulsion. It's a tedium of staccato stutters – oblivious to the complexities that can be created by angled clauses. In poetry a sentence can be made to do more than in prose.

Love poetry is the core of the enterprise – the hub of the wheel from which the other preoccupations radiate like spokes.

It's presumptuous to call oneself a poet. Anyone who begins a sentence 'As a poet, I' is probably not a poet. It's like calling yourself a saint. It's what I most want to be. Since I favour intensity of utterance and formal compression, you could say that I am trying to be a lyric poet.

One of the best things ever said to me about poetry was John Hewitt's off-hand remark: 'If you write poetry, it's your own fault'.

Poetry… is a vocation rather than a profession… I live from poem to poem, from hand to mouth. In 'Pascoli's Portrait' I say 'a poem's little more than a wing and a prayer'.

Biographies

Gary Allen was born in Ballymena, Co. Antrim. He has published eighteen collections, three novels and a collection of short stories. A new collection, *Bonfire Night*, is due out later this year from Greenwich Exchange Publishing, London. Widely published in international magazines including *Australian Book Review*, *London Magazine*, *The New Statesman*, *The Poetry Review*, *The Wild Court*. Highly recommended in The Forward Prize 2019.

Joseph Allen was born in Ballymena, Co. Antrim. He has published six collections, most recently, *Clabber Street Blues*, Greenwich Exchange Publishing. Published widely in magazines, including, *Acumen, Poetry Ireland Review*, *The London Magazine*, *Stand*.

Elizabeth Barton read English at Christ's College, Cambridge, after which she worked as a teacher and freelance writer. She has lived in Spain and the U.S. and now lives in Surrey where she is Stanza Rep for Mole Valley Poets. Her poems have appeared in magazines including *Agenda, Acumen, Orbis, South, The Curlew* and *The Frogmore Papers*.

William Bedford's poetry has appeared in *Agenda, Encounter, The John Clare Society Journal, London Magazine, The New Statesman, Poetry Review, The Tablet, The Washington Times* and many others. Red Squirrel Press published *The Fen Dancing* in March 2014 and *The Bread Horse* in October 2015. He won first prize in the 2014 *London Magazine* International Poetry Competition. Dempsey & Windle published *Chagall's Circus* in April 2019. His latest collection, *The Dancers of Colbek*, was published by Two Rivers Press in January 2020.

Colette Bryce is a poet from Derry, N. Ireland. She has published five collections including *The M Pages*, published by Picador in 2020. *Selected Poems* (2017) was a PBS Special Commendation and winner of the Pigott Prize for Irish poetry. She is the current editor of *Poetry Ireland Review*.

Nick Burbridge is an Anglo-Irish poet, playwright, and short story writer. He is the author of three poetry books: *On Call* (Envoi Poets, 1994), *All Kinds Of Disorder* (Waterloo, 2006) and *The Unicycle Set*, (Waterloo, 2011). *Undercover Work*, is scheduled for publication by The Wild Geese Press. His plays include *Dirty Tricks* (Soho Theatre), *Vermin* (Finborough), and *Cock Robin* (Verity Bargate Award Runner-up), and others broadcast on BBC Radio. He is also a successful songwriter.

Martin Caseley lives in Norfolk. His essays, articles and poems have appeared regularly in *Agenda*, *PN Review* and *The Countryman* on subjects as diverse as Bob Dylan, Thomas Hardy, Ronnie Lane, hares, Geoffrey Hill and ancient trees. He also contributes book reviews to the International Times and Stride Magazine websites.

Pratibha Castle's debut award-winning pamphlet, *A Triptych of Birds and A Few Loose Feathers* (Hedgehog Press, 2021) portrays the childhood and adolescence of an Irish Catholic emigré in1950s England. Her work appears in various magazines including *Sarasvati, Reach, Fly on the Wall Press*, and various anthologies. It is featured in various online sites *The Blue Nib*, *Words for the Wild*, and forthcoming with *Fragmented Voices*. Her poems have been broadcast regularly on West Wilts Radio in The Poetry Place. She graduated in in 2015 from The University of Chichester with a first-class honours degree in English and Creative Writing plus a Post Graduate Diploma in Creative Writing.

Originally from Co. Antrim, **Brendan Cleary** has published many collections from presses such as Bloodaxe, Wrecking Ball & Tall-lighthouse. His next collection *The Other Place* is due from Red Hen Press in September 2O21. He lives & writes in Brighton.

Belinda Cooke's translations include *Kulager* by Ilias Jansugurov (Kazakh N.T. A., 2018); *Forms of Exile: Poems of Marina Tsvetaeva* (The High Window Press, 2019); *Contemporary Kazakh Poetry* (C.U.P, 2019). Her own poetry includes *Stem* (the High Window Press, 2019) and her *Days of the Shorthanded Shovelists* forthcoming (Salmon Poetry). She is currently working on a memoir of her mother's life.

Kevin Crossley-Holland has just published his twelfth collection of poems, *Gravity for Beginners* (Arc, 2021). He is a well-known translator from Anglo-Saxon and author of *The Penguin Book of Norse Myths* and a memoir of childhood, *The Hidden Roads*. His books for children include *Between Worlds: Folktales of Britain and Ireland* as well as his *Arthur* trilogy (translated into 24 languages) and *Gatty's Tale,* and he has been awarded the Carnegie Medal, and the *Guardian* Children's Fiction Prize. Kevin has worked with many distinguished composers and artists, and is a Fellow of the Royal Society of Literature, and a patron of the Society for Storytelling and the Story Museum.

Hilary Davies has published four collections of poetry from Enitharmon: the latest, *Exile and the Kingdom*, was published in November 2016; most recently, she has been a co-contributor to Yves Bonnefoy's *Collected Prose*, (Carcanet, 2020) and co-editor of *Prophetic Witness. The Re-Imagining of the World*, (Routledge, 2020) . From 2012 to 2016 she was a Royal Literary Fund Fellow at King's College, London and in 2018-9 at the British Library.

Since his first collection *Sheltering Places* appeared in 1978, **Gerald Dawe** has published over twenty books of poetry and literary essays along with editing the anthology, *Earth Voices Whispering: Irish War Poetry 1914-1945*. He is Professor of English and Fellow Emeritus, Trinity College Dublin and has held academic and writing positions in various countries. Born in Belfast he lived for many years in the west of Ireland before moving to Dún Laoghaire, County Dublin in 1992.

Terence Dooley's translation of Mariano Peyrou's *The Year of the Crab* was a Poetry Book Society Recommendation for Spring last year. His translation of Eduardo Moga's anthology *Streets where to walk is to embark: Spanish Poets in London* and of *(Sur)rendering* by Mario Martín Gijón came out earlier this year, also with Shearsman Books, as has his *10 Spanish Contemporary Women Poets* which is the Poetry Book Society recommended translation. His own poems, *The Why of it*, are published by The Argent Press.

Leontia Flynn has published four collections of poetry with Jonathan Cape, most recently *The Radio* (2017), which was shortlisted for the T. S. Eliot Prize and won the Irish Times Poetry Prize. She has also received the Forward prize for best First Collection, the Rooney Prize for Irish literature and the AWB Vincent American Ireland Fund Literary Award. The Lifeboat Press published her pamphlet of Catullus translations, *Slim New Book*, in 2020. She lives in Belfast and is Reader at the Seamus Heaney Centre at Queen's University.

Naomi Foyle is a British-Canadian poet, science fiction novelist and essayist based in Brighton, UK. In 1994, encouraged by the late Belfast poet and journalist Mairtín Crawford, she took an Irish pen-name in honour of her great-grandmother, only to learn much later that genetically she is only 13.5% English, being also 60% Irish-Scottish and 20% Scandinavian, with her 6.5 % Iberian DNA likely also due to her Irish ancestry. Naomi Foyle's three poetry collections include *The Night Pavilion* (Waterloo Press), an Autumn 2008 PBS Recommendation, and *Adamantine* (Red Hen/Pighog Press, US/UK); her ten pamphlets include *No Enemy but Time* (Waterloo Press), an elegiac tribute to Mairtín Crawford and his quietly remarkable mother, Flo Crawford, that launched at the Belfast Book Festival in 2017.

Widely-published London-based poet, fourth-generation Irish-Australian **Katherine Gallagher**'s most recent collection is *Acres of Light* (Arc Publications, 2016) following her *Carnival Edge: New & Selected Poems* (Arc, 2010). www.katherine-gallagher.com

Cathy Galvin is a poet and journalist. Her awards include a 2021 Arts Council England DYCP bursary, a Hawthornden Fellowship, residency at the Heinrich Böll Cottage, Achill Island and shortlistings for the Listowel Poetry Collection Prize and Goldsmiths/Spread the Word Life-Writing Prize. Melos Press published her first two pamphlets of poetry, *Black and Blue* and *Rough Translation*. Her most recent work, *Walking The Coventry Ring Road With Lady Godiva*, was published by Cornwall's Guillemot Press. A graduate of the Writing MA at the University of Warwick, she is completing a poetry practice PhD at Goldsmiths College, University of London. She is founder and director of the UK's leading promoter of short fiction, the Word Factory, co-founder of the Sunday Times Short Story Award and an English PEN Trustee.

John Greening is a Bridport Prize and Cholmondeley Award winner: he has published over twenty collections, including *The Silence* (Carcanet, 2019), the recent *a Post Card to* (Red Squirrel Press, with Stuart Henson) and *The Giddings* (Mica). He has edited Grigson, Blunden and Iain Crichton Smith, along with several anthologies, notably the forthcoming *Hollow Palaces: Modern Country House Poems* (with Kevin Gardner, L.U.P.). His collected essays, *Vapour Trails*, have recently appeared.

Irish poet, **Vona Groarke**, has published seven poetry collections with Gallery Press, the latest being *Double Negative* (2019). Her *Selected Poems* won the 2017 Pigott Prize for best Irish poetry collection. A Cullman Fellow at the New York Public Library 2018-19; former editor of *Poetry Ireland Review* and selector for the Poetry Book Society, she teaches at the University of Manchester and otherwise lives in south Co. Sligo, in the West of Ireland. Her eighth collection, *Link*, is due in October.

Jeremy Hooker was born in Hampshire but has spent most of his working life in Wales. He has published two *Selected Poems*, with Enitharmon and Shearsman respectively, and his books of essays, on poetry, nature, and painting, and published journals include: *Poetry of Place*, *Imagining Wales*, *Ditch Vision*, *Art of Seeing*, *Welsh Journal* and *Openings: A European Journal*. His BBC 3 feature *A Map of David Jones* was first broadcast in 1995. He is a Fellow of The Learned Society of Wales and Emeritus Professor of the University of South Wales.

Joseph Horgan was born in England of Irish immigrant parents. He has lived in Ireland since 1999. He is the author of three full collections, *Slipping Letters beneath the Sea* (Doghouse, 2008), *An Unscheduled Life,*(with Brian Whelan) Agenda Editions, 2012, *The Year I Loved England,* (with Antony Owen) Pighog Press, *2014* and a pamphlet collection, *21 The Thing I Am,* Flarestack, 2019. He is also the author of a prose work, *The Song at your Backdoor,* Collins Press, 2010. His new book, *People That Don't Exist Are Citizens Of A Made Up Country,* is due out in April 2021. Amongst his credits is The Patrick Kavanagh Award.

Paul Jeffcutt's new collection is *The Skylark's Call* (Dempsey & Windle, 2020); his first collection, 'Latch', was with Lagan Press (2010). Recently his poems have appeared in *The Honest Ulsterman, The Interpreter's House, Magma, Orbis, Oxford Poetry, Poetry Ireland Review, Poetry Salzburg Review* and *Vallum.* He lives in Northern Ireland.

Ben Keatinge is a Visiting Research Fellow at the School of English, Trinity College Dublin. He is editor of *Making Integral: Critical Essays on Richard Murphy* (Cork UP, 2019) and his poems have been published, most recently, in *Cyphers, Irish Pages, The Stony Thursday Book, Orbis* and anthologised in *Writing Home: The 'New Irish' Poets* (Dedalus Press, 2019). He lectured in English literature for nine years at South East European University, North Macedonia and he has travelled widely in the Balkans.

Patrick Lodge lives in Yorkshire and is from an Irish/Welsh heritage. His work has been published in several countries and he has been successful in several poetry competitions including the Gregory O'Donoghue, the Leeds Poetry Peace Prize, Poetry On The Lake, Red House Poets, the Trim Festival and the Manchester Cathedral Poetry Competition in 2020 and he is Manchester Cathedral poet of the year for 2020. He has read by invitation at festivals internationally and reviews for several magazines. His latest collection, *Remarkable Occurrences* is published by Valley Press.

Edna Longley is a Professor Emerita at Queen's University Belfast. Her books include *Poetry & Posterity* (Bloodaxe, 2000), *Yeats and Modern Poetry* (Cambridge University Press, 2013) and *Under the Same Moon: Edward Thomas and the English Lyric* (Enitharmon, 2017). She has edited Edward Thomas: *The Annotated Collected Poems* (Bloodaxe, 2008); and co-edited (with Peter Mackay and Fran Brearton) *Modern Irish and Scottish Poetry* (Cambridge, 2011), and (with Fran Brearton) *Incorrigibly Plural: Louis MacNeice and his Legacy* (Carcanet, 2012).

John McAuliffe grew up in Co Kerry and has lived in Manchester since 2004. He has published five books with The Gallery Press, most recently *The Kabul Olympics,* which was a *Guardian* Poetry Book of the Month in June 2020 and *Irish Times* 2020 Book of the Year. His versions of the Bosnian poet Igor Klikovac, *Stockholm Syndrome* (Smith Doorstop), was a Poetry Book Society Winter pamphlet Choice in 2019. Gallery will publish his *Selected Poems* later this year. He is Professor of Poetry at the University of Manchester's Centre for New Writing and Associate Publisher at Carcanet Press.

Niall McDevitt is the author of three collections of poetry, *b/w* (Waterloo Press, 2010), *Porterloo* (International Times, 2013) and *Firing Slits, Jerusalem Colportage* (New River Press, 2016). He is also known for his poetopographical walks such as The William Blake Walk, An Arthur Rimbaud Drift, A London Chaucer Pilgrimage, and many others. In 2012 he read at Yoko Ono's Meltdown. In 2016, he performed his poetry in Iraq at the Babylon Festival. In 2020 he featured in THE BARD at Flat Time House. A new book *London Nation* is forthcoming. He occasionally blogs at poetopography.wordpress.com

Kathleen McPhilemy was born and brought up in Belfast but now lives in Oxford. She has published three collections of poetry, the most recent being *The Lion in the Forest* (Katabasis, 2005). Her poems have appeared in a wide range of print and online magazines and anthologies. She has recently retired after many years teaching in further education. Poetically, she owes a lot to the encouragement of James Simmons, Dinah Livingstone and John Rety. Currently, she is running a monthly Zoom Open Mic poetry evening in Oxford and home tutoring much of her extended family.

Sam Milne has recently published a series of plays in the Scots magazine, *Lallans.* He has a long poem and an essay on the Scottish poet Edith Anne Robertson coming out in the next issue of that magazine. He has just completed a translation of the *Iliad* in Scots, and translations of Racine's *Andromaque* and Sophocles's *Antigone.*

A. David Moody is an Emeritus Professor at the University of York and the author of *Thomas Stearns Eliot: Poet* (C.U.P., 1979, 1994), and *Ezra Pound: Poet. A Portrait of the Man & his Work* (O.U.P., 3 vols. 2007, 2014, 2015). With Mary de Rachewiltz and Joanna Moody he co-edited *Ezra Pound to his Parents: Letters 1895-1929* (O.U.P., 2010).

Hayden Murphy: born Dublin 1945. Poet, editor, arts journalist. Lives in Edinburgh with his wife Frances Corcoran. Latest publication *In the Ear of the Owl* (Roncadora Press, 2018).

Sean O'Brien teaches at the University of Newcastle upon Tyne. He won both the Forward Poetry Prize and the T.S Eliot Prize for his collection *The Drowned Book* in 2007. His collection of poems *Europa* and his collection of short stories *Quartier Perdu* were published in 2018. His tenth volume of poems, *It Says Here*, was published in September of last year.

Steven O'Brien is the editor of *The London Magazine*. He has published two collections of poetry, and is working on a collection of Arthurian poems.

Ruth O'Callaghan has 11 poetry collections. Her 23 interviews with the most eminent women poets throughout the world, *Without Skin*, is 'a very important contribution to world literary history.' (Professor Clare Brant, King's College, London.) Awarded a gold medal for poetry at the XXX WCP in Taiwan, an Arts Council award to visit Mongolia, she leads workshops, co-organises festivals and reads throughout Asia, Europe, and the U.S.A. Her two London poetry venues, where the famous and unknown read together, raise money for the homeless.

Bernard O'Donoghue was born in Cullen, County Cork in 1945 and he still lives there for part of the year. Since 1962 he has lived principally in England, and since 1965 in Oxford where he taught Medieval Literature for forty years at Magdalen and Wadham Colleges. He is now an Emeritus Fellow in English at Wadham. He has published seven volumes of poetry, including *Gunpowder* which won the Whitbread Poetry Prize in 1995. His *Selected Poems* was published by Faber in 2008. His most recent volume was *The Seasons of Cullen Church* (Faber, 2016), and his *Very Short Introduction to Poetry* was published by Oxford UP in 2019.

John O'Donoghue is the author of *Brunch Poems* (Waterloo Press, 2009) and *Fools & Mad* (Waterloo Press, 2014); the memoir *Sectioned: A Life Interrupted* (John Murray 2009); and the short story collection, *The King From Over The Water* (The Wild Geese Press, 2019). His writing has attracted a number of awards, including Mind Book of the Year 2010; the Irish Post Listowel Writers' Week Award 2016; and a Brookleaze Grant, also in 2016, from the Royal Society of Literature. He holds a PhD in Creative Writing from Bath Spa and lives in Brighton.

Caitríona O'Reilly is from Wicklow. She was educated at Trinity College, Dublin, where she completed a PhD in American poetry. She has published three collections with Bloodaxe Books: *The Nowhere Birds* (2001); *The Sea Cabinet* (2006); and *Geis* (2015). Her work has been translated into many European languages. Her books have been shortlisted for several major prizes and she is a recipient of the Rooney Prize in Irish Literature and the Irish Times Poetry Now Prize. Caitríona O'Reilly lives in Lincoln.

Maurice Riordan was born in Lisgoold, Co. Cork, and lives in London. His fifth collection from Faber, *The Shoulder Tap*, is due in October. Among his previous books are *The Water Stealer* (2013), *The Holy Land* (2007), *Floods* (2000) and *A Word from the Loki* (1995). He edited *The Finest Music* (Faber, 2014), an anthology of early Irish poetry in translation. He is Emeritus Professor of Poetry at Sheffield Hallam University.

Stephen Sexton's first book, *If All the World and Love Were Young* was the winner of the Forward Prize for Best First Collection in 2019 and the Shine / Strong Award for Best First Collection. He was awarded the E.M. Forster Award from the American Academy of Arts and Letters and the Rooney Prize for Irish Literature in 2020. He was the winner of the National Poetry Competition in 2016 and the recipient of an Eric Gregory Award in 2018. He teaches at the Seamus Heaney Centre at Queen's University, Belfast.

Gerard Smyth has published ten collections of poetry, the most recent of which are *The Sundays of Eternity* and *A Song of Elsewhere* (both Dedalus Press). *The Yellow River* (a collaboration with artist Seán McSweeney) was published by the Solstice Arts Centre, Navan. He is a member of Aosdána (Ireland's academy of arts and letters).

Seán Street was born in Portsmouth to an Irish mother. His most recent collection is *Camera Obscura* (Rockingham Press). Prose includes works on Gerard Manley Hopkins and the Dymock Poets, and a number of studies of sound poetics, including *The Sound Inside the Silence* (Palgrave, 2019). His latest book, *The Sound of a Room: Memory and the Auditory Presence of Place* is published by Routledge. He is Emeritus Professor of Radio at Bournemouth University.